American University Studies

Series II
Romance Languages and Literature

Vol. 76

PETER LANG
New York · Bern · Frankfurt am Main · Paris

Mystical Imagery

Elizabeth Teresa Howe

Mystical Imagery

Santa Teresa de Jesús
and San Juan de la Cruz

PETER LANG
New York · Bern · Frankfurt am Main · Paris

Library of Congress Cataloging-in-Publication Data

Howe, Elizabeth Teresa,
Mystical imagery.

(American university studies. Series II. Romance
languages and literature ; vol. 76)
Bibliography: p.
1. Teresa, of Avila, Saint, 1515–1582—Contributions
in mysticism. 2. John of the Cross, Saint, 1542–1591—
Contributions in mysticism. 3. Mysticism—History—
16th century. 1. Title. II. Series.
BV5075.H69   1987   248.2'2   87-22551
ISBN 0-8204-0614-7
ISSN: 0740-9257

CIP-Kurztitelaufnahme der Deutschen Bibliothek

Howe, Elizabeth Teresa:
Mystical imagery : Santa Teresa de Jesús and San
Juan de la Cruz / Elizabeth Teresa Howe. – New
York; Bern; Frankfurt am Main; Paris: Lang,
1988.
(American University Studies: Ser. 2, Romance
Languages and Literature; Vol. 76)
ISBN 0-8204-0614-7

NE: American University Studies / 02

BV
5075
.H69
1988

© Peter Lang Publishing, Inc., New York 1988

Printed by Weihert-Druck GmbH, Darmstadt, West Germany

TABLE OF CONTENTS

Works of Santa Teresa

V	Vida
CP	Camino de perfección (Roman numerals refer to chapters in both Escorial and Valladolid editions)
CPe	Camino de perfección (Escorial edition only)
CPv	Camino de perfección (Valladolid edition only)
F	Fundaciones
M	Las moradas del castillo interior
Med	Meditaciones sobre el Cantar de los Cantares
Ex	Exclamaciones
Cuentas	Cuentas de conciencia
A	Avisos
Carta ST	Carta of Santa Teresa

Works of San Juan de la Cruz

S	Subida al monte Carmelo
CE	Cántico espiritual (Cantico B: Jaen edition)
N	Noche oscura
Ll	Llama de amor viva
Dichos	Dichos de luz y amor (Compendium of Avisos y sentencias)
Cautelas	Cautelas a un religioso
Carta SJC	Carta of San Juan de la Cruz

With some exceptions, these abbreviations are those used by Luis de San José, O. C. D. in Concordancias de las obras y escritos de Santa Teresa de Jesús, 2nd ed. (Burgos: El Monte Carmelo, 1965), and Concordancias de las obras y escritos del doctor de la Iglesia, San Juan de la Cruz (Burgos: El Monte Carmelo, 1948).

INTRODUCTION

The quatercentenary celebration in 1942 marking the
anniversary of the birth of the Spanish Carmelite, San Juan de la
Cruz, saw the publication of a handful of articles and books
which unostentatiously initiated a new and important era in the
study of the works of both San Juan and his mentor, Santa Teresa
de Jesús. By no means the first studies devoted to the poetry
and prose of both authors, the critical works which appeared
during that anniversary year established the basis for the
discussion of the mystics' writings in the light of their
contributions to Spanish literature. Before the publication of
Damaso Alonso's pivotal work, La poesía de San Juan de la Cruz
(Madrid: C.S.I.C., 1942), the preponderance of the literature
devoted to the works of Santa Teresa and San Juan had dealt
almost exclusively with historical facts and doctrinal questions
pertinent to their roles as reformers of the Carmelite order and
as Doctors of the Church. Explanations and interpretations of
their mystical theology thus form the bulk of the scholarship
dealing with both authors. Nevertheless, among the historical
studies which treat of San Juan and Santa Teresa in particular
and Spanish mysticism in general, a few stand out as key
contributions to the critical work which was to follow.

In his acceptance speech on entering the Royal Spanish

Academy in 1881, Marcelino Menéndez y Pelayo chose as his subject "aquel género de poesía castellana por el cual nuestra lengua merecía ser llamada lengua de ángeles,"[1] his grandiloquent way of referring to mystical poetry. In a tour de force, he traced its presence through Spanish letters, ranging far afield in what he considered poesía mística.[2] Because of the time limitations of his speech, Menéndez y Pelayo was unable to develop in detail the importance of individual authors. This task was taken up with limited success by Pedro Sainz Rodríguez in his Introducción a la historia de la literatura mística en España (Madrid: Voluntad, 1927; reprt. Espasa-Calpe, 1984), a work intended to explain the influences at work in Spanish mystical literature as well as to delineate the unique contributions made by Spanish authors to the whole of mystical writing. The author augmented his original work with the publication of Espiritualidad española (Madrid: Rialp, 1961), which focused on the influence of Italian mysticism in Spain, the formation of Jesuit spirituality, and the contributions of Fray Luis de León and Fray Domingo de Valtanás to Spanish religious literature. While neither Menéndez y Pelayo nor Sainz Rodríguez branched out into extensive critical studies of the literary merit of the mystics' works, they did provide the historical perspective necessary for such studies. Continuing the work begun by his precedessors in the field, the British Hispanist, E. Allison Peers, began his own extensive work on Spanish mysticism with his two-volume Studies of the Spanish Mystics (London: The Sheldon Press, 1927-1930), which combined biographical, historical, doctrinal, and critical synopses of the major contributors to Spanish mystical literature. In numerous scholarly articles, critical studies,[3] translations,[4] and biographies, Peers contributed significantly to an overall understanding of the Spanish mystics in general and of Santa Teresa and San Juan in particular. More recently, the Fundación Universitaria Española has sponsored a great deal of scholarship focusing on the historical background of spirituality and mysticism in Spain. The studies produced draw attention to the continuum of religious writing in Spain, its debt to varied sources, and its contributions to the body of spiritual literature.[5]

Scholarship devoted to other than the strictly doctrinal or historical aspects of San Juan's works certainly preceded Dámaso Alonso's study. Jean Baruzi in Saint Jean de la Croix et le problème de l'experience mystique (Paris: Alcan, 1924), combined philosophical and psychological insights into the life and works of the poet and, especially, into the saint's original use of night as the pre-eminent symbol of his mystical experience. Fr. Crisógono de Jesús Sacramentado, O. C. D., in San Juan de la Cruz, su obra científica y su obra literaria (Madrid: Mensajero de Santa Teresa y San Juan de la Cruz, 1929), presented both doctrinal and literary studies in two separate volumes. Although both Baruzi and Fr. Crisógono attempted to combine doctrinal studies with literary analysis, their expertise rested more securely on their philosophical and theological training than on their literary formation. On the other hand, as part of the Turnbull lectures delivered at the Johns Hopkins University in Baltimore in 1937, the Spanish poet, Pedro Salinas, turned to the classics of Castilian poetry to discuss the topic of reality and the poet in Spanish poetry.[6] In a lecture entitled "The Escape from Reality," Salinas drew parallels between the lives and poems of Fray Luis de León and San Juan de la Cruz. In both poets he discerned movement--centrifugal in Fray Luis and centripetal in San Juan--beyond the physical confines of the prisons in which they created their lyrical masterpieces and beyond the bounds of creation to the central mystery of their religious experiences. He considered both men manifestations of the Spanish dynamism which marked the sixteenth century (p. 98). While Salinas compared the works of Fray Luis and San Juan in terms of their escape from reality, he also dealt with other poets and their perceptions or reactions to reality, among whom he included Calderón de la Barca, Garcilaso de la Vega, Luis de Góngora, and José de Espronceda. A similar juxtaposition of poets and their works around a central theme dealing with the poetic act occurs in subsequent studies by other critics. Regrettably, the same restrictions of time which prevented Menéndez y Pelayo from developing his insights more fully also limited the scope of Salinas' remarks.

On the foundation laid by his eminent predecessors as well as his own experience as a poet, Dámaso Alonso approached the poems of San Juan "desde esta ladera" (as he was to sub-title subsequent editions of his work), that is, as poetic rather than religious statements. He wished to "explicar lo explicable--sólo lo explicable--."[7] The task he set for himself was to fit San Juan's poems into the literary context of sixteenth-century Spanish letters by examining traditional, Biblical, and cultured sources influencing the mystical poet. Alonso's examination of sources showed San Juan's debt to Scripture and to Spanish poetry for many of his most effective images while the chapter on style explained the characteristics of his poems which set them apart from those of his literary predecessors and contemporaries.[8] Later expanded in Poesía española; ensayo de métodos y límites estilísticos (Madrid: Gredos, 1950), Alonso's analysis of style concentrated on four characteristics of San Juan's verse: great economy in the use of verbs, predominance of nouns at the expense of adjectives, a "sistema ondulatorio" of the adjectives which are used, and suppression of the epithet. Just as Salinas had done, Alonso included in his essay on methods and stylistics not only the poems of San Juan but those of other poets as well. Thus, his work also considered works by Garcilaso, Fray Luis de León, Góngora, Lope de Vega, and Quevedo. Within the limits of the critical task he set out to accomplish, Alonso produced a key work which heralded the appearance of purely literary studies in a number of works devoted either to source studies or to assessmments of the literary worth of the poems.

While Alonso dealt with three principal sources of literary influence in San Juan's poems, those who have followed his lead have attempted to limit the focus of their studies to one or two of those enumerated by their predecessor or to consider other, non-Spanish influences in the mystic's works. In a series of articles appearing in various journals between 1946 and 1952 and later collected in Estudios literarios sobre mística española (Madrid: Gredos, 1955),[9] Helmut Hatzfeld combined analysis of individual poems and style with considerations of the influence of other mystical writers on San Juan's works. While Alonso and Salinas had tied San Juan's poetry to the mainstream of Spanish literature, Hatzfeld suggested a similar connection with the great body of European mystical literature. The German scholar focused attention on the similarities of mystical language which he discerned between the Spanish mystics and the works of French and German mystical writers[10] as well as the fourteenth-century Catalán, Ramón Llull, and Dante. Although he considered questions of style in some essays, Hatzfeld's discussion of mystical sources centered on particular concepts and, in some cases, symbols common to the works of San Juan and other mystics. From 1940 on he directed a number of theses and dissertations at the Catholic University of America which advanced research in some areas suggested by his early works by focusing on the individual works of San Juan, and, more especially, on the major symbols in these works.[11]

Fr. Angel Custodio Vega, 0. S. A., expanded on the subject of Fray Luis de León's influence on San Juan de la Cruz suggested by both Dámaso Alonso and Pedro Salinas in Cumbres místicas; Fray

Luis de León y San Juan de la Cruz (encuentros y coincidencias) (Madrid: Aguilar, 1963). Vega did not limit himself to literary influences but considered as well the contact between the two men on other levels. In addition to their relationship as student and teacher, Vega discussed their similarities in doctrine, symbolism, and aesthetic interests. This study of the common doctrinal and literary ground shared by Fray Luis and San Juan was further augmented by Francisco García Lorca (De Fray Luis a San Juan; la escondida senda [Madrid: Castalia, 1972]), who discussed San Juan's debt to Fray Luis's translation of the Canticle of Canticles for many of his major symbols. García Lorca discounts the direct influence of Garcilaso's work on San Juan as well as that of Sebastián de Córdoba. He stresses instead the transmutation of much of Garcilaso's imagery in the works of Fray Luis, which, in turn, directly influenced San Juan's figurative language.[12]

The possible influence of Islamic mysticism on the works of both San Juan de la Cruz and Santa Teresa was first addressed by the Arabist, Miguel Asín Palacios, in a series of articles originally published in Al-Anadalus and later collected in his Obras escogidas I (Madrid: C. S. I. C., 1933). Luce López Baralt has continued this study in her work on San Juan de la Cruz y el Islam (Recinto de Río Piedras, P. R.: Universidad de Puerto Rico, 1985), which argues for direct and indirect Islamic influence on both style and imagery in the poetry of San Juan de la Cruz.

Concentrating on a single work, Jose L. Morales in El

Cántico espiritual de San Juan de la Cruz; su relación con el
Cantar de las Cantares y otras fuentes escriturísticas y
literarias (Madrid: Editorial de Espiritualidad, 1971), limited
his work to the poem and prose commentary of the Cántico
espiritual and its relation to the Canticle of Canticles. In a
strophe-by-strophe analysis he points out San Juan's debt to the
Biblical work while also summarizing the principal secular
sources the poet evokes. Morales also presents a valuable review
of the various critical opinions regarding individual strophes or
images through selective quotation but, unfortunately, adds
little of his own insight into San Juan's work.[13] In contrast,
Colin P. Thompson in The Poet and the Mystic: A Study of the
Cántico espiritual of San Juan de la Cruz (Oxford: Oxford
University Press, 1977) succinctly presents both the historical
background of the composition and influences at work in San
Juan's Cántico as well as an analysis of its literary merit and
its mystical content. Thompson approaches the work for the first
time as both literature and mystical treatise rather than from
one or the other perspective as has been the case heretofore.
Manuel Ballestero (Juan de la Cruz: de la angustia al olvido
[Barcelona: Ediciones Península, 1977]) provides a similar
analysis of the Subida del Monte Carmelo, foregoing the
historical perspective in order to concentrate on the literary,
psychological, and phenomenological aspects of negation in the
Subida.

Other distinguished poets evinced interest in literary

aspects of San Juan's three major poems, the Noche oscura, the Cántico espiritual, and the Llama de amor viva. In the Charles Eliot Norton lectures at Harvard University in 1957-1958,[14] Jorge Guillén discussed "The Ineffable Language of Mysticism" in the works of San Juan. Beginning with an analysis of each poem, Guillén initially put aside the saint's own explanations of his work in order to adduce the purely poetic statement of human love present in each. Next turning to the spiritual interpretations which accompanied the poems, Guillén showed the relationship which existed between San Juan's commentaries and their scriptural foundations. In addition, he, too, discussed San Juan's work in apposition to some of his literary predecessors and successors, such as Berceo, Góngora, Bécquer and Miró. Unlike other critics, he was not so much interested in tracing sources as he was in discerning the corroboration of San Juan's mystical experience in Biblical examples. Finally, he turned to the figurative language of the poems in order to discover the key with which to unlock the mysteries of a poetry which he described as "everything: illumination and perfection."[15]

Following the lead of his contemporaries, the poet Gabriel Celaya also devoted a chapter of his Exploración de la poesía (Barcelona: Seix Barral, 1964). to a consideration of "La poesía de vuelta en San Juan de la Cruz," an examination of the uniquely literary contributions of San Juan from a secular point of view, "desde esta ladera." His work includes as well essays on the poetry of Herrera and Bécquer. Describing San Juan's poetry, he insists that one must "distinguir entre la experiencia mística propiamente dicha y la operación poética que la plasma," yet, interestingly, he turns to San Juan's commentaries in order to discover the key to that poetic operation which creates a poem. From the poetic theory which he gleans from the commentaries, Celaya turns to the lyrics themselves and discovers what he considers the essence of San Juan's poetry: "esa Poesía sólo puede comprenderse como algo 'de vuelta': es decir, no como una marcha atrás sino como una recuperación dialéctica, cuyos términos quizás sea posible transparentar a través de la terminología doctrinal de nuestro autor."[16] Rather than the doctrine of nothingness usually associated with San Juan, Celaya sees the saint as a "Doctor de Todo."

Evident in much of the recent scholarship focusing on the literary merit of San Juan's poetry is the tendency to discuss it in relation to equally renowned poets. Alonso, Salinas, Guillén, and Celaya may pay homage to the mystical intent proposed by the poet, but they choose to concentrate on the saint's work as literature. In doing so, they juxtapose his poetic contributions with those of other poets whose works may manifest little or no religious sentiments. While Alonso does touch on the question of possible sources of influence in particular images present in San Juan's works, his primary purpose, like that of his fellow poets, remains the peculiar contribution of the mystic to the body of Spanish literature. When he and his contemporaries juxtapose San Juan's poems with those of others, their purpose is to compare, directly or indirectly, the works as works. Their essays are not source studies, therefore, but comparative criticism in its purest form. They show how different poets deal with reality, language, style, or poetry itself, employing in the process imagery and symbolism analogous yet distinct.

Numerous articles have followed these general discussions of San Juan's works and have dealt in turn with individual poems or individual images. The dominant imagery of night, flame, and light have received the greatest attention, as have the three principal poems. Unfortunately, careful consideration of San Juan's commentaries in conjunction with the poems has not often occurred. The highly doctrinal nature of the commentaries with their allegorical reading of the poems strikes many as too restrictive while an incomplete analysis of the poem, "En una noche oscura," found in the Subida-Noche diptych inhibits analysis of poem and commentary as a single unit. Nevertheless, as José Luis Aranguren observes in his study of San Juan's works:

> . . . las obras de San Juan de al Cruz no consisten ni
> en poemas ni en tratados de teología mística, sino en
> ese género único que es el poema-comentario . . . . La
> espléndida unidad poema-comentario se abre a la más
> amplia poesía-doctrina experiencia o vida (en
> comunidad).[17]

For a complete understanding of San Juan's message, therefore, consideration of poems and commentaries as units is essential.

Equally important to a study of both San Juan's and Santa Teresa's mystical and literary message is the necessity of looking at their imagery as a whole. Treating individual images

in isolation necessarily distorts the perception of the overall
effect achieved in the authors' works. In his study of the
romances of chivalry, Jessie L. Weston (<u>From Ritual to Romance</u>
[Garden City, N.Y.: Doubleday, 1957]) touches the heart of the
matter at issue in isolating individual images from the body of
the work in which they appear. He writes:

> . . . there is one point which I would desire to
> emphasize, <u>viz</u>., the imperative necessity for treating
> the Symbols or Talismans, call them what we will, on
> the same principle as we have treated the incidents of
> the story, i.e., as a connected whole. That they be
> not separated the one <u>from</u> the other, and made the
> subject of independent treatment, but that they be
> regarded in their relation the one <u>to</u> the other, and
> that no theory of origin be held admissible which does
> not allow for that relation as a primitive and
> indispensable factor. (p. 67)

What Weston says of the chivalric novels applies with equal force
to the works of the mystics. While night is without question a
dominant image in San Juan's work just as water is in that of
Santa Teresa, both writers incorporate these images into a much
broader aggregation of literary and mystical language. Only by
considering as far as possible the entire spectrum of their
imagery can the reader understand the multifaceted message they
wish to convey.

The lack of autograph manuscripts of San Juan's works,
however, adds a further complication to the critical
consideration of his poems and prose.[18] A question first posed
by Dom Philippe Chevalier, O.S.B., "Le Cantique spirituel de
saint Jean de la Croix a-t-il été interpolé?"(<u>BH</u>, 24 [1922],
307-42) and later answered by him in a series of articles

appearing in La Vie Spirituelle-Supplément from 1926 through 1931, has cast doubt on the authenticity of all but the first redaction of the Cántico espiritual (Cántico A). Debate concerning the different versions has produced a large body of scholarship devoted to this single topic which may be divided into three distinct groups. One group, made up primarily of Spanish Carmelites, accepts both redactions as equally authentic. A second, smaller group admits of three redactions (Cánticos A, A', and B) considered equally authentic. The third group, comprised chiefly of French scholars such as Chevalier and Baruzi, accepts the validity of only the first redaction and finds profound transformations in Cántico B.[19] The transformations noted by the third group concern the marginalia of the second redaction (B) but, more importantly, the rearrangement of strophes in Cántico B with accompanying changes in the commentary. While generally conceding with some reservations the clarification of the doctrinal presentation wrought by the changes of Cántico B, the supporters of Cántico A's exclusive authenticity decry the poorer poem which results from the transformations. Authors principally interested in San Juan's poetry have usually accepted the arguments of the proponents of Cántico A or have chosen to discuss this redaction alone since its authenticity is accepted by all groups.

Two critics who accept both redactions as equally authentic present cogent and convincing arguments in separate articles. Inez Isabel Macdonald in her article "The Two Versions of the

Cántico espiritual," (MLR, 25 [1930], 165-84), observes that "a purely literary consideration of the poem is out of place when we are dealing with a work the purpose of which is not literary perfection, but the advance of the soul in the mystic life." She goes on in her article to show that the second redaction is a "conscious improvement on the first as a mystical treatise." While Cántico A expressed San Juan's personal experience of mystical union, Cántico B presents a "well meditated scheme of life."[20] In a more recent article, Colin P. Thompson, in "The Authenticity of the Second Redaction of the Cántico espiritual in the Light of the Doctrinal Additions," (BHS, 51 [1974], 244-54), takes up the main points of Macdonald's presentation. After enumerating the changes in the order and number of strophes in the poem, Thompson considers the significant emendations in the text of the commentary. By relating the principal changes to San Juan's other works, Thompson shows that Cántico B is in harmony with San Juan's doctrine as presented in the other three commentaries. In a tone of exasperation he writes: "sometimes, reading Chevalier, one gets the distinct impression that San Juan was miraculously preserved from what is evidently the sin of changing his mind!" Save for this personal lapse, however, Thompson and Macdonald before him defend the authenticity of Cántico B by reminding their readers that San Juan is first a mystic and secondly a poet. As such, one sees in his second redaction "the mind of a systematic thinker applying itself to his earlier, more spontaneous lyrical creation, so rich in language, so evocative in atmosphere, expressing the inexpressible."[21] Since the present study intends to examine both the poetic and doctrinal aspects of San Juan's works, the second redaction of the Cántico espiritual will be used exclusively.

As in the case of San Juan, critical attention to the works of Santa Teresa de Jesús experienced a resurgence as a result of the four-hundredth anniversary commemoration of her death in 1982. Prior to that year, Santa Teresa's writings did not receive as much attention from literary scholars as those of her protégé. Although her works were published soon after her death (Salamanca: Guillermo Foquel, 1588), and subsequently appeared in numerous editions and translations, the literary criticism generated by them was less rigorous and less voluminous than that which deals with San Juan. Since the autograph manuscripts of her works have been preserved, no serious question comparable to that surrounding the Cántico espiritual arises concerning Santa Teresa's major prose works. Consequently, the bulk of the literature concerning Santa Teresa has dwelt on biographical, doctrinal, and devotional aspects of her life and works.

Source studies have tended to follow clues provided by the saint herself for possible influences from other authors or have concentrated on the cultural milieu in which she wrote. For the most part, the majority of critical studies on Santa Teresa's works have appeared only in the twentieth century. Although some nineteenth-century Spanish novelists such as Juan Valera and

Emilia Pardo Bazán[22] praised her as a writer, neither author examined her work in depth. In his article "Les Lectures de sainte Thérèse" (BH, 10 [1908], 17-67), Alfred Morel-Fatio reviewed the sources which Santa Teresa cited directly and suggested others which she may have known since copies or translations were available at the time she was writing. Gaston Etchegoyen expanded on Morel-Fatio's study in L'Amour divin; essai sur les sources de sainte Thérèse (Bordeaux: Feret et Fils, 1923), by tracing Santa Teresa's debt to other spiritual writers for some doctrinal concepts. Robert Ricard has devoted much of his research to the broader context of sixteenth-century Spain in order to show how Santa Teresa reflects the cultural and intellectual ambience of that age, while Luce López Baralt has suggested certain parallels between Santa Teresa's castle imagery in the Moradas and Islamic sources.[23] The Carmelite scholars, Efrén de la Madre de Dios and Otger Steggink, supplemented their introduction to the Obras completas (3rd ed. [Madrid: Editorial Católica, 1972]) with a longer study of the life and times of Santa Teresa.[24] They further expanded this aspect of their research in the three volume Santa Teresa y su tiempo (Salamanca: Universidad Pontificia de Salamanca, 1982-1984), a comprehensive study of the historical and cultural context of Santa Teresa's life and reform that draws on her works, correspondence, and other primary source material. The focus of both of these works, however, remains essentially biographical and historical rather than literary.[25]

The French scholar, Rodolphe Hoornaert, provided the first comprehensive study of Santa Teresa's entire literary production in Sainte Thérèse écrivain: son milieu, ses facultés, son oeuvre (Paris: Desclée de Brouwer, 1922). In it he attempted to correlate biographical and historical facts concerning the author with an analysis of style and influences present in her works. Hoornaert and some of his contemporaries in Teresian criticism, however, have tended more to enumerate and classify her images rather than to elucidate them.[26] While valuable as an introductory discussion, Ramón Menéndez Pidal's essay, "El estilo de Santa Teresa,"[27] does not examine in any detail her works or her figurative language. Nevertheless, it does provide a good overview of her style. In La poesía de Santa Teresa (Madrid: Editorial Católica, 1972) Angel Custodio Vega collected those poems penned by or attributed to Santa Teresá and attempted to compare them to some of San Juan's works in terms of common themes or images. As the author indicates, however, the doubtful attribution to Santa Teresa of so many of the poems necessarily constrains his discussion. More successful is Victor G. de la Concha (El arte literario de Santa Teresa [Barcelona: Ariel, 1978]), who synthesizes previous scholarship devoted to the saint's literary contributions by focusing on her esthetic, poetic, and rhetorical style in detail. Concha comes closest to examining the figurative language employed by Santa Teresa in many of her mystical works in order to discern the patterns present in her images and symbols. In contrast, John Welch, O.

Carm. (<u>Spiritual</u> <u>Pilgrims</u> [New York: Paulist Press, 1982]), approaches the major imagery of Santa Teresa's <u>Moradas</u> from a Jungian perspective with the intention of providing his readers spiritual direction rather than literary commentary. In the majority of cases, therefore, critics have limited themselves to studying the dominant images of castle and water, the colloquialisms and elliptical style of some of the saint's works, or specific didactic considerations.

In 1982 the quatercentenary commemoration of the death of Santa Teresa led to the publication of a diversity of works on Teresian subjects touching all aspects of the saint's life, works, and place in history as well as literature. International conferences published articles considering Santa Teresa in the broad context of her place in the history of mysticism and literature both inside and outside Spain.[28] In addition to the compendia of articles which came out of these conferences, individual works dealt with particular questions of her life and accomplishments. Rosa Rossi's <u>Teresa de Avila</u>. <u>Biografía de una escritora</u> (Barcelona: Icaria, 1984), originally published in Italian (Roma: Editori Riuniti, 1983), correlates events in the life of the saint with particular passages from her writings that enhance the personal dimension of her literary production. The authors of <u>Cinco ensayos de Santa Teresa de Jesús</u> (Madrid: Editorial Nacional, 1984) focus principally on sociological implications of her life and works, while José María Poveda Arino (<u>La psicología de Santa Teresa de Jesús</u> [Madrid: Rialp, 1984]), combines a psychological profile of the saint based on her autobiographical writings with an extrapolation of her psychological method gleaned from her didactic works. Nevertheless, no single significant study of Santa Teresa as literary figure appeared among these critical works.

As contemporaries, co-reformers of the Carmelite order, fellow mystics, Doctors of the Church, and friends, Santa Teresa de Jesús and San Juan de la Cruz understandably share a common historical and doctrinal ground. In spite of the voluminous bibliography available for both of these Spanish Carmelites, a comprehensive scholarly study of their common literary ground and their contributions to literary style is still lacking. Even though both writers shared a common interest in describing their mystical experience, few critics have attempted to deal with the similarities of imagery and symbolism present in their works. A study by Antonio Sánchez Moguel[29] failed to probe their works comparatively, while Arthur Symons' article, ("The Poetry of Santa Teresa and San Juan de la Cruz," Contemporary Review, 75 [1899], 542-51), dealt more with the spirit than the substance of either writer's work. Some brief articles have compared the glosses on the traditional song "Vivo sin vivir en mí" by both authors,[30] yet few have studied their shared problem of mystical expression. María Jesús Fernández Leborans (Luz y oscuridad en la mística española [Madrid: Cupsa Editorial, 1978]) compared both authors' use and development of light and darkness in their mystical works from a structuralist point of view.

While a thorough-going analysis of light and obscurity in their works, the study limited itself to these twin images without considering the whole of their literary language.[31]

By collating the mystical works of both Santa Teresa and San Juan de la Cruz, the manner in which each approaches the conundrum of adequately describing mystical union is more clearly discerned. Patterns of development in the use and complexity of figurative language appear which show the intricate interrelationship present in what, on the surface, appear to be isolated and divergent images. Beyond the dominant images of night, flame, light, and water, the prose and poetry of the saints use everyday human experience as the vehicles of the tropes by which they convey the whole of their mystical experience. Seen in conjunction with the tenors, however, the vehicles of their metaphorical writing articulate not only the mystical experience but also a world view which unifies the diversity of creation.

This work, therefore, analyzes the imagery derived from fauna, flora, objects, the social and physical body, activities, and the elements in order to discover the underlying message it conveys in the mystics' works. After considering the problems of expression confronting the mystical author and the solutions he or she utilizes in order to speak of mystical experience, the study next examines each group of images enumerated above. By means of intertextual comparison among the works of both writers, an overall perspective of the function and symbolic meaning attributed to individual images emerges. The debt of the Carmelite mystics to secular and spiritual sources that preceded their compositions demonstrates that, rather than writing in a literary vacuum, Santa Teresa and San Juan belong to a rich literary tradition which they incorporate into their mystical works. At the same time, their innovative use of imagery compares favorably with that of their poetic successors whether religious or secular, so that the mystics' elaboration of traditional imagery and consequent enrichment of it for subsequent generations broadens our understanding and appreciation of their contribution to Spanish letters. As the examination of the mystical imagery of both writers unfolds, it will be apparent that this figurative language articulates a statement at once simple yet profound concerning the mystics' apprehension of divinity in their individual experiences of union.

The inspiration, preparation, and publication of this work would not have been possible without the aid and encouragement of numerous individuals, institutions, and libraries. The original research opportunity was provided by the Fulbright-Hays committee who funded a year in Spain. Subsequent aid from the American Council of Learned Societies, Duke University, and Tufts University made it possible to complete research and bring the book to print. Among the libraries that provided me access to their materials and assisted in my investigations were the Biblioteca Nacional and the Consejo Superior de Investigaciones

Superiores in Madrid, the Teresianum in Rome, the Biblioteca Teresiana of Avila, Whitefriars Hall and the Catholic University of America in Washington, D. C., and the libraries of the University of California at Santa Barbara, Duke University, and Tufts University.

I am especially grateful to those individuals who encouraged and directed me in my studies. My thanks go to the late Arturo Serrano-Plaja for sparking my interest in Golden Age prose and José Luis Aranguren for directing my initial research in Spain. By graciously allowing me access to his private library, Don Pedro Sainz Rodríguez enabled me to pursue my interest in the mystics and to focus my work. A special word of thanks goes to Bruce W. Wardropper of Duke whose incisive comments and perceptive criticism of my work has provided invaluable direction in the formulation and writing of the final draft. I also owe a debt of gratitude to my sister, Maggie, who generously offered her time and expertise in the preparation of numerous drafts of the book. To my parents, Walter and Elizabeth Howe, who have aided me in ways I cannot begin to count but will always appreciate, I respectfully dedicate this work.

Introduction

NOTES

[1] "De la poesía mística en España. Discursos de recepción en la Real Academia Española," in San Isidoro, Cervantes y otros estudios (Madrid: Espasa-Calpe, 1941), p. 34.

[2] He includes in the term "poetry" the prose mystical treatises of Santa Teresa as well. See ibid., p. 61.

[3] The most important of which are collected in Saint John of the Cross and Other Lectures and Addresses 1920-1945 (London: Faber and Faber, Ltd., n. d.) and Saint Teresa of Jesus and Other Essays and Addresses (London: Faber and Faber, 1951.

[4] Besides his translations of the complete works of both San Juan and Santa Teresa (Complete Works of Saint John of the Cross, trans. from the critical edition of P. Silverio de Santa Teresa, O. C. D. and ed. by E. Allison Peers, 3 vols. [London: Burns, Oates and Washbourne, 1934-35] and Complete works of St. Teresa of Jesus, trans. from the critical edition of P. Silverio de Santa Teresa, O. C. D., ed. by E. Allison Peers, 3 vols. [New York: Sheed and Ward, 1946], Peers has also published two brief, but excellent biographies of both writers. See Mother of Carmel (London: SCM Press, 1945) and Spirit of Flame (New York: Morehouse-Gorman Co., 1945).

[5] Among the works of the Fundación pertinent to a study of the

Spanish Carmelites are: Melquiades Andrés Martín, Los Recogidos.
Nueva visión de la mística española (1500-1700) (Madrid:
Fundación Universitaria Española Seminario "Suárez", 1975);
Manuel Morales Borrero, La geometría mística del alma en la
literatura española del siglo de oro (Madrid: Fundación
Universitaria Española Seminario "Suarez", 1975); Daniel de
Pablo, Amor y conocimiento en la vida mística (Madrid: 1979);
Baldomero Jiménez Duque and Luis Morales Oliver, San Juan de la
Cruz, Conferencias pronunciadas en la Fundación Universitaria
Española los días 9 y 11 de diciembre de 1975 con motivo del
Tercer Centenario de su beatificación (Madrid: 1977); Pablo M.
Garrido, O. Carm., Santa Teresa, San Juan de la Cruz y los
Carmelitas españoles (Madrid: 1982); and Jeannine Poitrey,
Vocabulario de Santa Teresa (Madrid: Universidad Pontificia de
Salamanca y Fundación Universitaria Española, 1983).

[6] These lectures were later translated by Edith Fishtine
Helman and collected in Reality and the Poet in Spanish Poetry
(Baltimore: The Johns Hopkins Press, 1940). A second edition with
an introduction by Jorge Guillén appeared in 1966.

[7] Alonso, La poesía, 4th ed., 1966, p. 176.

[8] A very weak counter-argument to Alonso's thesis was
presented by Fr. Emeterio G. Setién de Jesús-María, O. C. D. in
Las raíces de la poesía sanjuanista y Dámaso Alonso (Burgos: El
Monte Carmelo, 1950), in which he disallowed secular influences
on the poet's works. Other critical opinion concerning San

Juan's works was loosely and subjectively collected by Fr. Sabino de Jesús, O. C. D., in San Juan de la Cruz y la crítica literaria (Santiago de Chile: Talleres Gráficos "San Vicente," 1942). Scanty and incomplete documentation as well as the lack of the author's own critical evaluation of the Carmelite mystic's works mar the study.

[9] A second edition with additional essays appeared in 1968.

[10] The influence of mystical writings from the Low countries on the Spanish mystics has been discussed Pierre Groult, Les Mystiques des Pays-Bas et la littérature espagnole du seizième siècle (Louvain: Uystpruyst, 1927), a study which Hatzfeld utilized in his comparison of the language of San Juan and Jan van Ruysbroeck. It has subsequently been translated into Spanish by Rodrigo A. Molina and republished as Los místicos de los países bajos y la literatura espiritual española del siglo XVI (Madrid: Fundación Universitaria Española, 1976).

[11] See for example, Tierney J. Cahill, "The Symbol of the Flame in the Works of San Juan de la Cruz," unpublished M. A. thesis: Catholic University of America, 1950; Eugene F. Kilkenny, "Analysis of the 'Cántico espiritual' of San Juan de la Cruz in the Light of the Biblical Canticum Canticorum," unpublished M. A. thesis: 1950; Sr. Mririam Therese Olabarrieta, S. C. N., "Simple Imagery in the Poems of St. John of the Cross," unpublished M. A. thesis: 1954; Sr. Mary Casimira Haduch, C. S. S. F., "Classification of Some Symbols and Similes in La noche oscura

del alma of San Juan de la Cruz," unpublished M. A. thesis: 1956; Olabarrieta, The Influence of Ramon Llull on the Style of the Early Spanish Mystics and Santa Teresa (Washington, D. C.: The Catholic University of America Press, 1963). Sr. Rosa Maria Icaza's study of the Cántico espiritual, The Sytlistic Relationship between Poetry and Prose in the "Cántico espiritual" of San Juan de la Cruz (Washington, D. C.: The Catholic University of America Press, 1957), considers both doctrinal and stylistic aspects in an analysis of the relationship between the poem and its accompanying prose commentary.

[12] José Manuel Polo de Bernabé, "Tensión metafórica y transmisión del lenguaje poético: de Garcilaso a San Juan," REH, 16 (1982), 275-85, continues the discussion of the relationship between Garcilaso's poetic language and that of San Juan.

[13] A student of Morales' at St. John's University of New York, Sr. Teresa Maria Benedicta of the Cross, O. C. D., in The Symbols of the Animals, Flowers and Fruits in the Poetry of the Spiritual Canticle of St. John of the Cross (Salamanca: Graf. Ortega, 1972), examines some of the images of the Cántico and reviews some of the scholarship regarding their interpretation.

[14] Later collected by the author in Language and Poetry: Some Poets of Spain (Cambridge: Harvard University Press, 1961). A Spanish edition, Lenguaje y poesía (Madrid: Revista de Occidente, 1962), is also available.

[15] Guillén, Language, pp. 93 and 121.

[16] Celaya, pp. 158 and 176.

[17] José Luis Aranguren, San Juan de la Cruz (Madrid: Júcar, 1973), pp. 41-42.

[18] For a resumé of the textual problems, see Fr. Silverio de Santa Teresa, O. C. D., the volume entitled Preliminares of Obras completas de San Juan de la Cruz, I (Burgos: El Monte Carmelo, 1929), pp. 172-84.

[19] A concise presentation of the main points of the debate can be found in the Dictionnaire de spiritualité, ascetique et mystique, doctrine et histoire, ed. Marcel Viller, S. J., et al., 11 vols. (Paris: Gabriel Beauchesne et Fils, 1937), s. v. St. Jean de la Croix. Eulogio de la Virgen del Carmen, O. C. D., in El Cántico espiritual. Trayectoria histórica del texto (Paris: Desclée, 1967), provides the first group's counter-arguments to Chevalier's conclusions while Jean Krynen in Le Cantique spirituel de saint Jean de la Croix commenté et refondu au XVIIe siècle. Un regard sur l'histoire de l'exégese du Cantique de Jaen in Acta Salmanticensia: Filosofía y letras, III (Salamanca: Universidad de Salamanca, 1948), summarizes the theses of the third group. Fr. Eulogio's book also contains a comprehensive bibliography of articles and books dealing with both sides of the discussion. Recent editions of the Cántico and of San Juan's poetry continue the debate. Cristóbal Cuevas García reiterates

the textual arguments in his edition of the poem and prose commentary (Cántico espiritual. Poesías [Madrid: Alhambra, 1979]), finding all three versions authentic. Eulogio Pacho presents an exhaustive intertextual analysis and comparative edition of Cántico A and A' (Cántico espiritual [Madrid: Fundación Universitaria Española, 1981]), while in his edition of San Juan's poetry (Poesía [Madrid: Cátedra, 1984]), Domingo Yndurain repeats the conclusions of Pacho and Cuevas García before indicating his preference for Cántico B. Additional comments on yet other variants of the Cántico question appear in Roger Duvivier, "De l'ineffabilité mystique à la confusion critique? Un Débat de méthode à propos de la genèse du Cántico espiritual" in Wayne H. Finke, ed., Estudios de historia, literatura y arte hispánicos ofrecidos a Rodrigo A. Molina (Madrid: Insula, 1977), pp. 109-27; and André Berthelot, "Sobre la 'Oncena lira' del Cántico espiritual de San Juan de la Cruz," PSA, 86 (1977), 115-26, who finds a variant of Cántico A which includes the disputed strophe 11.

[20] Macdonald, pp. 166 and 180.

[21] Thompson, "The Authenticity," pp. 252 and 254. Thompson repeats and expands his defense of Cántico B in The Poet and the Mystic, pp. 21-59.

[22] Valera's defense of her literary contributions came in the form of an address to the Royal Spanish Academy, "Elogio de Santa Teresa de Jesús," in 1897, which was later reprinted in Nuevos

estudios críticos, III (Madrid: M. Tello, 1888), pp. 387-416. Pardo Bazán included Santa Teresa among the four authoresses she considered in Lecciones de literatura. Cuatro españolas (Madrid: Ibero-Americana, 1914).

[23] Ricard's interest is especially evident in his essay, "Notas y materiales para el estudio del 'socratismo cristiano' en Santa Teresa y en los espirituales españoles," which appears in Estudios de literatura religiosa española (Madrid: Gredos, 1964), pp. 22-147. In Etudes sur sainte Thérèse (Paris: Institut d'Etudes Hispaniques, 1968), he considers sources and symbolism. Like the earlier Estudios, these essays first appeared as articles in French and Spanish publications prior to being collected. Although López Baralt has examined Islamic influences on San Juan in greater depth, she has also addressed similar questions in regard to Santa Teresa in "Santa Teresa de Jesús y Oriente: El símbolo de los siete castillos del alma," Sin Nombre, 13 (4) (July-Sept. 1983), 25-44.

[24] Tiempo y vida de Santa Teresa (Madrid: Editorial Católica, 1968).

[25] So, too, does the Introducción a la lectura de Santa Teresa (Madrid: Editorial de Espiritualidad, 1978), a collection of articles examining historical, biographical, and doctrinal questions surrounding her literary works.

[26] See for example, Fr. Luis Urbano, O. P., "Las alegorías

predilectas de Santa Teresa," Ciencia Tomista, 28 (1923), 52-71, and "Las analogías predilectas de Santa Teresa de Jesús," Ciencia Tomista, 28 (1923), 364-83 and 29 (1924), 350-70, who lists the major images present in her works but offers little analysis beyond an occasional comparison with similar examples in other writers.

[27] While part of the essay first appeared in Escorial in 1941, the entire text was later published in La lengua de Cristóbal Colón, El estilo de Santa Teresa, y otros estudios sobre el siglo XVI (Madrid: Espasa-Calpe, 1942), pp. 119-142.

[28] As their titles indicate, the Actas del Congreso Internacional Teresiano Salamanca 4-7 Octubre 1982, ed. Teófanes Egido Martínez, Victor García de la Concha, y Olegaro González de Cardenal, 2 vols. (Salamanca: Universidad de Salamanca, 1983); and Santa Teresa y la literatura mística hispánica. Actas del I Congreso Internacional sobre Santa Teresa y la mística hispánica (Madrid: Ediséis, 1984); are compendia of articles and papers presented at international colloquia held in Spain. At the same time, the journals, Carmelite Studies (Centenary of Saint Teresa, ed. John Sullivan, O. C. D. [Washington, D. C.: ICS Publications, 1984]) and Letras de Deusto (IV Centenario de Santa Teresa (1582-1982) 24 [Julio-Diciembre 1982]), published special editions devoted solely to Teresian studies. All of these anthologies combined studies of religious dimensions of the saint's works with those focused on her contributions to

literature.

[29] El lenguaje de Santa Teresa de Jesús. Juicio comparativo de sus escritos con los de San Juan de la Cruz y otros clásicos de su época (Madrid: 1882. Published posthumously in Madrid; Clásica Española, 1915).

[30] See for example Helmut Hatzfeld, "Two Types of Mystical Poetry (Santa Teresa and San Juan de la Cruz)," American Benedictine Review, 1 (1951), 421-62, and Hilario S. Saenz, "Notas a la glosa 'Vivo sin vivir en mí' de Santa Teresa y de San Juan de la Cruz," MLQ, 13 (1952), 405-408.

[31] Recently, María Jesús Mancho Duque, El símbolo de la noche en San Juan de la Cruz (Salamanca: Ediciones Universidad de Salamanca, 1982), examined the symbol of night in its lexical and semantic context within San Juan's works. An unpublished doctoral dissertation by Mary Lou Smitheram ("The Symbol of Night in the Works of Santa Teresa de Jesús and San Juan de la Cruz" Ph. D. Diss., University of California: Santa Barbara, 1977), compared the use of night in the works of both mystics. Studia Mystica 8 (1985), 38-75, published a group of articles focusing on the use of night in the works of Osuna, Santa Teresa, San Juan, and secular love poetry of the siglo de oro.

Chapter 1

THE PROBLEM OF MYSTICAL EXPRESSION

The problem of mystical expression begins with the word
"mystic" itself. Rooted in the Greek mysterion, the term remains
as elusive as the secrets of the mystery sects who gave it its
name. Consequently, mysticism elicits a variety of definitions
among the many writers who address the subject.[1] While the
principles of mystical thought in the West were first enunciated
in the works of Plato, Dom Edward Cuthbert Butler points out that
in the Latin Church the term used was not "mysticism" but
"contemplation". It is only in the Middle Ages that the
dissemination of the Divine Names and the Mystical Theology of
Pseudo-Dionysius, the Areopagite, lent popular currency to the
terms "mystic" and "mystical" in Christianity.[2] Like so much
verbal currency, however, the term mystic has suffered a
devaluation of meaning through the years, leading one writer to
deplore the current situation where "popular speech seized upon
the word and used it to designate a man carried away with any
irrational and enthusiastic idea: one hears of a mystique of
sport . . . that has no longer any relation to the word's
original meaning."[3] As a result, even the briefest review of

works devoted to mysticism reveals that the definitions of mystic and its related terms are as numerous as the books devoted to the subject.

In his study of Christian mysticism, William Inge traces the etymology and history of the term mystic in the west. Later in the same work he defines mysticism as "the attempt to realize, in thought and feeling, the immanence of the temporal in the eternal, and of the eternal in the temporal."[4] In contrast, Butler suggests a more specific understanding of mysticial union, wherein "the soul, already in this life, enters into conscious, immediate relationship with God" (p. 135). In his series of essays detailing the varieties of religious experience among which he included mysticism, William James cautions that the words "'mysticism' and 'mystical' are often used as terms of mere reproach, to throw at any opinion which we regard as vague and vast and sentimental, and without a base in either facts or logic."[5] Nevertheless, he does examine mystical experience, distinguishing its characteristics and reducing them to four. He describes it as noetic, transient, passive, and ineffable (pp. 367-38). In a wholly different vein, the Spanish philosopher and novelist, Miguel de Unamuno, writes in the prologue to Niebla: "y luego hay la mística, una metafísica de la religión que nace de la sensualidad de la combatividad."[6] At the same time, Unamuno also authored a more serious reflection on mysticism which he describes as a desire for the absolute and perfect made substance, an introduction to the Beatific Vision, and a longing to arrive at the ideal of the universe and of humanity.[7] Finally, in her seminal study of mysticism, Evelyn Underhill writes:

> Mysticism is seen to be a highly specialized form of that search for reality, for heightened and complete life, which we have found to be a constant characterisic of human consciousness. It is largely prosecuted by that 'spiritual spark,' that transcendental faculty which, though the life of our life, remains below the threshold in ordinary men.[8]

What is evident from this brief catalogue of definitions is the elusiveness of the term mystic, which today is actually applied almost indiscriminately to any and all writers, works, experiences, or sects whose exact nature eludes definition. The essential mystery of the mystic and his experience makes him fascinating to a society seeking a key with which to unlock the meaning of the universe. In the modern idiom, therefore, a mystic seems to be any one whose life or work remains a mystery; one who possesses or claims to possess some secret knowledge; or, quite simply, one who is just difficult to comprehend. If the word is to retain any significance, however, a more precise application is in order.

As noted, the definitions of a mystic are as numerous as the books written about mysticism, yet from the wealth of definitions, some general characteristics can be adduced. In the present study, mysticism may be understood as a desire on the part of certain spiritually advanced individuals for union in this life with the Absolute, God. In the experience of this union, the mystic claims to receive certain knowledge of ultimate truth which, by its very nature, is essentially incommunicable. This ineffable aspect is what cloaks mystical writings in their apparent obscurity; for, as San Juan de la Cruz remarks: "no hay vocablos para declarar cosas tan subidas de Dios como en estas almas pasan" (Ll. II, 21).[9]

The ultimate goal of the mystic quest is a permanent union with the object of the soul's desire, which for the Christian is God. Since that end can only be fully realized in eternity, the proximate goal while still on earth is both the unitive experience, which is necessarily a passing phenomenon, and an increase in love. Hence, "the locus of the mystical experience is the will rather than the intellect."[10] This is true not only in the preparatory stages through which the mystic may pass in his quest for union, but also in the act of will that manifests itself in love. What is equally evident is that mystical experience does not always or necessarily result in an act of explanation to others, because the mystic feels no inherent need to describe union to anyone. In point of fact, most mystical literature results from requests made to mystics by religious superiors or would-be initiates to describe to them both union and the means of attaining it. While we are familiar with those mystics who responded to such requests, there are undoubtedly others who, for whatever reasons, did not commit their mystical insights to writing. Whether a mystic writes or not, it is important to remember that the experience of union does not bestow on him the literary acumen necessary to such a task.

Rather, as Henri Bremond contends:

> It is not the normal function of the mystic in the Church to teach. The lights they receive in contemplation not only do not impose on them the duty of consecrating themselves to that task, but--and this is the important point--they do not themselves give them the means of doing so.[11]

Few dispute that San Juan and Santa Teresa de Jesús are mystics. In the four centuries which have passed since their deaths, theologians and literary critics alike have ascribed the appelation to both of them. For their spiritual works, they are both called Doctors of the Church, while San Juan has earned the added title of mystical doctor. Spurred on by obedience to a confessor, as in the case of Santa Teresa, or the inquiries of initiates in the contemplative life, as in San Juan's, the mystical writer attempts to clarify the steps to union for those who would follow his example. The mystic's intention is to elucidate the via mystica, not to obfuscate. The obscurity which seems to cloud their writings derives from the ineffability of their experience and the inadequacy of finite language exactly to express the infinite. The mystics face what Jorge Guillén calls insufficient language.

Aware of the almost insurmountable problem of mystical expression, San Juan de la Cruz, in the prologue to the Cántico espiritual, summarizes the essential difficulties facing the mystical writer in a series of questions:

> . . . Porque ¿quién podrá escrebir lo que a las almas amorosas donde El mora hace entender?, ¿y quién podrá manifestar con palabras lo que las hace sentir?, ¿y quién finalmente, lo que las hace desear? Cierto,

nadie lo puede; cierto ni ellas mesmas por quien pasa
lo pueden; porque ésta es la causa por qué con figuras,
comparaciones y semejanzas, antes rebosan algo de lo
que sienten y de la abundancia del espíritu vierten
secretos y misterios que con razones lo declaran. (CE.
Prólogo, 1)

In these few sentences San Juan touches the heart of the mystic's
difficulty in writing of his experience. This dilemma is not,
however, unique to the mystical writer. Assuredly all writers
grapple with the inadequacies of the language and their own
deficiencies as authors in trying to express themselves.
Nevertheless, the very subject matter of mysticism creates unique
obstacles for the writer who would tell of the steps to union.
The mystic's is a difficult task. He is attempting to translate
an essentially incommunicable experience into understandable
form. Knowing, as he does, that this experience is the province
of very few, he cannot be assured that his readers will
understand his meaning fully. Only those who actually experience
similar union can comprehend all of the ramifications of what the
mystic writes. On the other hand, the deficiencies of the author
who chooses human love as his theme may be minimized by his
readers who are able to relate what he says to their own
experience.

In a special sense the mystic shares with the poet the
insufficiency of language noted by Guillen as well as by Celaya
and Salinas in their respective essays on Spanish poetry. The
mystic and poet both struggle "with words, and words have many
weaknesses and limitations."[12] The similarities are not
confined to expression alone, however; for, like the mystical,

the poetic experience partakes of the transcendent and the ineffable at times. Thus, the poet imitates the mystic writer when he seeks to translate his experience of a higher reality into comprehensible terms. Nevertheless, even though poetic vision may resemble the mystical, yet if differs from it in degree. In effect, "what art seeks and sometimes finds, mystical experience knows, and it knows by affinity and love."[13] Jacques Maritain denotes fundamental differences in the very nature of poetic and mystical experience, explaining that "poetic experience is concerned with the created world and the enigmatic and innumerable relations of beings with each other; mystical experience with the principle of things in its own incomprehensible and supramundane unity."[14] When poetic and mystical experience converge, as they do in some writers, a blending of those twin concerns occurs.

Just as poetic and mystical experience differ in nature, so, too, does the poet differ significantly from the mystic in his reaction to his heightened perception of reality. Expression of the experience in the form of the literary work is essential to the poet but not to the mystic, for the "poet is not truly a poet until he has composed and achieved."[15] Patrick Grant refines the distinction further when he explains that

> the mystic has much in common with the poet, but with this difference: the poet is not essentially concerned with man's ultimate destiny, and the perfection he seeks is that of the poem he writes. Likewise, the mystic is not essentially concerned with art, but pronounces his vision of an ultimate synthesis in the One Source of all manifestation, within which our partial creative efforts will be taken up and made whole. (16)

Thus, while the poet's objective is to distill the experience in as pure a form as his talent and language allow, the mystic's goal is the experience itself with no concomitant necessity to express it in words. For the mystic, the experience of union is its own end. He feels no inherent need to describe it to others, for his function in the Church is not to teach but to aspire to and to realize union with the infinite. The mystical experience, therefore, does not automatically result in an attempt to explain or define it. Rather, the mystic writes as a "result of superabundance, a generous attempt at communication."[17]

However inadequate human language may be to deal with the infinite, it is the only language with which the mystic may work. Following the logic of St. Thomas Aquinas, all knowledge of the spiritual must be expressed in terms of the sensible. Thus, the mystic relies on "figuras, comparaciones y semejanzas" from the material world in order to reveal the mysteries of union with an infinite God. By analogies expressed in familiar language, the mystic, in the words of Jean Baruzi, "aspire à nommer et à definir ce qu'il aperçoit."[18]

In aspiring to name what he perceives, the mystical writer is really no different from any other author. It is the subject matter which sets the mystic apart from his secular counterpart. Nevertheless, he shares the same difficulties of expression. The vehicle a particular mystic chooses to convey his message depends largely on his or her background and abilities. St. Bernard of

Clairvaux and Meister Eckhart, for example, favor the sermon. The Victorines and Ruysbroeck rely on theological treatises while Ramon Llull cloaks his doctrine in the vocabulary of the romances of chivalry. Santa Teresa shows a predilection for colloquial prose. As more than one critic has pointed out, however, there are few true mystics who are also true poets, for rarely are the heights of mystical experience ascended by an unquestionably gifted poet. Although, in San Juan de la Cruz that combination of mystic and poet converges, nevertheless, one critic describes the crux of the poet-mystic's dilemna in expressing the inexpressible when he writes:

> Jean de la Croix n'écrit point de la poésie pour, au sens le plus noble du terme, 'faire de la littérature', comme un Luis de León, par exemple, mais parce que le langage poétique est le seul capable de lui permettre de tenter un extériorisation 'propédeutique' de son expérience mystique. Il tentera ensuite d'expliciter, non cette expérience--ce n'est pas humainement possible, seul de poème 'inspiré' pouvant en donner une approximation--mais les termes choisis ou subsconsciemment encontrés pour l'exprimer et surtout la communiquer, la faire partager à ses desciples, sans aucunement solliciter leur admiration littéraire.[19]

While the bulk of Santa Teresa's mystical writings are in prose, she no less than San Juan also struggles with the inadequacy of language to convey accurately to her readers the essence of her mystical experiences. In one instance she laments: "riéndome estoy de estas comparaciones, que no me contentan; mas no sé otras" (M. VII, 2, xiv).[20] Whether their mystical works are prose or poetry, however, both Spanish Carmelites seek an appropriate idiom for elucidating the steps to union as they invite their readers to consider the depths of God's infinite love. It is equally a divine mystery plumbed by chosen souls at God's discretion who, while he holds out to them the promise of union, does not guarantee literary acumen as well. Thus, each mystic who chooses to write approaches the problem with diverse literary tools derived from divergent educational backgrounds, aware that he or she is attempting to put in human terms the essence of an ineffable apprehension of ultimate reality.

For Santa Teresa, the tireless reformer who often wrote hurriedly to an unlettered audience, a simple, direct, colloquial prose style best served her literary ends. Although Menéndez Pidal remarks on her disinterest and even opposition to "todo lo que se puede llamar literatura," she is, nevertheless, "una brillante escritora de imágenes."[21] What she herself terms "harto groseras comparaciones" are, in fact, very effective similes based on the everyday experiences of sixteenth-century Castilian life. In massing image upon image, however, she creates what Helmut Hatzfeld describes as a garland of metaphors which ties together disparate images into multivalent statements concerning the mystical experience.[22]

Where Santa Teresa is the colloquial, ingenuous writer who boasted of rarely re-reading what she had written, San Juan is the careful craftsman of "symbolic-concrete poetry" and "direct-abstract prose."[23] While ostensibly intended as explanations of his mystical poems, the four prose commentaries differ from each other in organization and content. The Subida

del Monte Carmelo and the Noche oscura del alma use the same poem
as a point of departure for a doctrinal explanation of the
purgative stages of mystical advancement. Both works are only
partial commentaries on the poem. On the other hand, the Cántico
espiritual and the Llama de amor viva combine the doctrinal
message with a strophe-by-strophe allegorical analysis of the
poems on which they are based. Even at his most theological,
however, San Juan remains a poet, so that "there is no
understanding anything he says unless one brings to it the
imaginative breadth and the willingness to expand that great
poetry demands."[24]

As a poet, San Juan speaks through the medium of metaphor
and symbol. At times he suppresses the first term of comparison,
thus converting metaphor into symbol especially in the Cántico
espiritual.[25] In contrast, Santa Teresa relies heavily on
simile. Both writers turn to nature and personal experience for
their examples. They draw upon sources as divergent as Scripture
and the popular folk songs of their day, transmuting these
allusions into symbolic expressions which touch the very heart of
the mystic experience. Strictly speaking, the figurative
language they employ is not original, for it often imitates that
of their literary and mystical predecessors. Nevertheless,
imitation does not preclude originality. It is not the discovery
of effective comparisons which makes the works of the Spanish
Carmelite mystics valuable but, rather, the uses to which this
figurative language is put. Both writers integrate familiar

imagery into their doctrinal messages thereby transmitting it to later generations of authors in a form enriched by the symbolic meanings which they add to it. At the same time, however, they find as countless writers before and after them have discovered, that "there exists no word, no idea, that can contain the reality of God."[26] Similarly, none is adequate to contain the reality of union with God. Consequently, the mystics find open to them essentially two ways of both approaching God and describing the steps to their union with him. One is the way of affiliation, while the other is a way of denial. Cursory examination of the works of the Spanish Carmelites might lead to the conclusion that San Juan advocates the second way while Santa Teresa presents the first; yet, as Thomas Merton further points out: "these two ways are not offered for us to select according to our own taste. We have to take both. We must affirm and deny at the same time" (p. 94). Thus, both Santa Teresa and San Juan manifest in their imagery a similar polarity between affiliation and denial in describing the approach to God as well as mystical union with him. They affirm and deny at the same time.

Despite the essential incommunicability of the mystical experience, the mystics do attempt to put in writing what they have encountered in union. Whether the form they choose be poetry or prose, a tendency to employ symbols and images is evident. The elusiveness of the symbol is its strength to the writer of mysticism, for it offers a glimpse "per speculum in aenigmate" (I Cor. 13;12) of the divine luminescence beheld by the mystic in union. The symbol remains open to possibilities of deeper understanding. It reveals and suggests more about mystical union as it is less restricted and circumscribed. Herein lies its value to the mystic searching for analogies to define his spiritual experience. All mystics, therefore, have recourse to images and symbols drawn from the sensible world to speak analogously of the spiritual. Regardless of the genre employed, this tendency is present. Hence, in the poetry and prose commentaries of San Juan de la Cruz as well as the prose works of Santa Teresa de Jesús, the reader discerns a marked preference for symbol and image to convey meaning. Before embarking on a detailed analysis of the particular images and symbols used by the Carmelite reformers, some consideration must be given to the meaning of the terms utilized.

While both San Juan and Santa Teresa employ the term imagen, they usually use it in the biblical sense of man made in the image of God (Gen. 1:27) or in the sense in which Covarrubias later defines it:

> llamamos imágenes las figuras que nos representan a Christo Nuestro Señor, a su benditíssima Madre y Virgen Santa María, a sus apóstoles . . . en quanto pueden ser imitados y representados, para que refresquemos en ellos la memoria y que la gente ruda, que no sabe letras, les sirvan de libro.[27]

In neither author does imagen appear as a strictly literary term to designate comparisons they make. Whereas image is confined to a visual representation, either physical or mental, of a specific event or person in the mystics' lexicon, the term símbolo occurs not at all. The reason for this omission may lie in the restricted sense in which the term was then understood, or simply in the fact that the motivating force behind the mystics' writing is doctrinal rather than literary. It is the literary meaning which interests us here, however, and which controls the use of the terms symbol and image in this study.

Although the visual element in imagery still predominates in most definitions of the term, literary analysis allows a broader application of it, using it as a reference to any simile or metaphor which appeals to one or more of the five senses. C. Day Lewis believes that every poetic image is "to some degree metaphorical [because] it looks out from a mirror in which life perceives not so much its face as some truth about its face."[28] Writing in the Encyclopedia of Poetry and Poetics, Northrop Frye defines an image as "the reproduction in the mind of a sensation produced by a physical perception."[29] On the other hand, in her study of Shakespeare's imagery, Caroline Spurgeon offers a comprehensive yet succinct definition of image, calling it:

> any and every imaginative picture or other experience, drawn in every kind of way, which may have come to the poet, not only through any of his senses, but through his mind and emotions as well, and which he uses, in the forms of simile and metaphor in their widest sense, for the purposes of analogy.[30]

Although in basic agreement with the other critics, Spurgeon goes further than they in defining imagery. Her definition encompasses the sensual base of imagery while making allowance for other possibilities more difficult to categorize. In this discussion, Spurgeon's definition is the controlling one.

The dividing line between imagery and symbolism is a fine one easily traversed by the literary critic. The difficulty of distinguishing these two terms lies in their basic interrelationship. Image and symbol are not antithetical concepts. Rather, the symbol derives naturally from the image in the order of meaning, a distinction which may be illustrated with an example. If we construct a phrase such as "a flag tugging fitfully at its mooring," the reader may conjure up a mental picture of a bit of colored cloth flapping in a breeze. Such a description fufills its image-making potential when the reader reconstructs mentally the sense impression implied by the phrase. No symbolic meaning need be discerned unless the author, within the broader context of his narrative, implies additional meaning. Thus, if the flag so described flies from the masthead of the Victory at Trafalgar, it may symbolize the might of the Royal Navy or the last, dying breaths of Nelson. On the other hand, if this flag is in the process of being hauled down by anti-war protestors bent on immolating it, still more meanings accrue. Both protestors and police see in the flag symbolic meanings far deeper than its mere physical reality. The initial mental image, therefore, gives way to a wealth of symbolic meanings within the context of the work.

Imagery thus serves as a building block to symbolism in a literary work. While it can be used to create sense impressions of place and mood, it can also acquire symbolic meaning beyond its intrinsic meaning. It achieves this symbolic attitude in a variety of ways. As an image recurs in a work, it may take on the characteristics of a symbol. On the other hand, an image may be introduced in a work with a specific symbolic meaning attached. The function of a symbol is to "push forward the frontiers of knowledge and to grasp the reality of things, the real nature of life, the stuff of existence itself,"[31] or, as another writer would have it, the symbol serves as "a visible or audible sign or emblem of some thought, emotion or experience, interpreting what can be really grasped only by the mind and imagination by something which enters into the field of observation."[32] For example, since the time of the Pseudo-Dionysius, mystical writers have used darkness for its symbolic possibilities. The effect on the reader is twofold. Initially, darkness evokes a mental impression based on the reader's sense perception of this state we call darkness. If he reads "en una noche oscura," he forms a mental conception of a dark night as perceived through sense impressions. The mystic, however, also uses darkness as a symbol for the union he experiences with a transcendent God. It becomes a divine darkness in which, paradoxically, the mystic is illuminated. The image is the imaginative recreation of darkness in the mind of the reader, while the symbol transcends this primary meaning, pointing to some other reality.

A symbol, therefore, is a word or group of words which stands for something outside of or beyond its own intrinsic meaning. It brings together two realities which are related to each other (e.g., flag and patriotism) but which are not necessarily limited to a single interpretation or definition. As Urban observes: "It is precisely the nature of the symbol that it takes the primary and natural meaning of both objects and words and modifies them (in some cases we speak of 'distortion') in certain ways so that they acquire a meaning relation of a different kind."[33] The symbol fulfills the analogical function which makes the spiritual world perceptible to the material. It relates an object from this material reality to something beyond in order to provide an insight into the non-material realm. Thus, Dunbar considers the insight symbol an attempt "to look beneath the datum of experience to its relationships in the universal pattern and in consequence to set forth, not only the particular fact, but also that fact in its fundamental relationships."[34] The symbol serves man in his grappling to apprehend and express fundamental truths. Nevertheless, the symbol can never reach the truth. If it were truth, it would no longer be (or need to be) a symbol. It is the means by which we attempt to speak of truth.

The symbol which seeks to express some aspect of ultimate truth is the religious or philosophical symbol. Paul Tillich considers the symbolic language of religion "an expression of man's actual relation to that which concerns him ultimately."[35] He goes on to call the symbol the very language of religion. Since religion is man's means of relating to the transcendental reality beyond his sensible world, it is through symbol that he strives to make that spiritual realm perceptible. Theology itself, and mystical theology especially, must inevitably rely on symbol to convey meaning. Although it seeks to systematize our conceptions of God and his attributes, only through analogy with the world of sense can the truths of the spirit be comprehended. Thus, St. Thomas reiterates St. Gregory the Great's four methods of interpreting the Scriptures. The literal, allegorical, tropological, and anagogical interpretations seek ever deeper meanings for the symbols of Scripture. The last and most profound of the four, the anagogical, is used "when the things that lie ahead in glory are signified".[36]

The mystic's claim is that he has experienced something of that glory which lies ahead while still in this material world. Hence, the mystical symbol seeks to express that transcendental experience of union with ultimate truth. It is related to the religious symbol since it deals with ultimate truth. Its meaning, however, is more restricted, for it tries to express the essence of union with the transcendent, ultimate reality (which we call God). Only those symbols which refer to union are rightly called mystical symbols. In addition, the mystics use symbols in their works not properly called mystical since they refer to concepts other than the unitive experience.

Symbol and image are at the heart of the mystics' attempts to write about the via mystica. Indeed, only through imagery and symbolism can they hope to show what that way means. San Juan's "figuras, comparaciones y semejanzas" and Santa Teresa's "groseras comparaciones" become the very flesh and bones of mystical expression. Whether this expression takes the form of poetry or prose commentary, both San Juan and Santa Teresa return again and again to imagery and symbolism drawn from the sensible world to try to unveil some of the secrets of that "tertium coelum" to which St. Paul alludes (2 Cor. 12:2).

The chapters which follow will examine specific imagery which San Juan and Santa Teresa draw from various sources and which they utilize in individual ways. Just as the mystical writers tap the varied yet rich sources of imagery available to them in order to capture the essence of their experience in words, so, too, do subsequent generations of poets draw on the accumulated wealth of poetic language in creating new works of literature. The literary relationship between the mystics and their secular counterparts has been the focus of much recent scholarship, beginning with Alonso's study of San Juan's poetry and continuing in the works of Menéndez Pidal, Celaya, Guillén, Salinas, and others who juxtapose the mystics' works with those of other Spanish authors. Whether authors such as Lope de Vega, Calderón de la Barca, Quevedo, Góngora, Sor Juana Inés de la Cruz, and others consciously employ the mystical language of their predecessors, nevertheless, each offers his own unique contribution to the store of poetic imagery. Although he writes of Baroque poetry in general, still Lowry Nelson touches the heart of the matter concerning influences exercised by one writer on another when he states:

> The question of direct influences and borrowings is an
> important one, though not conclusive; for the
> relationship between 'emitter' and 'receptor' is often
> more oblique than mere verbal parallels would suggest.
> Much more important, and historically more conclusive,
> are the similarities among national traditions in the
> way metaphor is used as an element of structure.[37]

Thus, how each author utilizes specific images and symbols also found in the works of Santa Teresa and San Juan shows the vital links in the chain of poetic language which extends through generations of poets and prose writers. Through their figurative language the mystics seek to penetrate the very heart of the mystery they have experienced, to offer a glimpse of that glory which is to come. In doing so, they alter incalculably the literary language of Spain.

Chapter 1

NOTES

[1] An excellent summary of definitions from the principal writers on the subject may be found in John Ferguson, Encyclopedia of Mysticism and Mystery Religions (New York: Crossroad, 1982), pp. 126-27.

[2] Dom Edward Cuthbert Butler, Western Mysticism (New York and London: Constable, 1951), pp. 4 and 135. Andrew Louth, The Origins of the Christian Mystical Tradition. From Plato to Denys (Oxford: Clarendon Press, 1981), traces the history of mystical thought in the West from Plato through the Fathers of the Church to the Pseudo-Dionysius. He appends an additional chapter as well dealing with Saint John of the Cross (pp. 179-90).

[3] A. Ple, "Mysticism and Mystery," in Mysticism and Mystery (London: Blackfriars, 1956), p. 11.

[4] William Ralph Inge, Christian Mysticism (New York: Meridian Books, 1956), pp. 3 and 5.

[5] William James, The Varieties of Religious Experience (New York: New American Library, 1963), p. 366.

[6] Miguel de Unamuno, Niebla (Nívola) (Madrid: Espasa-Calpe, 1914), p. 14.

[7] Miguel de Unamuno, "De mística y humanismo," in En torno al

casticismo in Obras completas, I (Madrid: Escelicer, 1966), p. 840.

[8] Evelyn Underhill, Mysticism (New York: E. P. Dutton and Co., 1961), pp. 93-94.

[9] San Juan de la Cruz, Vida y obras de San Juan de la Cruz, ed. Fr. Crisógono de Jesús, O. C. D. y Lucinio Ruano, O. C. D. (Madrid: Editorial Católica, 1973). All references to the works of San Juan are taken from this edition. Abbreviations listed on p. vii will be used within the text to refer to specific works. Aldo Ruffinatto, "Los códigos del eros y del miedo en San Juan de la Cruz," Dispositio, 4 (1979), 1-26, summarizes critical consideration of ineffability in the works of San Juan before examining in detail its manifestation in the Llama de amor viva.

[10] Harold L. Weatherby, The Keen Delight: The Christian Poet in the Modern World (Athens: University of Georgia Press, 1975), p. 101.

[11] Henri Bremond, Prayer and Poetry (London: Burns Oates & Washbourne, 1927), p. 157.

[12] C. M. Bowra, Inspiration and Poetry (Cambridge: Cambridge University Press, 1951). p. 26.

[13] E. Jennings, "Poetry and Mysticism: on re-reading Bremond," Dublin Review, 234 (1960), 87.

[14] Jacques Maritain, Creative Intuition in Art and Poetry (New

York: Meridian Books, 1955), pp. 172-73.

[15] W. A. Fowlie, "Poet and Mystic," Clowns and Angels (New York: Sheed and Ward, 1943), p. 131.

[16] Patrick Grant, Literature of Mysticism in Western Tradition (New York: St. Martin's Press, 1983), p. 8.

[17] Jacques and Raissa Maritain, The Situation of Poetry (New York: Philosophical Library, 1955), p. 34.

[18] Jean Baruzi, "Introduction à des recherches sur le langage mystique," Recherches Philosophiques, (1931-1932), 75.

[19] André Berthelot, "Sur la traduction de la poésie de S. Jean de la Croix," RHS, 53 (1977), 118.

[20] Santa Teresa de Jesús, Obras completas, ed. Efrén de la Madre de Dios, 0. C. D. and Otger Steggink, 0. Carm. (Madrid: Editorial Católica, 1972). All references to the works of Santa Teresa are taken from this edition unless otherwise noted. Abbreviations listed on p. vii will be used within the text to refer to specific works.

[21] Menéndez Pidal, La lengua de Cristóbal Colón, p. 21.

[22] Hatzfeld, Estudios literarios, 2nd ed., 1968, p. 21. Elias Rivers, "The Vernacular Mind of St. Teresa" in John Sullivan, ed., Centenary of Saint Teresa (Washington, D. C.: ICS Publications, 1984), p. 120, holds that Santa Teresa

"deliberately refused to imitate the new style of classical Spanish prose [and] in a true patristic spirit, she invented her own vulgar style of substandard written Spanish, a style that is clearly anti-academic and even anti-rational."

[23] Icaza, The Stylistic Relationship, pp. 50-1.

[24] Barrv Ulanov, "Shakespeare and Saint John of the Cross: De contemptu mundi," in Sources and Resources: The Literary Tradition of Christian Humanism (Westminster, Md.: Newman, 1960), pp. 172-73.

[25] Judith B. McInnis, "Eucharistic and Conjugal Symbolism in The Spiritual Canticle of Saint John of the Cross," Ren, 36 (1984), 123, so describes San Juan's technique.

[26] Thomas Merton, The Ascent to Truth (New York: Harcourt, Brace and Co., 1951), p. 92.

[27] Sebastián de Covarrubias Horozco, Tesoro de la lengua castellana o española, ed. Martín de Riquer (Barcelona: S. A. Horta, 1943), p. 732. The current definition given by the Real Academia Espanola reflects both San Juan's "figuras, comparaciones y semejanzas" as well as Covarrubias' definition. See Diccionario de la lengua española, 19th ed. (Madrid: Espasa-Calpe, 1970), p. 731a.

[28] C. Day Lewis, The Poetic Image (London: Jonathan Cape, 1947), p. 18.

[29] Northrop Frye, "Imagery" in Alex Preminger, ed., Encyclopedia of Poetry and Poetics (Princeton: Princeton University Press, 1974), p. 363.

[30] Caroline Spurgeon, Shakespeare's Imagery (Cambridge: Cambridge University Press, 1935), p. 5.

[31] Thomas Fawcett, The Symbolic Language of Religion (London: SCM Press, 1970), p. 30.

[32] As cited in Everett M. Stowe, Communicating Reality through Symbols (Philadelphia: The Westminster Press, 1966), p. 92.

[33] William Marshall Urban, Language and Reality (London: Geo. Allen and Unwin; New York: Macmillan, 1939), p. 405.

[34] H. Flanders Dunbar, Symbolism in Medieval Thought and Its Consummation in the Divine Comedy (New York: Russell and Russell, 1961), pp. 17 and 134.

[35] Paul Tillich, "The Word of God," in Ruth N. Anshen, ed., Language: An Enquiry into Its Meaning and Function (New York: Harper and Row, 1957), pp. 132-33. Two additional essays by Tillich on the subject of religious symbolism as well as replies and criticism of his theories are reprinted in Religious Experience and Truth, ed. Sidney Hook (New York: New York University Press, 1961).

[36] St. Thomas Aquinas, The Summa Theologiae (Cambridge: Blackfriars, 1964-1976), Ia, Iae, x. McInnis, "Eucharistic," p.

58

121, believes that in his exegesis in relation to the four-fold tradition, San Juan "suppresses almost completely the literal level, assumes the figural level, and concentrates on the tropological level which is the most adaptable to the justification of his own images and doctrine."

[37] Lowry Nelson, Jr., Baroque Lyric Poetry (New Haven and London: Yale University Press, 1961, p. 12. Ciriaco Morón-Arroyo, "'I will give you a living book': Spiritual Currents at Work at the Time of St. Teresa of Jesus," in John Sullivan, ed., Centenary of Saint Teresa, p. 97, insists that comparison of Santa Teresa's work with that of other spiritual treatises should emphasize differences rather than similarities.

Chapter 2

FAUNA

In a study of the transmission and recreation of Greco-Latin themes in Spanish poetry of the Renaissance, María Rosa Lida finds that the poets of this and later periods in Spanish letters, while incorporating themes and images drawn from traditional sources, still give an individual stamp to them:

> individual es la elaboración del contexto a que se ajusta, por ejemplo, un símil heredado, o el nuevo sentido con que se llena un molde transmitido; individual y no menos reveladora, la reducción o la complicación de un motivo, su realización más alta o su forma malograda; y cada una de esas expresiones individuales no sólo reflejan al poeta que las pensó, sino que también retratan en conjunto el sector de la historia cultural a que pertenecen.[1]

Just as their literary predecessors had done, the Carmelite mystics turned to classical and traditional sources in order to draw comparisons between the animal kingdom and their mystical experiences. Present in their works are images and symbols drawn indirectly or directly from Greek and Latin literature, traditional myths and beliefs concerning fauna catalogued in part by writers such as Pliny and Isidore of Seville, the folk traditions of the _romancero_ and the bestiaries, and, of course, the Bible. Their reliance on these sources is no less

significant than that of other medieval and Renaissance writers.
Whether the image be based on a classical allusion or on a humble
comparison drawn from day-to-day living, "by it ordinary
experience of everyday life was brought into touch with religious
experience. The analogy of religion could be perceived in all
places and all times. There was no shutting off religion into an
isolated compartment, from which ordinary feelings and actions
were excluded."[2] It is not, however, the mere inclusion of
imagery based on these sources which is of interest, but rather,
as Lida has observed, the individual stamp which the authors put
on it--the recreation and elaboration of familiar themes. At the
same time, the concatenation of sources as well as their novel
application in deeper symbolic meanings is of equal interest in
both mystics' works. From simple similes to complex, multivalent
symbols, San Juan and Santa Teresa not only perpetuate
traditional themes but revitalize and reinterpret them as well.

Although Lida is principally concerned with the literary
forces at work in the use of traditional imagery and symbolism,
theological and philosophical reasons also compel San Juan and
Santa Teresa to turn to the natural world for examples to explain
their mystical experiences. San Juan holds that once the soul
has studied itself it must begin to "caminar por la consideración
y conocimiento de las criaturas al concocimiento de su Amado,
criador dellas" (CE. IV, 1). For both San Juan and Santa Teresa,
"las criaturas del orden sensible son, pues, un medio necesario
para el hombre en su ascensión a Dios. No puede prescindirse de

ellas."[3] However necessary creatures are to man's progress to God, they are kept in perspective, since the soul must continually remember that it is the Creator to whom it directs its attention "porque el amor hace semejanza entre lo que ama y es amado" (S. I, 4, iii).

Even as San Juan's division of creation into "criaturas, así terrestres como celestiales," "racionales [e] irracionales", and "superiores [e] inferiores", suggests the Ptolemaic conception of the universe, no conscious ordering of the specific animals and plants which serve as symbols of various aspects of the mystic experience appears evident in either San Juan's works or in Santa Teresa's. This is not to suggest that the Carmelite mystics did not conceive of the world order in Ptolemaic terms, but, rather that they do not impose such a schematic on their imagery. Rather, they choose any of the creatures in the "great chain of being," whether humblest or mightiest to serve their ends with either positive or negative connotations.[4] None are used only to be discarded. All are eventually divinized or "mysticalized."

In a familiar analogy derived from the Bible and the Imitatio Christi, Santa Teresa compares herself to a "gusanillo". By implication she uses the term to emphasize a sense of her unworthiness in the face of God's grace, further underscoring this sense with such qualifying phrases describing the gusano such as "tan podrido" (V. XX, 7).[5] When she specifically describes the silkworm however, she clearly establishes the correlation between the gusano and the purgative state.

In the fifth Morada, Santa Teresa considers the life cycle of the silkworm from "simiente . . . a manera de granos de pimiento pequeños," as she believed, to "una mariposica blanca muy graciosa" (M. V, 2, ii). With the exception of the rather fanciful belief that the worm begins as a seed, her description is faithful to that of Pliny and Isidore. The spinning of the cocoon by the worm is analogous to building "la casa adonde ha de morir," which is Christ. Thus, the passage from larval to pupal stage is equivalent to passage through the ascetic practices necessary to advancement. Similarly, just as the worm is hidden in the cocoon so the soul is hidden in Christ.[6] As the soul constructs its cocoon-mansion, God joins with it to complete and perfect it. The use of morada in connection with the silkworm's cocoon further extends her comparison by associating the gusano symbol with that of the building and castle imagery present in the whole of Las moradas.

Once the worm dies to the world, "sale una mariposita blanca," a symbol of the soul as it enters the illuminative and unitive states. Since the mariposa may still engage in restless flight "porque no halla su verdadero reposo," the emerging moth does not stand for union alone. More important than the passage through definite stages from ugly worm to beautiful moth is the creature's attraction to light, for, just as the moth is inevitably attracted to the light, so the mystical soul draws nearer to God until, like the mariposica, it succumbs in spiritual marriage. Rather than a symbol of destruction, however, the moth's self-immolation symbolizes the fulfillment of the mystical quest: life in Christ. Like Quevedo's "pintado amante," its epitaph reads: "Aquí goza, donde yace."[7]

In the hands of the mystics, therefore, the symbol of the moth not only embraces the general connotations of purification by fire and resurrection but also the specific concept of the mystic soul drawn to the symbolic light of Christ where union is realized in immolation of the will. While subsuming the tradition, the mystics also extend it to the temporal experience of the unitive state which is a foretaste of heaven. Thus, San Juan and Santa Teresa turn a traditionally religious symbol to more specifically mystical ends.

While insects represent generally positive aspects of the mystical experience, reptiles serve contrary functions. Since Christian art and literature often associate a negative connotation with serpents and lizards, Santa Teresa's and San Juan's reflection of this traditional association is not surprising. Actual snakes, vipers, and serpents as well as their mythical counterparts, the dragon and the basilisk, therefore, fittingly symbolize the mystic's classic enemy, the devil.

San Juan and Santa Teresa both support the literary tradition surrounding reptiles, subtly injecting into it variations which broaden its scope. Thus, Santa Teresa places sabandijas, largatijillas, serpientes, culebras, víboras, and poisonous things outside the walls of her interior castle, equating these poisonous creatures with "pensamentillos que proceden de la imaginación" (M. V, 1, v). The would-be mystic must prevent these creatures from entering the castle if he or she wishes to progress in prayer. Traditionally, "it was customary to fill the castle moat with vicious and poisonous creatures as an added deterrent to enemies."[8] At first glance, therefore, Santa Teresa seems to adhere faithfully to the medieval conception of the castle fortified within and without against the enemies of the inhabitant. Nevertheless, her comparison is more complex than it first appears.

According to Paschal of the Blessed Sacrament's observtions, the poisonous creatures are placed in the moat by the inhabitant of the castle to keep enemies out. If Santa Teresa intends this meaning, therefore, once again she suggests that the soul's greatest enemy is not an external force symbolized by the devil, but its own faults and failings. Since the castle symbolizes the soul, by implication the "cosas emponzoñosas" have been placed in its way by its own weakness. Rather than keeping out enemies, the poisonous distractions and worldly concerns prevent the soul from entering its own abode. By tradition the reptiles "en el cerco del castillo" may symbolize the temptations of the devil, but by implication they stand for the soul's own failings. Thus, Santa Teresa suggests that the greatest enemy to the mystic's progress is herself.

The only instances in which reptiles assume positive

connotations in the works of both authors offer unusual interpretations of familiar references. When San Juan equates the unworldliness necessary for spiritual advancement with "la prudente serpiente, que tapa sus oídos por no oír los encantadores" (S. III, 23, iii), he presents an interesting reversal of the traditional exegesis of one of the psalms (Ps. 58:5-6). By citing the positive example given by the serpent, San Juan derives a moral lesson quite at odds with that of other hermeneutical authors. St. Augustine, for one, considers the asps of the psalms examples of agnostics who stop up their ears in order not to hear the word of God.[9] For San Juan, however, the serpent represents the soul which shuts out the distractions and temptations which come through hearing so that it might become recollected for prayer.

On the other hand, Santa Teresa compares the soul to a "tortuga cuando se retir[a] hacia sí." While the tortoise chooses its moments of retirement, the soul achieves recollection only with God's grace. Although the turtle's withdrawal into its shell is a defensive maneuver, the action of the soul in turning inward signifies an advance toward union rather than a retreat from it. Like San Juan, Santa Teresa reverses the usual significance of the reptile in question by ascribing a positive rather than a negative meaning to its action.

From Plato's description of the soul as a winged creature through Keats's Ode to a Nightingale, birds, whether actual or mythical, general or specific, have often symbolized spiritualization and are commonly found as symbols of the soul all over the world. Thus it is with both Carmelite mystics who employ birds as symbols of the soul or of aspects of mystical advancement. To Santa Teresa the beginner in prayer resembles a fledgling which must learn to fly by imitating its elders, yet whose range of flight is restricted because of its immature spiritual wings. If the spiritual exercises it undertakes prove too strenuous, it is returned to its nest for rest. Only when it has acquired "las alas para bien volar" (V. XX, 22) is it capable of ascending to the heights where the divine bird, which is God, waits to be seized in mystical union. Although an important part of the appeal in the comparison of souls to birds lies in the fact that "ad sublimia remigio alarum conscendant,"[10] it is by no means the only reason.

On three occasions San Juan expands on the image of the "pájaro solitario" suggested by the psalm (101:7-8). Extrapolating from the adjective solitario, he virtually ignores the literal sense of the line and considers instead the five attributes he discerns in the bird which he deems worthy of emulation by the contemplative soul. In contrast to St. Augustine who devotes a great deal of attention to the three birds and their habitats in this same psalm,[11] San Juan concentrates on only one and then says nothing about its habitat. Rather, he turns his attention to the passer solitarius which builds its nest in the eaves of a roof. From these few details he discusses physical characteristics and habits not explicitly stated in the context of the psalm. Besides its love of solitude, he ascribes to the bird a lack of distinguishing color, soft singing, an ability to soar, and a tendency to fly into the wind.[12] Like the bird, the contemplative must seek solitude, do the wll of God, and, with the aid of the Holy Spirit, contemplate His glory rather than the things of earth. While the references in the Dichos and the Subida refer directly to the "alma contemplativa," the one in the Cántico espiritual stands, instead, for knowledge and spirit. Despite this change of reference, however, the points of the comparison remain unchanged. In contrast, Santa Teresa cites the passer solitarius of the psalm as an example of the experience of the enraptured soul that feels itself to be removed from contact with the world. She emphasizes that "con esta comunicación [que tiene el alma en el arrobamiento] crece el deseo y el estremo de soledad en que se ve" (V. XX, 10). The experience is at once pleasurable and painful, for the soul both feels that "no está . . . en sí, sino en el tejado o techo de sí mesma y de todo lo criado" yet realizes that a perfect union with the Amado eludes her. While neither San Juan nor Santa Teresa equates the passer solitarius with the final state of mystical union, yet each utilizes the symbol in an individual manner.

When they turn to specific types of birds, whether real or imaginary, the elaboration of themes noted by Lida is most apparent in the works of both mystics. The mythological phoenix is a case in point. This fanciful bird, which has the power to

die in flames and then to rise from its ashes, is a traditional
symbol of both Christ's death and resurrection and, by extension,
the death and resurrection of all Christians. In the hands of
San Juan and Santa Teresa, the ave fénix undergoes a subtle
metamorphosis as a symbol. According to San Juan, its immolation
in flame and subsequent rebirth is like the soul "abrasando en
fuego y llama de amor, tanto que parece consumirse en aquella
llama y la hace salir fuera de sí y renovar toda y pasar a nueva
manera de ser" (CE. I, 17). Santa Teresa considers it a symbol of
the death of the "hombre viejo de faltas y tibiezas" so that
another, newer man may arise. For both writers, therefore, the
phoenix stands for the soul which has attained union and is
forever transformed by the love it experiences. The phoenix's
self-immolation recalls that of the moth's yet, at the same time,
extends it. Whereas the moth is completely consumed by the
flame, the ave fénix rises from the ashes to live again.

A far more complex symbol than the phoenix to both San Juan
and Santa Teresa is the eagle. For example, San Juan notes the
paradox of the "águila real muy subida" which allows itself to be
snared by a lesser bird representing the soul (CE. XXXI, 7),
while Santa Teresa reverses the comparison and marvels at the
"águila caudalosa" which captures souls with its wings (V. XX,
3). In both comparisons, the eagle symbolizes the Bridegroom.
Yet, in another part of the Vida, Santa Teresa compares souls
enjoying rapid advancement in prayer to soaring eagles. The
eagle, then, may represent God or the mystic soul.

Santa Teresa's use of the eagle reveals a tacit understanding of the bird's actual and mythic characteristics. In all save one instance, she describes the creature as caudalosa. This adjective, coupled with the description of the bird's activities, suggests its power, majesty, and rapidity of flight. When she joins a plea to be cured of her spiritual blindness with a reference to the powerful eagle of God's majesty, she unwittingly recalls another of the eagle's attributes which is expounded in the bestiaries. On the one hand, Isidore asserts that the eagle derives its name from the acuity of its vision.[13] Thus, it is fitting to think of the eagle when desirous of remedying blindness. On the other hand, tradition holds that when the eagle's sight begins to fail in old age, it soars toward the sun in order to burn away the clouds in its eyes, then returns to earth renewed.[14] Hence, the juxtaposition of blindness and eagle takes on a deeper meaning when considered in the light of traditon. In another work, Santa Teresa develops the comparison more fully. Writing of ecstasy, she says:

> mas llegada aquí [the state just prior to ecstatic union], que le da este Sol de Justicia que la hace abrir los ojos, ve tantas motas que los querría tornar a cerrar, porque aún no es tan hija de esta águila caudalosa que pueda mirar este Sol de en hito en hito, mas, por poco que los tenga abiertos, vese toda turbia. (V. XX, 29)

The saint's comparison is a complicated one which produces multivalent symbolic meanings. While the "águila caudalosa" refers to the Bridegroom, it is clear that so does the "Sol de

Justicia." The associaton of the eagle with the element of air, high altitudes, and the sun makes it an apt symbol for spiritual aspirations as well as for Christ, the Sun of Justice. Similarly, the reference to the mote-filled eyes suggests the traditional mythology regarding the eagle's flight to the sun in order to renew its sight. Santa Teresa suggests all of these readings and more in this comparison. Although remarking that the soul is not yet "tan hija de esta águila caudalosa," nevertheless, she implies that it is within its power to become such a daughter through ecstatic union. Thus, while suggesting the exaltation of mystical ecstasy by comparing it to the eagle's flight toward the sun, she also interposes the soul's humbling realization of its own unworthiness with the references to motes. At the same time, she implies that union will transform the soul into a child of God who will one day be able to look at the sun without blinking. While the goal of union still eludes the soul in this reference, the possibility of its attainment is real.

When the context of this reference is broadened to encompass the paragraph which follows in the Vida, the layers of possible meanings increase. In the next paragraph, Santa Teresa compares the soul to a "palomita" dazzled by the brightness of the sun and blinded by the clay of its own faults. Since the dove also has the peculiarity of recovering its lost sight, the juxtaposition of the eagle which soars toward the sun in order to be renewed with the humble dove blinded by both earthly concerns and the rays of the "divino Sol" implies an interchange of the attributes between aguila and palomita.

Santa Teresa's comparison of the soul to a palomita in this selection from the the Vida clearly refers to a bird. In the Moradas, however, it is not a bird, but rather the moth to which she refers.[15] When the saint's works are considered as a whole, therefore, the connection of mariposa-palomita-águila presents a layering of symbolic meanings. Since both moth and eagle are attracted to the flame, whether candle or sun, both creatures are fitting symbols of the mystic, who desires union with the Sun of Justice. While the moth immolates itself, the eagle returns renewed as the mystic must return from its unitive experience to the ordinary world. Yet, to achieve union and to continue in the world of men, the mystic soul must also possess the humility of the dove.

Drawing on the eight references in the Canticle of Canticles to doves, San Juan reduces the number to two in the Cántico and so combines, compresses, and extends their meaning as to create a powerful symbol of promise fulfilled. On the surface, the first reference to paloma appears as little more than a term of endearment in strophe XIII of the Cántico. Nevertheless, the stanza is a turning point in the unfolding action of the entire poem. Besides being the first direct communication between Bridegroom and Bride, the strophe also closes the first section of the poem dealing with search while opening that which considers the espousals and eventual spiritual marriage. The poet accomplishes this effect in a number of ways. By reintroducing the figure of the stag initially mentioned in the opening strophe, he ties this symbol of the Amado to that of the Amada represented by the dove. The parallel structure of direct address in the exchange between Bridegroom and Bride as well as the transference of wounding from the abandoned soul to the "ciervo vulnerado" further knits the diverse strands of imagery into a tapestry of references which will become more intricate as the work progresses. The combination and repetition of these images "help to determine a spiraling form of development of the poem as a whole."[16]

The Esposa addresses a command to the Esposo which has its counterpart in the Canticle of Canticles (6:4). While the "Apártalos, Amado" is spoken by the Bride, that of the Canticle is uttered by the Bridegroom. Yet the Biblical request reflects the beauty of the Bride "terribilis ut castrorum acies ordinata" (Cant. 6:3) after her espousals and marriage. In San Juan's version, however, the soul wishes the Amado to withdraw the "ojos deseados" which she longs to see reflected in the spring's waters and which are already "en [sus] entrañas dibujados" (CE. XII). The very possibility of seeing these desired eyes reflected in the spring's waters leads the Bride to the verge of ecstasy. Only the Bridegroom's counter-command, "Vuélvete, paloma," prevents the soul's ecstatic flight. Its premature desire for union is thus forestalled.

Even though he states that both spring and dove signify

faith, San Juan does not specifically mention the eyes of the dove. Yet, implicit in his reference to fuente, ojos, and paloma are the "oculi tui columbarum" of the Canticle of Canticles, for the eyes which the soul actually sees in the waters of the spring are its own. To Origen and Saint Bernard of Clairvaux, the dove's eyes symbolize faith and understanding of spiritual mysteries. Thus, San Juan evokes both the Biblical references to the dove's eyes and the allegorical interpretations of them in a series of related images without even mentioning them directly.

When he refers more directly to the Canticle (2:10), he makes another slight, yet significant, change. Where the Bridegroom exhorts the Biblical Bride to arise and come, the command in the Cántico is to return. The Esposo restrains the soul from a precipitous flight of ecstasy before it is spiritually prepared. Although the soul imitates the dove in its quest for a rapid ascent as well as in its love and simplicity, it must follow the example of the Esposo, who, like the wounded stag, seeks the solitude and refreshment of the high mountains. Together they will achieve union.

In the second appearance of the paloma, the bird alluded to is the dove sent from the Ark by Noah which returns with the olive branch. The successful flight of this dove inevitably recalls the failed flight of the earlier reference. San Juan further strengthens the connection between the two references in a number of ways. Besides the repetition of parallel images he also establishes a relationship between the paloma and another bird, the tórtola. At the same time, San Juan links the two doves in his commentary. In both the first reference and the second, he compares the paloma to that sent forth from the Ark. The first dove, however, returns from its flight over the waters of "las fatigas y ansias suyas de amor" to the Ark of Noah's caridad y amor" without the branch (CE. XIV-XV, 1). In contrast, the "blanca palomica" flies over the waters of sin and imperfection. When God permits these waters to recede, the second dove finds the olive branch which represents the "premio y paz conseguida en la victoria de sí misma" (CE. XXXIV, 4). For the soul, this victory is both a triumph over its own imperfections with the aid of grace and, more importantly, union with the Amado.

The description of the dove in the commentary also combines a number of characteristics of the bird derived from or suggestive of traditional sources. San Juan calls the dove white, "no morena como ella se llamó," thus paraphrasing the Biblical source and the Bride's self-description (CE. XXIV), while also evoking the traditional morena songs of Spanish poetry. The dove's blancura symbolizes the soul's state of grace, while the simplicity, gentleness, and "ojos claros y amorosos" of the bird represent the highest state of contemplation reached by the soul. San Juan thus applies the characteristics of the dove noted by the naturalists to an explanation of advanced mystical states.

With his repeated references to the dove's eyes, San Juan

recalls the Canticle of Canticles and the first appearance of the bird in the Cántico. Whereas the eyes of that reference are actually those of the Amado, which the Bride wishes to see reflected in the spring, they suggest the eyes of the dove itself. The Bridegroom now gazes on the Bride with "los ojos como ella se lo ha pedido" (CE. XXXIV, 1). What represented the hope of eventual union at the beginning of the Cántico symbolizes the fulfillment of the mystic quest at the conclusion.

Just as he associated the paloma with the ciervo in the first series of references, so San Juan juxtaposes the dove with another bird in the later strophe. Related in the natural order, the dove and the turtledove are further joined by the poet as a single, multivalent symbol by means of a series of stylistic devices. The repetition of the diminutive -ica, the parallel grammatical structures of verbs and prepositional phrases, and the shared sense of victorious discovery present in the actions described, all serve to show the interrelatinship of paloma and tórtola. The turtledove's preference for drinking from muddy waters has been interpreted as an attempt "to avoid seeing its own reflection, which would remind it of its absent mate."[17] Yet, this characteristic of the bird, coupled with the repetition of the adjective deseado, also recalls the "ojos deseados", which were the object of longing for the Bride. The reunion of the turtledove with its mate thus symbolizes the realization of the soul's wish for union first expressed at the outset of the poem

With the introduction of the turtledove, San Juan continues

the interplay of qualities and attributes among the various symbolic animals of the Cántico. First by implication, then by juxtaposition he intertwines the qualities of one with another. The Bride is "con gemido" and "herid[a]" because the Amado, symbolized by the stag, has left her. By juxtaposing the paloma with the ciervo vulnerado, San Juan shows that both soul and Bridegroom share the pain of separation and the wounding of love. The widowed turtledove incorporates not only a sense of longing at separation from its mate and the wounding of love but also a predilection for solitude in the mountains and constant fidelity to its missing lover. It is not widowhood, however, but absence and solitude that San Juan stresses in the turtledove.

Drawing on traditional lore surrounding the turtledove, San Juan establishes a series of correspondences betwen bird and soul which he interprets symbolically. The bird's attraction to barren branches, its avoidance of clear, cold water and shade, and its solitary nature correspond to the contemplative's disinclination for "algún deleite . . . , alguna honra y gloria del mundo . . . , algún favor y amparo de criaturas" and its attraction to "la soledad de todas las cosas" (CE. XXXIV, 5). Only by leaving all worldly interest can the soul hope to find the Amado. Once reunited with him, the soul delights in him, drinking the clear waters of "alta contemplación" beneath the shade of his "favor y amparo" and secure in his continued companionship.

The mystic accomplishes his objective of union only by

withdrawing from all worldly concerns and living in solitude. The poet underscores the essential nature of solitude to realization of the mystic quest in a single, remarkable strophe (CE. XXV) in which he repeats soledad and a solas five times in the space of five brief lines. Although the strophe follows that which deals with the reunion of Bride and Bridegroom, San Juan's use of imperfect and present perfect tenses strongly suggests that solitude is a necessary pre-condition to union. The strking effect of this litany to solitude recalls a similar though more abbreviated repetition in an earlier strophe. The "no sé qué que queda balbuciendo" (CE. VII) catches in form and content the soul's inarticulateness when faced with the first intimations of the advanced state of mystical experience. Finally, in solitude the wound of love which the soul received in its first encounter with the Amado is now shared by him who is ".también en soledad de amor herido" (CE. XXXV).

San Juan's reference to the turtledove's nest, which he considers a symbol of the "descanso y reposo" that the soul finds in union, raises an interesting problem. According to Pliny, doves "abandon not their own nests unless they be in a state of single life or widowhood by the death of their fellow."[18] Since the emphasis on solitude presupposes the loss of the mate, San Juan seems to err in his grasp of the nature of the bird. The construction of the nest in solitude by his turtledove, however, indicates a hope of reunion and a strong inference of absence from the mate rather than widowhood for the tórtola.

In contrast to the many references to the dove in the
Cántico, those to the turtledove are far fewer. San Juan's
inclusion of the dove of the Canticle in his poem is implicit
rather than explicit. With the turtledove, however, the poet not
only includes the Biblical connotation of the bird but also
intercalates the traditional lore surrounding the tórtola.
Besides using the turtledove as a touchstone of the Bride's
beauty, the Biblical author considers the bird principally as a
harbinger of spring. While suggesting the latter function of the
turledove by introducing it in a topos reminiscent of both
natural and supernatural rebirth, San Juan furthers extends the
meaning of the voice of the turtledove by broadening its symbolic
meanings through association with another bird not drawn from the
Biblical source but from classical tradition.

Following as closely as it does the reunion of soul and
Amado, the strophe which introduces the "canto de la dulce
filomena" (CE. XXXIX) offers a classical allusion which continues
the animal symbolism of the Cántico while also adding to its
complex interrelationship. That San Juan intends a connection
between the two birds is clearly evident in the commentary. Even
without the commentary, however, the relationship between tórtola
and filomena becomes apparent. Like the turtledove, the
nightingale has enjoyed a rich and varied literary history. San
Juan's choice of Filomena in his reference to the bird ties him
to both the classical accounts of the Philomela legend as well as
to the reintroduction of the theme in Renaissance literature.

Although he stands squarely in the center of the literary tradition surrounding the nightingale, he uses it in a unique way.

In her brief review of the history of the ruiseñor, Lida traces it from the Roman poets to San Juan. In the process she notes the dual nature of the symbol. Initially, the ancient myth saw in the bird, "el eco de una pena humana."[19] According to Eugenio Asensio, the nightingale's song represented sadness in the Renaissance and joy in the Middle Ages.[20] The ambivalent symbolism of the bird from classical literature through medieval and Renaissance Spanish poetry is reflected in San Juan's use of it in the Cántico. In addition, besides being a harbinger of spring, the nightingale also "heralds the dawn of a new day with her song," an aspect of the bird's nature emphasized by its Latin name, luscinia.[21] In the broader context of San Juan's poetry, the nightingale thus incorporates the charged symbolism of night as well as the other meanings given it in literary tradition.

While in the Canticle of Canticles the voice of the turtledove announces the end of winter and the coming of spring, it is also the voice of the Bridegroom inviting the Bride to espousal and marriage. By placing the only reference to the tórtola of his poem in a vernal setting, San Juan implies the sense of the Biblical passage. Having established a setting and events, such as the discovery of the "socio deseado," charged with the promise of union, the poet follows with the "canto de la dulce Filomena," which offers the soul the "actual comunicación y transformación de amor" of spiritual marriage. The winter of ascetical and purgative stages has passed as have the nights of senses and spirit. The nightingale's song heralds the passing of these trying states of mystical practice and invites the soul to the dawning of mystical union. The soul's complete transformation in love is apparent because "como dulce filomena da su voz con nuevo canto de jubilación de Dios" (CE. XXXIX, 8).

In the Cántico espiritual, therefore, the nightingale embodies the qualities of those birds which precede it. Implicit in its song are the pain and longing which characterize the soul's state at the outset of the poem, sensations epitomized by the turtledove as well as by the dove. Explicit is its function as a symbol of the fulfillment of union at the close. Yet, it also combines the nature imagery based on fauna and seasonal change with that of night which figures so importantly in San Juan's other poems. Rather than individual references serving specialized and separate purposes in the various parts of the poem, the birds of the Cántico espritual enjoy a close interrelationship of characteristics and symbolic meaning all associated with the soul.

The intertwining of symbolic meanings and consequent transfer of qualities from one bird to another in the Cántico also encompass other animals and other works by both San Juan and Santa Teresa. As noted above, the introduction of the dove in San Juan's poem is inextricably linked with that of the ciervo which becomes in the poem a symbol as complex as that of the birds; for, like the turtledove and the nightingale, the stag has enjoyed a literary history of varied symbolic meanings.

The initial reference to the stag in the first strophe of the Cántico espiritual calls attention to its absence rather than its presence. Addressing an anguished query to the missing Amado, the Bride asks why "como el ciervo huiste,/habiéndome herido" (CE. I, 16). In a reversal of roles, the stag has wounded the Bride "más de amor con [su] flecha," then fled to the mountains (CE. I, 16). In order to assuage her wound of love, the Bride is compelled to follow. Although San Juan's comparison derives from the Canticle of Canticles, it differs from it. The Biblical account describes the Bridegroom coming to the Bride over the mountains like a stag rather than fleeing from her. The action of the ciervo calls attention to the animal's preference for solitude and to "la presteza del esconderse y mostrarse". By alternately hiding and showing himself, the Amado impels the soul to greater longing and, thus, to greater love.

In its second appearance in the poem, however, the ciervo shares the soul's wound of love, for the Amado describes it as "vulnerado" (CE. XIII). Both the mutual wounding of love and the Biblical source to which San Juan turns in order to explain the symbol broaden the meanings which can be applied to the stag. By associating the stag of Psalm 41:2 with that of the Canticle of Canticles, San Juan increases the multivalent possibilities of an already rich symbol. He also interconnects the symbol of the stag with those of the paloma and the cristalina fuente. The alternating convergence and separation of soul and Bridegroom is symbolized as much by the dove's attraction to the spring waters with their hoped-for reflection and its aborted ecstatic flight from those "ojos deseados" as it is by the "esconderse y mostrarse" of the stag.

Wounded by its first encounter with the Bridegroom, the soul pursues him "encendida en amor de Dios" (CE. XII, 7). In looking to the cristalina fuente for refreshment and relief from its wound of love, it imitates the action of the hart which is similarly vulnerado. Lida explains that "por su posición inicial en el encuentro; por la proporción dentro del breve parlamento del Amado, se echa de ver en forma material que el ciervo herido que busca las aguas no es para el Santo poeta una decoración caprichosa, sino un símbolo que guarda relación viva con el pensamiento y la arquitectura del poeta."[22] While the transfer of symbolic meaning of the ciervo from soul to Bridegroom reflects a similar transference in the Canticle, the poet also underscores the correspondence of soul and Amado through love. The stag does flee to the mountains when it is frightened or wounded, but "si oye quejar a la consorte y siente que está herida, luego se va con ella y la regala y acaricia" (CE. XIII, 9). Thus, "God is figured by the wounded stag, but the soul also is, since each is both pursuer and pursued."[23]

Two subsequent poets utilize a similar combination of fauna for different effects from those achieved by San Juan. In the lira "Que expresan sentimientos de ausente,"[24] Sor Juana Inés de la Cruz alludes to the "tórtola gemidora" and the "ciervo herido" as symbols of the poetess suffering in her separation from the "Amado dueño [suyo]." While the details of Sor Juana's turtledove and stag echo San Juan's Cántico, absent from the lira is the intricate interconnection of the symbolic animals and the concomitant sharing of attributes between Amado and amada. Her anguish may resemble San Juan's, but its distillation in the poem falls short of his expression. On the other hand, in the Fábula de Polifemo y Galatea, [25] Góngora juxtaposes in the space of three strophes (vv. 177-200) a number of symbolic references also present in San Juan's work.

Galatea's languourous repose at the spring's edge accompanied by the song of the nightingale contrasts with the Bride of the Cántico anxiously searching the spring's surface for a sign of the missing Bridegroom. Similarly, the description of Acis's arrival at the locus amoenus in search of a cooling drink suggests the stag's desire for refreshment at the mountain spring and its flight from the hunters. Nevertheless, while San Juan captures the anguished search and ecstatic impulse of the Esposa in the initial strophes of the Cántico only to lead the mystical lovers further afield in his poetic landscape, Góngora creates a scene of sensual beauty in the initial meeting of his mythical lovers. For San Juan the interconnecting lines of symbolism initiated in the opening strophes of the Cántico eventually coalesce in a multifaceted symbol of the lasting union achieved by the mystical lovers. In the Polifemo, however, the initial union of the lovers at the spring will prove fleeting, for it eventually distintegrates as they flee Polifemo's wrath. Acis's death and absorption by the sea is a paradoxical symbol, because it irrevocably separates him from Galatea even as it unites him symbolically to the scene of the lovers' first encounter and with Galatea's mother, Doris, the sea. Góngora manifests not only the techniques of multivalent associations present in San Juan's works, but an even more complex layering of detail and allusion embellishing a relatively simple narrative line.

In the broader context of the Cántico espiritual, it is evident that both God and the soul are figured by the paloma, the tórtola, the ruiseñor, and the ciervo. While San Juan may explicitly compare either soul or Amado to one of the creatures in question, implicit in each comparison is the fact that it applies equally to the other. The stag is one with the deer as the turtledove is one with its mate. In fact, each of these symbolic animals searches for and eventually finds its missing mate. The ciervo and tórtola accomplish this in solitude and faithfulness. All four are impelled by love and rewarded in a spiritual springtime of union with the amados. Through the juxtaposition of these varied symbols San Juan shows the multivalent complexity of the love which germinates and grows between the mystic and God, flowering finally in mystical union. Yet, it is Santa Teresa who effects a convergence of the symbolic animals of the Canticle in her description of the fulfillment of union. In the seventh Morada:

. . . aquí se dan las aguas a esta cierva que va
herida, en abundancia.   Aquí se deleita en el
tabernáculo de Dios. Aquí halla la paloma que envió
Noe a ver si era acabada la tempestad, la oliva, por
señal que ha hallado tierra firme dentro en las aguas y
tempestades deste mundo" (M. VII, 3, xiii).

A perusal of the animal imagery present in the works of San
Juan and Santa Teresa shows not only the debt to the classical
and traditional sources available to them but also their
individual preference for certain types of imagery and
elaboration of it. Through selection and extension of animal
images the mystics join their literary predecessors in
transmitting themes while adding to the tradition with the
individual stamp each puts on the subjects chosen. Further study
of the imagery indicates as well the literary background and
stylistic skill each writer brings to his or her subject.

Although Santa Teresa incorporates some classical and
Biblical references into her works, the majority of her
comparisons have as their base the everyday experiences of
sixteenth-century life and the great store of conventional folk
wisdom. E. Allison Peers observes that "she draws less profit
from the great sights of Nature . . . than from Nature's
accidents."[26] Certainly in her choice of animal imagery she
shows a decided preference for the ordinary, the domestic, and
the humble. On the other hand, San Juan's choice and elaboration
of animal images reflects a broader grasp of classical and
traditional sources as well as the ability to develop and sustain
the comparisons he does make, especially in the Cántico
espiritual. By means of stylistic devices such as juxtaposition

and repetition of key phrases or words as well as combinations of
shared characteristics and habits, he combines the images of the
stag, dove, turtledove, and nightingale in a symbol of the soul
and God in various phases of the mystical experience. This
charged symbol not only evokes the classical and traditional
wisdom surrounding each of the animals, but also compresses and
extends the significance of each to the others.

Nature imagery more than any other accentuates the
differences between San Juan and Santa Teresa in both background
and ability. San Juan's literary and theological training is
apparent in his selection of images as well as his utilization of
them, while Santa Teresa's lack of the same is also apparent.
While she "en tire des comparaisons utiles à son explication,"
San Juan "livre son âme dans le symbolisme éperdue de l'Epouse
comblée dans sa recherche."[27] The intention may be the same,
but the execution is uniquely individual.

Chapter 2

NOTES

[1] María Rosa Lida, "Transmisión y recreación de temas greco-latinos en la poesía lírica española," _RFH_, 1 (1939), 21. Rept. in María Rosa Lida de Malkiel, _La tradición clásica en España_ (Barcelona: Ariel, 1975), pp. 35-99.

[2] E. M. Wilson, "Spanish and English Religious Poetry of the Seventeenth Century," _Journal of Ecclesiastical History_, 9 (1958), 40.

[3] Fr. Crisógono de Jesús, _San Juan de la Cruz, el hombre, el doctor, el poeta_ (Barcelona: Labor, 1935), p. 71.

[4] Arthur O. Lovejoy, _The Great Chain of Being_ (Cambridge: Havard University Press, 1936), discusses the concept in detail. By negative and positive I do not wish to suggest a value judgment or a moral attitude on the part of the mystics regarding certain images. Rather, negative refers to that which impedes or inhibits progress to union or is in contradistinction to union. Positive, therefore, refers to that which encourages progress to union or symbolizes union itself.

[5] "Ego autem sum vermis, et non homo" (Ps. 21:12) and _Imitatio Cristi_, Bk. III, Ch. 3. The reading of the _Imitatio_ is required by the _Constituciones_ (I, 13). Otis H. Green, _Spain and the Western Tradition_, III (Madison: University of Wisconsin Press,

88

1965), p. 139 calls attention to the comparison in the Cancionero de Baena as well. See also S. Gregorius Magnus, Moralium in Patrologiae Latinae, LXXVI, col. 560.

[6] Santa Teresa paraphrases the Biblical quotation: "Mortui enim estis, et vita vestra est abscondita cum Christo in Deo. Cum Christus apparuerit, vita vestra; tunc et vos apparebitis cum ipso in gloria" Col. 3: 3-4. Her paraphrase of this particular Biblical passage both in the context of the silkworm and in light of her own religious profession is intriguing. During the vow ceremony for religious women in some congregations, the nuns prostrate themselves before the altar and are covered by a black, funeral pall. While funeral candles are lit, this scriptural passage is sung. The liturgy thus graphically demonstrates to the congregation the rebrith in Christ exemplified by religious profession. Whether Santa Teresa has this in mind in addition to the obvious resurrection symbolism and the mystical significance of the soul's transformation by love is, of course, a matter for speculation. It does, however, suggest another layer of meaning to a fairly complicated comparison on the saint's part.

[7] See Francisco de Quevedo, "Túmulo de la mariposa," in Antología poética, I (Madrid: Castalia, 1969), pp. 391-392.

[8] Paschal of the Blessed Sacrament, "A Visual Aid to the 'Interior Castle'," Ephemerides Carmeliticae, 13 (1962), p. 568, note 5.

[9] St. Augustine, PL, XXXVIII, col. 1432.

[10] Saint Isidorus of Seville, Etymologiarum sive originum. Libri XX, ed. W. M. Lindsay (Oxonii: Clarendoniano, 1911), XII, 7, iii.

[11] St. Augustine, Expositions on the Book of Psalms, trans. Members of the English Church in A Library of Fathers of the Holy Catholic Church, V (Oxford: John Henry Parker; London: F. and J. Rivington, 1853), pp. 9-11.

[12] While the translation of the psalm identifies the passer as a sparrow, San Juan simply refers to it as a pájaro. Corominas cites the derivation of pájaro: "Del lat. passer, -eris, gorrión, pardillo, vulgarmente passer 'pájaro' in Breve diccionario de la lengua castellana, 3rd ed. (Madrid: Gredos, 1973), p. 433. The attributes San Juan ascribes to the pájaro solitario seem to describe the swallow more than the sparrow. Given the preponderance of swallows that nest in Spanish cloisters, it is possible that the mystic had these birds in mind; however, Luce López Baralt, "Para la génesis del 'pájaro solitario' de San Juan de la Cruz," RPh, 37 (1984), 409-424, expanded in San Juan de la Cruz y el Islam, pp. 269-271, suggests Islamic sources for the image.

[13] Isidorus, Etymologiae, XII, 7, x-xi.

[14] Theobaldus Episcopus, Physiologus, ed. P. T. Eden, Mittellatenische Studien und Texte, Bd. 6 (Leiden: Brill, 1972).

The Physiologus notes only the eagle's attraction to the sun (II, p. 31).

[15] Fidele de Ros, "La 'palomica' des Moradas: papillon ou colombe?",BH, 46 (1944), 233-36, explains the derivation of the term and the errors made by translators of Santa Teresa's works. See also M. V, 3, i; v, i; VI, 2, i and 11, i, where she uses palomica (-ita) interchangeably with mariposa (-illa).

[16] Peter Marlay, "On Structure and Symbol in the 'Cántico espiritual'," in Homenaje a Casalduero (Madrid: Gredos, 1972), p. 365.

[17] Marlay, p. 368. Marcel Bataillon, "La tortolica de 'Fontefrida' y del Cántico espiritual," NRFH, 7 (1953), 302, notes that "lo de enturbiar el agua clara figura con menos constancia en el retrato de la tórtola viuda que lo de sentarse en rama seca."

[18] Pliny, The Natural History of Pliny, trans. John Bostock and H. T. Riley (London: Henry G. Bohn, 1855), Bk. X, Ch. 35.

[19] Lida, "Transmisión," p. 22.

[20] Eugenio Asensio, Poética y realidad en el cancionero peninsular de la Edad Media (Madrid: Gredos, 1957), p. 249.

[21] The Bestiary. A Book of Beasts, trans. T. H. White (New York: G. P. Putnam's Sons, 1960), p. 139.

[22] Lida, "Transmisión," p. 48.

[23] Marlay, p. 366. McInnis, "Eucharistic and Conjugal Symbolism," p. 130, recalls Thiebaux's account of St. Eustace and the deer.

[24] In Sor Juana Inés de la Cruz, Obras completas, ed. Francisco Monterde (Mexico: Porrúa, 1969), pp. 167-169.

[25] In Poems of Góngora, ed. R. O. Jones (Cambridge: Cambridge University Press, 1966), p. 77.

[26] Peers, Studies, I, p. 172.

[27] Maryvonne Bonnard, "Les Influences réciproques de sainte Thérèse et de saint Jean de la Croix", BH, 37 (1935), 143.

Chapter 3

FLORA

While animals and birds have enjoyed a complex symbolic
development throughout the history of literature, due in part to
the anthropocentric possibilities attributed to them, vegetation
has served more limited, but no less important, literary ends.
Like fauna, flora imagery pervades secular and religious
literature derived from classical as well as traditional
sources. Santa Teresa and San Juan draw on the rich sources of
plant images available to them, thereby perpetuating a poetic
tradition while also extending it to serve their mystical
purposes. Not only does flora imagery thus integrate the
mystics' works into the tradition of western poetry, but it also
ties these works to the broader tradition of religious myth found
in all cultures.

The extension of plant imagery beyond mere description to
symbolic representation begins in classical and traditional
sources. Flowers, fruits, trees, and gardens figure in
literature from the Bible, Greek and Latin poetry, medieval
literature, the cancionero and mystical works which immediately
precede those of the Spanish Carmelites. Vestiges of these

sources are evident in the works of San Juan and Santa Teresa whether by direct citation, by evocation of the pastoral poems of Garcilaso and Luis de León, or by implicit knowledge of the treatises of Llull and Osuna. The mystics are not so much interested "in what nature _is_ but rather in what it signifies.[1] Nevertheless, landscape in both authors "no tiene ciertamente más naturalismo que el logrado por cualquier novela o poesía pastoril del tiempo."[2]

Imagery based on flora provides a sensual adumbration of the soul in preparation for and in enjoyment of the experience of mystical union. Both authors often cull their plant imagery from that surrounding the topos of the locus amoenus, which Ernst Robert Curtius calls the principal motif of all nature description.[3] Present in varying degrees in the landscapes described by San Juan and Santa Teresa are the essential ingredients of the locus amoenus: the shady, natural setting of a meadow with trees, flowers, birdsong, and spring or brook. The same elements which constitute the classical topos are evident in the Biblical landscape of the Canticle of Canticles, as well as in the secular and religious poetry of Spain. San Juan and Santa Teresa tap the varied sources integrating the locus amoenus as part of their description, thus transmitting it to a future generation of writers in a form divinized by their mystical expression.

In Spanish literature, the presence of the pleasant place occurs in the works of a number of the predecessors of the

mystics. For example, Berceo introduces the Milagros de Nuestra
Señora with a description of an allegorical garden symbolic of
the Virgin Mary and replete with the elements of the locus
amoenus. Similarly, Garcilaso often incorporates the topos in
his descriptions of the trysting places of his poetic lovers. In
both medieval and Renaissance poets there exists an easy mixture
of open spaces similar to Virgil's Elysian fields and the more
confined concept of the garden. Later Christian poets divinize
the classical pagan description by converting it into a vision of
Paradise so that the "locus amoenus can also enter into the
poetical description of gardens," as Curtius observes (p. 200).
Nor does the topos of the pleasant place cease with the works of
the mystics, since it is certainly integral to the pastoral novel
in the hands of Lope de Vega or Cervantes. Similarly, the locus
amoenus figures prominently, although in quite distinct fashion,
in Sor Juana Inés de la Cruz's auto sacramental, El divino
Narciso.

In Christian literature, the Bible itself is a sufficient
source of garden imagery rich in symbolic possibilities. From
the earthly paradise of Eden (Gen. 2:5-17) to the enclosed
garden of the Canticle (4:12 and 5:10) and Gethsemane (Matt.
26:36), the garden has figured as an important, yet ambivalent
symbol in scripture. San Juan and Santa Teresa discuss each of
these scriptural gardens separately and jointly in their
consideration of the journey to union. San Juan departs from
traditional exegesis surrounding the "hortus conclusus, fons

signatus" of the Canticle (4:12), which held that "the monastic life is a return to paradise. The garden of paradise was an enclosed garden. The monastery is likewise a hortus conclusus separated from the world and closed again on God."[4] Rather, San Juan compares the "hortus conclusus" to interior recollection where the faculties of the soul are attuned to spiritual matters rather than worldly distractions in order to probe more deeply the truths revealed in contemplation. Similarly, he also turns to the Gospel account of the Magdalene's search for Christ in the garden after his resurrection as an example of "esta embriaguez y ansia de amor" (N. II, 13, vii) and of the will's search for the Bridegroom (CE. X, 2).

On the other hand, Santa Teresa is especially interested in Gethsemane, the scene of Christ's passion and betrayal. She often suggests it as a starting point in meditation or as a consolation in tribulation. Her description of interior recollection owes as much to the Gospel account as it does to her own fondness for meditating on the Passion: "Porque allí metida consigo mesma, [el alma] puede pensar toda la pasión y representar allí al Hijo y ofrecerle a el Padre y no cansar el entendimiento andándole buscando en el monte Calvario y al huerto y a la coluna" (CP. XLVII/XXVIII, 1). Once the soul achieves interior recollection, it passes from the particulars of meditation to the heart of the contemplation, an understanding of the Passion itself.

The combination of Biblical gardens in the works of the

mystics continues in those poets who follow them. Quevedo juxtaposes the figures of Adam and Christ in the contrary settings of Eden and Gethsemane in his sonnet, "Refiere cuán diferentes fueron las acciones de Cristo Nuestro Señor y de Adán." Like Santa Teresa's view of Gethsemane, Quevedo utilizes the comparison for meditation in a work which draws a moral lesson in the final tercet: "El dejó error, y vos dejáis memoria, / aquél fue engaño ciego, y ésta venta. /¡Cuán diferente nos dejáis la historia!"[5] Unlike the mystics' works, however, Quevedo evinces no interest in advancing further to an appreciation of the garden as a simile for mystical union. His remains a meditative rather than a mystical poem.

Of greater importance than the references to specific Biblical gardens, however, is the comparison of the soul to a garden of flowers and fruit trees which each author develops in similar, yet distinct ways. The four-fold method of watering the garden of the soul is probably Santa Teresa's most famous comparison. By utilizing a concept familiar to her readers she translates the complexities of contemplation into readily understandable terms. Summarizing the comparison early in the discussion, she explains the four ways to water the garden:

> . . . con sacar el agua de un pozo, que es a nuestro gran travajo; u con noria y arcaduces, que se saca con un torno (yo lo he sacado algunas veces), es a menos travajo que estotro y sacase más harta la tierra de agua y no se ha menester regar tan a menudo, y es a menos travajo mucho del hortolano, u con llover mucho, que lo riega el Señor sin travajo ninguno nuestro, y es muy sin comparación mijor que todo lo que queda dicho. (V. XI, 7)

Water represents both prayer and the grace to engage in it. By implication, the garden flourishes with virtue as the prayer life of the soul deepens. Initially, the soul struggles to pray just as the gardener must manhandle a bucket of water from a well without benefit of crank or pump. The amount thus drawn is beneficial even if it is miniscule. As the soul advances in prayer, the task becomes easier until, in the last stages, God waters the garden with rain.

In addition to the progressive nature of contemplative prayer suggested in the comparison, Santa Teresa also implies both the decreasing activity of the soul as it advances as well as the increasing activity of God in leading it toward union. Her equation of the second water with the prayer of quiet, however, is not as successful as another water image she uses in the Moradas. In the later work she likens the prayer of quiet to "dos fuentes con dos pilas que se hinchen de agua" (M. IV, 2, ii). The basin slowly filling with water describes more accurately the passive qualities of this state than does the second water of the Vida. While the watering comparison succeeds in describing the progress of the soul in prayer and the increasing passivity it experiences, it does not succeed in distinguishing between union and the final stages of betrothal and spiritual marriage. The final mystical experience requires a different sort of comparison.

Santa Teresa's simile in the Vida depends on no specific source for its development but rather derives almost wholly from the author's own imagination and observation of the cultivation of household and convent gardens. On the other hand, San Juan's poetic garden in the Cántico espiritual intercalates the spiritual source of his inspiration with his own individual interpretation of the characteristics of the topos which enhance the mystical message he reads in it. His emphasis lies in the flowering and fruition of the spiritual garden rather than in the preparation of infertile and weed-choked ground.

The initial reference to garden in the Cántico suggests the Biblical source, especially when the poet addresses the wind in strophe XVII, first as "Cierzo muerto" and then as "Austro".

> Detente, Cierzo muerto,
> Ven, Austro, que recuerdas los amores,
> Aspira por mi huerto,
> Y corran tus olores,
> Y pacerá el Amado entre las flores. (CE. XVII)

According to the commentary, the garden is "la misma alma". No mention of preparation of the ground occurs. Rather, San Juan's garden of spiritual espousals finds God opening "estos cogollos de virtudes" and emitting "estas especias aromáticas" (CE. XVII, 6). Even as he evokes the Canticle in this strophe, San Juan also deftly links two images of both the Biblical source and his poetic rendering of it. The reference to the Amado grazing among the flowers of the garden suggests the lines from the Canticle of Canticles: "Dilectus meus descendit in hortum suum ad areolam aromatum, ut pascatur in hortis, et lilia colligat" (Cant. 6:1). Both the evocation and the use of the verb pacerá further recall the image of the stag from the earlier strophes of the poem. In contrast to the pain of loss and wound of love shared by both Bride and Bridegroom symbolized in the anguished search for the ciervo vulnerado, the calmer, almost languorous description of this pastoral setting underscores the peace which accompanies union. That the enjoyment of betrothal and marriage is not yet consummated in this strophe is evident in the future tense of the verb.

In the strophes which follow, appetites and powers of the soul are systematically quieted, thereby readying the mystic for the longed-for consummation of spiritual marriage. By entering the "ameno huerto deseado," the Bride reaches the locus amoenus where she figuratively reclines "sobre los dulces brazos del Amado" (CE. XXII) in transforming union. This transformation by love is further underscored by the ambivalent significance of the term huerto, which initially referred to the soul, but here is taken to mean God. In union they become one.

A poetic successor to the Spanish Carmelites, Sor Juana Inés de la Cruz evokes both the Biblical Canticle and San Juan's poem in the setting and language of her auto sacramental, El divino Narciso. The brief description of the setting of the third act, "un paisaje de bosque y prado; y en su extremo, una fuente,"[6] enumerates the elements of the locus amoenus. Elaborating on the details of the setting, Sor Juana echoes both Canticle and Cantico in the plaintive cries of Naturaleza Humana:

> ¡Oh Ninfas que habitáis este florido
> y ameno prado, ansiosamente os ruego
> que si acaso al Querido
> de mi alma encontraréis, de mi fuego

> Le noticiéis, diciendo el agonía
> con que de amor enferma el alma mía!
> (Cuadro 3, Escena vi)

Through the dramatic character, Sor Juana demands of the listeners: "Decidme donde está El que mi alma adora / . . . que Lo voy buscando." [7] The subsequent search for the Beloved inevitably leads the character of Narciso to the edge of the spring where he pleads:

> ¡Ven, Esposa, a tu Querido;
> rompe esa cortina clara:
> muéstrame tu hermosa cara,
> suene tu voz a mi oído! (Cuadro 4, Escena ix)

The plea recalls a similar request in the Llama de amor viva, where the soul demands of the flame: "Rompe la tela deste dulce encuentro" (Ll. I).

Sor Juana adds levels of interpretation to her imagery not fully developed in her predecessor's work. The search and eventual union of Narciso and Eco represent on one level the Incarnation of Christ and, by extension, the life of the Christian in Christ. Linked to the Incarnation is the Eucharist which forms the theological base of the auto sacramental. By extension, Sor Juana suggests vestiges of mystical union as well, for the physical union of Christ with human nature and the believing Christian with the sacramental presence in the Eucharist mirror mystical union. Consciously or not, she may wish to suggest the Patristic notion of the term "mystical" which discerns no difference between mystical and sacramental union. By effectively utilizing the mystical language of her literary and religious predecessors in combination with the classical myth of Narcissus and Echo, Sor Juana creates a symbolic garden setting equally as rich in source and evocative in significance.

In her study of mystical symbolism, Mary Anita Ewer compares progress and garden imagery, finding in the latter "an attempt to express a growth which is largely, though not wholly, an increase in ethical ideas and practices." Unlike progress, however, the garden focuses more clearly on the goal of union and in so doing it "does tend to overshadow the course."[8] While the mystical garden of the soul presented by San Juan and Santa Teresa does emphasize the unitive aspect of the mystical experience, a consideration of the plant imagery in all of the ascetical-mystical works of both writers reveals an organization which corresponds to the other stages of mystical advancement as well. Santa Teresa's admonition to uproot the weeds of imperfection in the garden of the soul finds an echo in San Juan's warning not to allow the "raíz de imperfección e impureza" to take hold. Once imperfection takes root, it is difficult to dislodge.

In explaining the traditional symbolism of flowers, Pliny writes in the Natural History:

> as for the flowers and their perfumes, Nature has given them birth for but a day--a mighty lesson to man, we see, to teach him that that which in its career is the most beauteous and the most attractive to the eye, is the very first to fade and die.[9]

The transitoriness of both life and love finds symbolic expression in the brief life of flowers which secular and religious writers incorporate into their works. Present in European poetry since the time of Horace, the theme of carpe diem draws an analogy between the rose's brief life and the evanescence of beauty, love, and human existence. In an a lo divino rendering of carpe diem, San Juan admonishes his readers to follow the spiritual way: "Mira que la flor más delicada más presto se marchita y pierde su olor." The saint's is not an encouragement to partake of earthly pleasures but to forsake them for the "dulzura y paz en abundancia" of eternity (Dichos XLII).

In the natural order flowers signal the arrival of spring and, thus, rejuvenation and rebirth after the death of winter. Along with the song of the turtledove and the passing of the rains, the Canticle of Canticles (2:11-13) includes flowering fields among the harbingers of spring. In a passage reminiscent of the Canticle, Garcilaso places Salicio in a pastoral setting rich in vernal imagery (Eg. II, 1146-1153).[10] Much of the vernal imagery present in Garcilaso's Egloga appears as well in San Juan's Cántico where he combines classical elements drawn from this poem as well as the Canticle. The interrelationship of the turtledove and nightingale noted above indicates that the two birds combine the roles of heralds of the passing of the winter of purgation and the mystical nights with the announcement of the soul's spiritual springtime in union (CE. XXXIX, 8). Unlike Garcilaso's turtledove, San Juan's does not moan. Rather, it rejoices in reunion with its mate "en las riberas verdes" (CE. XXXIV), just as his nightingale "es el ruiseñor enamoradizo de la canción popular, voz del mundo florido y renaciente."[11] The green banks recall the strophe which describes the stringing of garlands by Bride and Bridegroom which, in turn, evokes an earlier strophe dealing with the flowering vine. Since the flowering vine is also one of the harbingers of spring cited in the Canticle of Canticles (2:10-13), the intricate interconnection of symbols which San Juan achieves in the poem by association, evocation, or repetition becomes apparent.

For both mystics, flowers primarily represent the virtues which the soul receives "para sí y para los otros" (V. XXI, 8). Santa Teresa stresses God's generosity in bestowing virtues and His desire to sustain them in the soul, even as she implies that any cutting or picking of the flowers of virtue in the mystical garden comes at the hands of the soul and not the Beloved. On the other hand, in traditional song, plucking blossoms or fruits in the maiden's garden by the caballero usually symbolizes her deflowering. While San Juan implies this traditional symbolism in the Bride's query regarding "el robo" early in the Cántico, subsequent imagery in the poem as well as the explanation of the commentary emphasize fulfillment rather than loss. In fact, San Juan carefully notes in the commentary on the verse that "pacerá el Amado entre las flores." He calls special attention to the preposition entre. The Amado does not consume the flowers, but rather, grazes among them for "lo que pace es la misma alma transformándola en sí" (CE. XVII, 10).

Although the equation of virtues with blossoms is the

dominant comparison of both San Juan and Santa Teresa, it is not the only symbolic meaning which flowers enjoy in their works. The same ambivalence present in much of their imagery is shared by flowers in both general and specific references. For example, the initial allusion to flowers in the Cántico occurs in a negative context. When the esposa states that in her search for the Amado she will not pick the flowers, she disdains to pick "los gustos y contentamientos y deleites que le pueden ofrecer en esta vida" (CE. III, 5). In the next strophe, however, San Juan reverses the polarity of the symbolic significance of flores by placing them in the wholly positive context of the trees and bushes "plantadas por la mano del Amado".

Even though San Juan's highly allegorized reading of strophe IV limits the possible interpretations for the individual images in the commentary, it is unequivocally positive in the meanings attributed to each image. Thus, he explains that the soul having turned from distractions and temptations is now ready to consider God through reflection on his creation. San Juan makes a transition from nature to the source of being in union with the Creator. To him the "bosques y espesuras" represent the elements of the physical world, while the "verduras" refer to celestial things and the "de flores esmaltado" to the angels and saints (CE. IV, 6). Nevertheless, his interpretation of the strophe in the commentary seems forced when one considers the pastoral context of the poem. That the Bride, in her search for the Beloved, sees his presence reflected in the countryside through

which he has passed needs no further explanation than that
offered by the verse which notes that all is planted by his
hand. Furthermore, the inclusion of the artificial ordering of
creation needs no more explanation than that God is discernible
in the beauties of nature. San Juan acknowledges that fact when
he cites Saint Paul's observations in Romans 1:20. The attempt to
force a correlation between each of the images in the strophe and
a particular link of the hierarchical system of the great chain
of being is strained.

When all is ordered within the soul, it is ready to enter
the "ameno huerto deseado" of union with the Bridegroom.
Consummation of their love takes place on the "lecho florido".
Thus, the promise symbolized in the flowering vine is fulfilled
on the flowering litter, an interrelationship which San Juan
suggests by repetition of both the adjective florido and the
first person plural nuestro in each strophe.[12] As he does with
fauna, so also with flora San Juan elaborates an interconnection
of events and concepts in mystical progress within the Cántico
espiritual through a series of stylistic devices. Just as he
wove a tapestry of repetition and evocation of imagery in the
references to animals in the poem, so, too, does he tie together
the disparate imagery based on flora with the slender threads of
grammatical form and subtle similarity to show their intricate
interrelationship in the warp and woof of the entire poem. For
example, the exterior landscape described as "de flores
esmaltado" through which the Bride passes in her search for the

Amado becomes part of the interior landscape of the soul festooned with virtues symbolized by the descriptive phrase "de flores y esmeraldas". The repetition of the prepositional phrase as well as the initial sound correspondence between "y esmeraldas" and "esmaltado" subtly evoke the earlier strophe. The Bride's question addressed to the "bosques y espesuras" ("Dezid si por vosotros ha pasado") (CE. IV), finds an implied reply in both the union of the Amado and Amada on the "lecho florido" as well as in the mutual work of braiding garlands (CE. XXX). San Juan frames the movement of the soul to union with the repetition of very similar phrasing and content. "Hacemos una piña" (CE. XVI) is reiterated later in "Haremos las guirnaldas" (CE. XXX) which links the decision to make "una piña a esta junta de virtudes", with the intention of Bride and Bridegroom to string garlands of flowers and emeralds on a thread of hair. Since the pinecone traditionally symbolizes fertility while garlands represent the ordering of the higher emotions and virtues, San Juan subsumes the traditional meanings in his use of piña and guirnalda. It is love that prompts the construction of both and a "cabello de amor" that binds together the flowers of the mystical garland.

In a lengthy passage in the commentary, San Juan further specifies the blossoms in the garden of the soul by considering specific flowers in conjunction with disparate images drawn from earlier sections of the Cántico. He thus creates a multilayered symbolic effect by juxtaposing images from different parts of the poem:

> acaecerá que vea el alma en sí las flores de las
> montañas que arriba dijimos, que en la abundancia y
> grandeza y hermosura de Dios; y en estar entretejidos
> los lirios de los valles nemorosos, que son descanso,
> refrigerio y amparo; y luego allí entrepuestas las
> rosas olorosas de las ínsulas estrañas, que decimos ser
> las estrañas noticias de Dios y también embestirla el
> olor de las azucenas de los ríos sonorosos, que
> decíamos era la grandeza de Dios que hinche toda el
> alma. Y entretejido allí y enlazado el delicado olor
> del jazmín del silvo de los aires amorosos, de que
> también dijimos gozaba el alma en este estado, y ni más
> ni menos todas las otras virtudes que decíamos del
> conocimiento sosegado, y callada música, soledad sonora
> y la sabrosa y amorosa cena. (CE. XXIV, 6)

The evocation of concepts hinted at in the other grammatical and
lexical repetitions is here made explicit. The soul slowly
interiorizes the reflection of the Beloved's presence in the
visible works of creation and the crystalline spring as it
approaches union so that the promise held out in the opening
strophes is now fulfilled in the flowers which bloom in the
mystical garden. The catalogue of nouns which serve as metaphors
for "Mi Amado" (CE. XIV-XV) and which sound a virtual paean of
joy in the Bride's initial rediscovery of the Bridegroom
foreshadows this final consummation. San Juan ties the disparate
symbols together with the thread of his commentary.[13]

The juxtaposition of the rose as a symbol of love with the
"azucena" in the commentary as well as the description of the
Bride's repose on the "pecho de su Amado" (CE. XVI, 8) recalls a
similar setting in the Noche oscura (VIII). To Agustín del
Campo, the azucenas of the Noche "marcan la línea terrenal, el
suelo florido hacia el que todo desmayo converge."[14] In the

broader context of San Juan's total work, however, rose and lily symbolize the flowering of love between mystic and God which is both passionate and pure. The beauty of the two flowers is neither fleeting like that of the woman's in Garcilaso's sonnet (XXII), nor is the love they represent debilitating like that of the rejected lover of the Egloga II (v. 1258).

In contrast to confinement implied in the symbol of the garden, San Juan refers to open spaces reminiscent of the Elysian fields of the Georgics and the pastoral poems of the Renaissance. Early in the poem, the Bride passes through the "prado de verduras" in search of the Amado. Once she emerges from the "la interior bodega/de [su] Amado," she gazes on "toda aquesta vega" (CE. XXVI), realizing that the knowledge attained in ecstatic union surpasses that perceptible to the senses. In both references, the open space signifies the exterior world where the soul finds the visible signs of its Beloved in the works of creation.

Just as the prado and the vega frame the central section of the Cántico espiritual, so, too, do the soto and bosque. The combination of open space suggested by the prado with the density of the soto or espesura is a familiar topos in classical and Renaissance poetry. San Juan's initial reference to grove and forest suggests the classical interplay of open and closed space (CE. IV). Soto, bosque, espesura all appear in the first catalogue of creation presented in the poem. The highly allegorical meaning attached to them in the commentary restricts rather than broadens the multivalent possibilities which their presence in the poem suggests, for San Juan carefully assigns to each of the references a fixed symbolic meaning in support of his thesis that "las cosas invisibles de Dios, de el alma son conocidas por las cosas visibles criadas e invisibles" (CE. IV, 1).

In the penultimate strophe of the poem, the "soto" changes from a symbol of creation into a symbol of the Creator. In contrast to the dense forest which blocks the sun's rays, San Juan combines the obscurity of the grove with the sun of justice. The paradoxical combination occurs in the juxtaposition of "el soto y su donayre" with "la noche serena" (CE. XXXIX). While soto signifies God, noche represents contemplation which leads to mystical union. Similarly, the espesuras, which were first mentioned in conjunction with forest and grove, now signify "la deleitable sabiduría de Dios" (CE. XXXVI, 2). San Juan wholly interiorizes the exterior landscape of creation in union with the Creator.

Just as the carefully tended jardín produces beautiful flowers so, too, does the huerto produce fruit-bearing trees. For both mystics, fruit and flower represent virtue. At the same time, Santa Teresa and San Juan also equate the tree with the soul, for it, too, blossoms before bearing fruit. While the bearing of fruit like the flowering of the garden primarily pertains to the symbolism of union, the mystics do employ tree imagery to speak of earlier stages of mystical progress. Thus,

in purgation, Santa Teresa advises her readers to guard against
blights in the form of "puntos de honor" which might harm the
fruit-bearing capabilities of the tree-soul. On the other hand,
San Juan considers advancement in purgative practices to the
point of the spirit's control of the flesh comparable to the hold
"el árbol [tiene] a una de sus hojas" (N. II, 19, iv).

As an integral part of the locus amoenus, the tree often
appears in conjunction with flowers, a breeze, and a clear
spring. Such a traditional description occurs in Garcilaso's
Egloga II (vv. 64-76) as well as in Góngora's Polifemo. Santa
Teresa recalls a similar setting in describing the soul in union
"plantada; que ansí como el árbol que está cabe las corrientes de
las aguas, está más fresco y da más fruto" (M. VII, 2, xii). As
long as the source of the tree's refreshment is "esta fuente de
vida", it need not fear the fruits it will bear. The trysting
place of the mystical lovers remains the soul itself.

While the tree in general signifies the soul, specific trees
include and broaden this basic comparison. The Canticle of
Canticles provides some points of comparison on which both
mystical writers elaborate. Although cedars, palms, and apple
trees figure prominently in the Biblical account, only the last
actually appears in San Juan's Cántico. Nevertheless, both San
Juan and Santa Teresa do employ these Biblical references in
other works. For example, in the Noche oscura San Juan creates a
strophe (VI) rich in visual imagery which describes soul and
Amado joined in union. Following as it does the climactic

exclamations to night, its more measured pace and tranquil picture effectively summarize the peace the soul experiences. Since the commentary on the Noche oscura does not extend to strophe VI, San Juan's interpretation of these verses must be gleaned from other works which deal with similar points of mystical union. The interconnection of lexical and grammatical items present in the first verse and the "lecho florido" has already been noted above, so that the reference to "cedros" in the context of the Noche oscura recalls similar circumstances in the Cántico. Since the cedars of Lebanon figure in the Biblical source as both a description of Solomon's litter and of the Bridegroom, the relationship of the "pecho florido" and "lecho florido" is strengthened. Similarly, when San Juan echoes yet another comparison from the Canticle, he understands "por las tablas cedrinas las afecciones y accidentes de alto amor" (CE. XX-XXI, 2), which the soul enjoys in spiritual marriage.

As an evergreen, as a touchstone of beauty in the Canticle (1:9), and as a Messianic symbol (Ezech. 17:22), the cedar has traditionally represented both Christ and the incorruptibility of the soul. San Juan not only includes this traditional symbolism in his use of the image, but he also extends it by utilizing it only in references to spiritual marriage. Since the cedar represents both soul and Beloved in the Noche and the Cántico, the poet conveys the sense of an interchange of attributes between the partners in mystical union. At the same time, the peaceful setting and tone of the strophe from the Noche suggest

the peace the soul now enjoys while the presence of the evergreen
implies its lasting nature.

Although cedar figures minimally as a symbol, the apple tree
plays a much more important role in the works of both
Carmelites. Traditionally, of course, the apple tree has been
understood as the forbidden tree of Eden (Gen. 3:3) even though
the Genesis account does not specify it as such. In the Canticle
of Canticles, however, such an assignation is implied in the
verse: "sub arbore malo suscitavi te; ibi corrupta est mater tua
ibi violata est genetrix tua" (Cant. 8:5). Nevertheless, the
Canticle (2:3) also uses the apple tree as a simile for the
Bridegroom. Faced with these diverse yet related symbolic
readings, San Juan subsumes all of them in his single allusion to
the manzano in the Cántico espiritual (XXIII). In the
commentary, he suggests the dual symbolism of the "manzano" when
he observes that human nature "fue violada" beneath the tree of
Eden but "[fue] reparada" by that of Calvary (CE. XXIII, 3).
While the presence of the "manzano" in the "ameno huerto deseado"
strongly suggests the Genesis account, the context of betrothal
and marriage in which it occurs stresses the redemptive aspect of
Calvary. In her Meditaciones sobre el Cantar de los Cantares,
Santa Teresa makes a similar comparison when she considers the
"manzano" a symbol of the cross whose fruits the soul enjoys
because Christ through his passion "[ha regado] este árbol con su
sangre preciosa" (Med. V, 7).

The "árbol" of the sonnet "Un pastorcico" is a similar

evocation of the cross, deftly presented in a pastoral poem a lo divino which transforms the individual shepherd pining for his lost lover into the Good Shepherd suffering crucifixion to redeem human nature. It is a transformation which occurs as well in Lope de Vega's sonnet addressed to the crucified Christ: "Pastor que con tus silbos amorosos." Like his mystical counterpart, Lope converts the shepherd to the Good Shepherd and his crook to the wood of the cross. Nevertheless, while the terms are similar, Lope narrows the devotional focus to the particular salvation of the individual sinner rather than the broader redemption of mankind implied in San Juan's poem.

Related in nature and in tradition to the apple is the pomegranate, which in the Canticle of Canticles, serves as a point of comparison for the Bride's beauty (4:3 and 6:6) as well as an indication of the flourishing love between her and the Bridegroom (4:13 and 6:10). In the poem, it is not the fruit of the pomegranate but the juice pressed from it that San Juan considers, a "mosto" which is "la fruición y el deleite de amor de Dios" (CE. XXXVII, 8). While San Juan limits his consideration of the significance of the pomegranate to two brief explanations in the commentary, a closer scrutiny of the allusion in the context of the entire Cántico espiritual reveals the same repetition of terms and concepts present in other symbols which serves to tie the imagery in a united whole. For example, the verb "entraremos," which precedes the reference to the "mosto de granadas," recalls the entry of the Bride into the "ameno huerto deseado" (CE. XXII) as well as the call to enter further "en la espesura" (CE. XXXVI). Similarly, both the verb and the reference to spiced wine recall the implied entrance of the Bride into "la interior bodega," where she drinks deeply of the Amado before leaving (CE. XXVI). The cellar spoken of in this strophe "es el último y más estrecho grado de amor en que el alma puede situarse en esta vida" (CE. XXVI, 3), while the wine is "sabiduría y ciencia de amor". The soul figuratively leaves the cellar because it cannot sustain ecstatic union indefinitely. Thus, strophe XXXVII serves as a culmination of imagery suggesting the interiority of the mystical journey and the mutual enjoyment by Bride and Bridegroom of the spiced wine symbolic of their knowledge and love of one another in union.

Aromatical spices and rich unguents whose odors permeate the literary setting also characterize both mystical and Biblical gardens. The Canticle of Canticles is replete with references to spices, incense, and sweet-smelling oils which provide the Biblical account with redolent appeals to the sense of smell in harmony with the equally numerous appeals to the senses of sight and touch. The Canticle includes these references in the catalogues of comparisons which describe the beauty of both Bride and Bridegroom or as products of the garden. San Juan selectively chooses from the various Biblical references to sweet-smelling spices and herbs, using only a few in a highly individual way. In two instances, however, he introduces two resinous substances which do not appear in the Canticle. Balsam, which Pliny calls "the most valuable of them all . . . [when treating of] the unguents,"[15] appears in the Cántico espiritual in the phrase "emisiones de bálsamo divino" (CE. XXV) which draw the Bride to the "interior bodega". In the commentary, San Juan calls these aromas the inward acts of the will which respond to the graces of God. In the Llama, however, the sweetness of union far surpasses that of balsam. Similarly, San Juan finds expensive, gold-hued amber a fitting symbol of the spirit of the Esposo who dwells in the soul, acting on its faculties and virtuous inclinations. Like the visual signs of the Beloved's presence, the aromas of these sweet-smelling resins permeate the poetic world created by San Juan as subtle enticements to the Bride to continue her pursuit of the Bridegroom.

While the works of both San Juan and Santa Teresa include landscapes strewn with flowers or thick with trees, these concrete images convey the underlying spiritual nature of the garden, forest, or plain which each author describes. The authentic landscape of both mystics is the interior one of the soul through which the contemplative passes and in which he discovers God. Like fauna, flora transcends the specific and concrete to form a symbolic representation of the complete mystical reality. Both writers use plant imagery to represent "una serie de ideas, símbolos y abstracciones que [ellos habían] unido a la palabra o imagen de una forma tan continuada e insistente que el término había adquirido para [ellos] una suma de significados o representaciones."[16] This concatenation of images points inevitably to a union in which not only soul and God are joined as one, but the individual attributes of nature are wholly and harmoniously united.[17]

Although Santa Teresa is justly famous for her extended comparison of mystical advancement to the cultivation of a garden, the variety of her flora imagery is relatively limited. As is true of much of her imagery, she relies on the familiar and the commonplace to make her points. While effective in a limited context, these comparisons do not evidence the complexity and diversity present in San Juan's works. Perusal of the poetic world which he created and commented on reveals a unique way in which nature in the form of plant imagery serves him. It becomes a complex symbol of the mystical experience as a whole, evidenced by the careful ordering of images in the Cántico espiritual. Such an approach leads both reader and Bride from exterior reality to the interiority of union even as it emphasizes a harmonious vision of the universe. What in their literary predecessors existed as a reflection of the poet's state of mind or emotion becomes in the Spanish Carmelite mystics a symbol of the substance of their experience. The locus amoenus of classical tradition with its varied elements is transformed into multivalent symbols for both the soul and, more importantly, the very ground of its being, God.

Chapter 3

FLORA

NOTES

[1] Etienne Gilson, The Spirit of Medieval Philosophy, trans. A. H. C. Downes (New York: Chas. Scribner's Sons, 1940). pp. 364-65.

[2] Eugenio D'Ors, Estilos del pensar (Madrid: Ediciones y Publicaciones Españolas, n. d.). pp. 251-52.

[3] European Literature and the Latin Middle Ages, trans. Willard B. Trask (New York: Harper and Row, 1953), p. 195.

[4] Joseph F. Chorpenning, "The Monastery, Paradise, and the Castle: Literary Images and Spiritual Development in St Teresa of Avila," BHS, 62 (1985), 247. On the other hand, McInnis, "Eucharistic and Conjugal Symbolism," pp. 122-123, demonstrates San Juan's ability to "transfer characters, scenes, and episodes from the Song of Songs into the world of Renaissance pastoral [in order] to develop a unified poem [the Cántico espiritual] with a clearer narrative progression."

[5] In Quevedo, Antología poética, p. 32-33.

[6] Sor Juana Inés de la Cruz, Obras completas, ed. Francisco Monterde (México: Editorial Porrúa, 1969), p. 392. Marie-Cecile Benassy Berling, Humanisme et religion chez Sor Juana Inés de la Cruz (Paris: Editions Hispaniques, 1982), pp. 224-25, contends

that Sor Juana was probably familiar with San Juan's poetry but not his commentaries.

[7] Alfonso Méndez Plancarte, San Juan de la Cruz en México (Mexico: Fondo de Cultura Económica, 1959), pp. 42-44, comments on the similarity of terms used by Sor Juana and San Juan.

[8] Mary Anita Ewer, A Survey of Mystical Symbolism (London: S. P. C. K.; New York: Macmillan, 1933), p. 79.

[9] Pliny, Bk. XXI, Ch. 1.

[10] Garcilaso de la Vega, Obras completas con comentario, ed. Elias L. Rivers (Columbus, Ohio: Ohio State University Press, 1974), p. 117.

[11] Asensio, p. 250.

[12] Louise M. Salstad, "The Garden of God: Metamorphoses of Paradise in Religious Verse of Sixteenth-Century Spain," Durham University Journal, 71 (1979), 203, discusses the dual symbolism San Juan ascribes to the garden as both God and the soul.

[13] In "El divino Narciso" Sor Juana (Cuadro 5, Escena xvi) again provides an analogous summation of the wonders of nature when the character of Gracia virtually summarizes salvation history for Eco by utilizing the entire spectrum of nature imagery. While reminiscent of San Juan's poetic language, Sor Juana's scene maintains its Eucharistic focus rather than suggesting mystical union.

[14] Agustín del Campo, "Poesía y estilo de la Noche oscura," RIE, 3 (1943), 54-55.

[15] Pliny, Bk. XXIII, Ch. 47. See also Covarrubias, p. 188, who reiterates its worth as a medicinal ointment and its use as holy chrism.

[16] Emilio Orozco Díaz, "La palabra, espíritu y materia en la poesía de San Juan de la Cruz," Escorial, 9 (1942), 319.

[17] Umberto Eco, Art and Beauty in the Middle Ages (New Haven and London: Yale University Press, 1986), pp. 56-57, explains that "it was John Scotus Eriugena, following the Pseudo-Dionysius, who gave to the Middle Ages the most fruitful formulation of metaphysical symbolism. For Eriugena the world was a great theophany, manifesting God through its primordial and eternal causes, and manifesting these causes in its sensuous beauties." He goes on to cite Eriugena's Super Hierarchiam Caelestem, Chap. 1 in PL, 122, col. 128.

Chapter 4

FAMILIAR OBJECTS

In seeking comparisons based on the ordinary experiences of
everyday life, the Spanish Carmelite mystics often turn to the
familiar objects, both large and small, which fill their
day-to-day lives. Analogies constructed around that which is
most familiar to themselves and to their intended audience thus
translate the experience of mystical progress into very human
terms. Evidence of the predilection for central images based on
the mundane presents itself in the very titles of their mystical
treatises which suggest controlling images of road, ascent, or
castle. In thus turning commonplace objects to their mystical
ends, San Juan and Santa Teresa perpetuate a tradition present in
their mystical predecessors.

Among the familiar objects which Santa Teresa and San Juan
include in their works are particular types of buildings, rooms,
furnishings, and the art of building itself. Santa Teresa's
work, Las moradas del castillo interior, certainly suggests that
the castle will serve as a controlling image in a work which
bears its name. Nevertheless, this is by no means the only
occasion on which she turns to buildings as apt comparisons for

points of doctrine she wishes to elucidate. Nor is the concept of building unknown to San Juan. Rather, both employ the image in remarkably similar fashion.

Undoubtedly taking her cue from the Gospel (ML. 7:26 27). Santa Teresa urges her readers to build on firm ground, constructing a foundation on humility, and laying the cornerstone of good conscience. Without a firm foundation "todo el edificio va falso" (CP. VIII, 8/V, 4), for the soul builds in order to construct a temple worthy of God's presence. At the conclusion of the Moradas, she exhorts her readers to build with "buenos cimientos . . . puniendo piedras tan firmes que no se os caya el Castillo" (M. VII, 4, ix). Although San Juan does not use building as extensively as Santa Teresa, he does emphasize the need for experienced confessors by warning: "fácilmente encontrará [el alma] con algunas personas que antes le destruyan el alma que la edifiquen" (S. II, 30, v). God is the "artífice sobrenatural" who constructs in each soul the building he desires. By disposing itself through its operations and natural affections, the soul enables this supernatural construction to take place. Even though they approach the comparison from different points of view, both writers are in essential harmony. Each agrees that God's grace and the soul's cooperation with it are necessary if advancement in the mystical life is to be realized. Thus, while San Juan considers God's action in building the soul, Santa Teresa emphasizes the soul's activity in constructing the interior castle.

As Cirlot observes, the castle is a complex symbol, for it combines numerous concepts of equal symbolic power. For example, it subsumes the idea of house and the enclosed city as well as the mountain, since it is often constructed on a hill or mountain top. It symbolizes "embattled spiritual power, ever on the watch," while the castle of light represents redemption. The implication of fortification and height thus stands for the soul aspiring to spiritual growth and aversion to sin.[1]

To Santa Teresa the castillo of Las moradas represents the soul. In the opening paragraphs of Las moradas, she states her intention of utilizing the castle as the controlling image of the work by equating it with the soul. It is still a fortification within which are many "aposentos" and "moradas" situated at different levels and encircling a central mansion "adonde pasan las cosas de mucho secreto entre Dios y el alma" (M. I, 1, iii). Having established the comparison, she then develops the analogy. In a seeming contradiction, she points out the necessity for the soul to enter the castle. That is, the soul must figuratively enter itself in interior recollection. Unfortunately many remain "en la ronda del Castillo" unaware that they can penetrate the wall through the entryway of prayer and move from mansion to mansion. Outside the castle one finds neither peace nor security. Only after entering can the soul progress through the moradas and eventually approach the seventh which is the center.

In its passage through the first mansions, the soul relies

on its own powers to progress. As it continues its movement
toward the central mansion, however, a subtle shift of activity
occurs as God takes a more active part in the soul's
advancement. As God begins to rule the interior castle, the
bellicose nature of the building recedes while the palatial
aspect of the innermost mansion comes to the fore. At the center
of the soul, the seventh mansion is actually a _palacio_ inhabited
by a great king. From the beginning, the central mansion has
been referred to as "la pieza u palacio donde está el Rey" (M. I,
2, viii), thus implying that the soul's inward journey is one of
discovery, not just of itself but, more importantly, of God. In
the sixth mansion, Santa Teresa equates God with "una Morada u
palacio muy grande y hermoso" (M. VI, 10, vi). As it approaches
the center, therefore, the soul strengthens its own "image and
likeness of God." Although her emphasis in the seventh _morada_ is
on the peace which reigns in the _palacio_ the nature of the
fortification which surrounds it is never wholly forgotten, for
war still rages outside.

While Santa Teresa divides her work into seven sections or
moradas, she emphasizes that many more mansions exist than those
she chooses to describe. The first six stages are always
referred to in the plural in order to emphasize this fact. Each
of the _moradas_ serves as a stage of the mystical experience
through which a soul may pass before reaching the last mansion.
Not all souls, however, pass through all of the preliminary
stages she describes. Some advance only partially; others

experience mansions she has not visited. Nevertheless, the final mansion is singular, for it is the "sétima morada" where God places those who attain spiritual marriage. At the same time, in contrast to some of her literary predecessors, Santa Teresa stresses the accessibility of the seventh mansion to those souls chosen by God for the final stages of mystical union. Thus, in his poem, "A Felipe Ruíz," Fray Luis de León relegates to "la más alta esfera / las moradas . . . de espíritus dichosos."[2] Evident in Fray Luis' poem is a Ptolemaic world view whose spheres encompass all forms of life from lowest to highest. The poet's desire to reach the highest reflects Santa Teresa's aspiration to attain the seventh mansion. Fray Luis' moradas, however, are reached only in eternity, while Santa Teresa's are accessible to mystics in this life.

The mansion in Las moradas serves primarily as a controlling image around which Santa Teresa constructs her doctrinal message rather than as the basis of a full-blown allegory for the mystical experience. Although some symbolic meaning is ascribed to parts of the mansions, by and large these parts do not take on a detailed allegorical sense at all. Santa Teresa writes of progress from one mansion to another on both a vertical and a horizontal plane, of skipping some of those she describes, and of returning to ones entered earlier. Nevertheless, the moradas in their sketchy descriptions remain essentially vague constructions, way stations on the inward journey to union.

San Juan also perceives the soul as a palace, a temple and a fortress. As he describes the soul in the Cántico espiritual, he reflects the fortress comparison utilized by Santa Teresa. The wall surrounding the fortified city of the soul is "el cerco de paz y vallado de virtudes y perfecciones" (CE. XX XXI, 10). Outside the walls are the cares of the world besieging the soul fortified by virtue. The suburbs of the city represent "la porción inferior o sensitiva" of the soul while the city itself is "la parte racional, que tiene capacidad para comunicar con Dios" (CE. XVIII, 7).

In both San Juan and Santa Teresa the image of a fortress, whether castle or city, is initially a symbol of the soul which, through mystical experience, finds within itself God dwelling in anticipation of union. The struggle to enter and to persevere to the center is manifest in the descriptions of the obstacles to progress. Peace and security are to be had only in the state of spiritual marriage realized in the final state of union.

On a humbler level than the castle or palace, San Juan compares the soul to a house in the Noche oscura. In his commentary on the lines "salí sin ser notada, / estando ya mi casa sosegada", he considers the passage a metaphor; for he equates those sleeping in the house with the powers of the soul asleep at the moment of ecstasy (N. II, 14, i). It is a "dichosa ventura" to free the soul from the "casa de sensualidad". On the other hand, Santa Teresa's references to casa are more varied than those of San Juan. In most cases, she uses the term to refer to the convents she has founded or to her own home. On one occasion, however, she does liken the Eucharist to the entry of Christ into "casa tan pobre como la suya" (CP. LXI, 4/XXXIV, 8) and the role of "entendimiento" in the prayer of quiet to one "como en casa ajena por huesped y buscando otras posadas adonde estar."[3] Understanding also resembles a mill grinding uselessly in thought when it should be completely recollected (M. IV, 1, xiii).

San Juan's references to the casa de sensualidad and Santa Teresa's to the moledor both imply negative meanings for the respective buildings. The comparisons utilizing castle, palace, and city, on the other hand, maintain essentially positive connotations for each. In a startling departure from the predominantly positive imagery utilized in most of her works, however, Santa Teresa describes a terrifying vision of hell which she experience:

> Ello fue en brevísimo espacio; mas aunque yo viviese muchos años, me parece imposible olvidárseme. Parecíame la entrada a manera de un callejón muy largo y estrecho, a manera de horno muy bajo y escuro y angosto; el suelo me parecía de un agua como lodo muy sucio y de pestilencial olor, y muchas sabandijas malas en él; a el cabo estava una concavidad metida en una pared, a manera de un alacena, adonde me vi meter en mucho estrecho. (V. XXXII, 1)

This vision is the antithesis of the interior castle "todo de diamante u muy claro cristal" (M. I, 1, i). The dominant impression is of darkness and confinement. The room resembles an oven from whose wall is hewn a cavity like a closet "adonde me vi en mucho estrecho." This distorted and frightening picture is all the more effective when juxtaposed with the spacious and regal buildings which serve as symbols for stages on the way to mystical union. Similarly, in the very concreteness of detail it is a more effective negative image than the casa or moledor which are described hardly at all.

Since entry into a building or city is usually achieved by means of a doorway or gate, entrance into the various stages of the mystical life is compared to passing through a door. Thus, to Santa Teresa entry to the interior castle is gained when the soul passes through the door of prayer (M. I, 1, vii). San Juan sees Christ as the doorway to mystical prayer even as he describes the door to union as "la cruz, que es angosta" (CE. XXVI, 13). In the purgative stage, however, San Juan likens the five senses and the three powers of the soul to doors which must systematically be closed if the soul wishes to advance. In contrast, in the unitive state "no ay puerta cerrada" for either mystic since God invites the soul to an intimate union. Only the mystic's continued life on earth prevents him from passing through the final door which allows access to an eternal union.

The door, therefore, symbolizes both entry into the mystical way through prayer and the final passage from union in this life to union with God in eternal bliss. Between these two doors are a myriad of others which must open or close if passage to union and eventual eternal happiness is to be achieved. While representing passage from one stage to another in the inward mystical journey, the door also serves as a traditional comparison of the physical senses to the "doors" or "windows" of the soul through which perception of the natural world enters. Since these sensual "doors" are closed on the passage to union, the mystics strongly imply that their knowledge comes through some other, non-sensual door.

Taking their cue from the Canticle of Canticles (1:3 and 2:4), both San Juan and Santa Teresa devote a great deal of attention to the bodega or wine cellar. To Santa Teresa the bodega symbolizes ecstatic union in which the powers of the soul and senses of the body are so overwhelmed that the mystic feels overcome by an "embriaguez divina". On the other hand, San Juan distinguishes seven moradas through which the soul progresses. Just as few are admitted to the chamber of the king, so also few attain the seventh "bodega" of "matrimonio espiritual".

In the Cántico the entrance of the Bride "en la interior bodega" of the "Amado" emphasizes the interiority of the soul's experience while recalling, yet subtly changing, the Biblical source. In the Canticle it is the king who "introduxit me in cellam vinariam" (Cant. 2:4), while San Juan's use of the first person verbs implies the Bride's action rather than the Bridegroom's. With the addition of Covarrubias' definition of bodega as a "cueva donde se encierra cantidad de vino", (p. 224) further complexity of the symbol occurs. As noted earlier, the repeated entrances as well as the reference to the "mosto de granadas" ties the bodega to strophe XXXVII of the poem. The interrelationship is sealed with the similarity between the cave-like wine cellar and the "subidas cavernas de la piedra", where the Bride finally receives the wish which initially impelled her on her search.

Just as the casa de sensualidad indicated the limitations impeding the soul's progress to union, so too does the cárcel carry a negative connotation in the mystics' works. In their comparisons of the body or life itself to a jail, both Santa Teresa and San Juan continue a traditional metaphor present in secular and religious literature. Limited to the "cárcel" of the body and its senses, the soul cannot ascend to God; but freed from this jail in ecstasy, the mystic does experience union. Conversely, Santa Teresa compares souls in a state of sin to chained prisoners in a dark jail, while her harrowing vision of hell resembled a "cárcel tan tenebrosa" from which God spared her. Conversely, San Juan considers cárcel an apt symbol for the soul passing from the night of the senses to the night of the spirit. For him, leaving the first is like being freed from jail.

If jail is primarily a negative image in the mystics' works, the idea of imprisonment is not. Although the cárcel impedes union, in the Cántico a "prisión tan preciosa" describes spiritual marriage, for the prisoner joined to the soul "por amor en un cabello" is Christ (CE. XXXI, 8). A similar ambivalence surrounds the use of cárcel and prisión in the works of some of the literary predecessors of San Juan and Santa Teresa. In two of Fray Luis de León's poems, for example, prisión like cárcel is a negative image connoting earthly existence.[4] Conversely, in

Llull's mystical libro de caballería, "estaba preso el amigo en la cárcel de amor."[5] In the Spanish Carmelite mystics, however, the reversal of symbolism provides an interesting contrast. The body as cárcel confines the soul, fettering it through the senses to worldly concerns. The soul freed from this incarceration in the enjoyment of mystical union wishes to imprison its divine Lover. While they perpetuate some of the traditional concepts surrounding both cárcel and prisión, San Juan and Santa Teresa also create a more complex symbolic meaning for both images. While cárcel represents the negative aspects of purgation, prisión symbolizes the positive enjoyment of union. The same Amado who frees the soul from the cárcel of worldliness becomes the willing prisoner of the same soul in union.

Further complicating the symbolism of imprisonment is the mystics' treatment of captivity. To San Juan the body represents a kind of "cautiverio", since the soul after original sin is like a "cautiva en este cuerpo mortal" (S. I, 15, i). Yet it is a blessed captivity when the soul allows God to reign over it as Santa Teresa observes in a passage reminiscent of conceptista prose:

> El reine y sea yo cautiva, que no quiere mi alma otra libertad. ¿Cómo será libre el que del Sumo estuviere ajeno? ¿Qué mayor ni más miserable cautiverio que estar el alma suelta de la mano de su Criador? Dichosos los que con fuertes grillos y cadenas de los beneficios de la misericordia de Dios se vieren presos e inhabilitados para ser poderosa para soltarse. (Ex. XVII, 3)

Captivity in earthly concerns is a hindrance to advancement in religious life; yet, paradoxically, mystical union is a captivity also. Union is a state from which the soul does not wish to be freed, however, for that liberty from the chains which bind it to God is a worse captivity still.

When Plato's allegory of the cave is juxtaposed with the imagery of the Spanish mystics, further complications of meaning result. While ecstasy provides a temporary escape from the "cave" of the body, union and eventual spiritual marriage bring the soul peace in this life and harmony between soul and body. The ideal of union occurs in the "interior bodega," "más profundo centro," and, finally, the "subidas cavernas." Whether consciously or not, the mystics have turned the Platonic escape from the cave to an escape to the highest cavern or profoundest center of the soul, thus achieving complete liberty by binding themselves firmly to God's will. As death is their life, so captivity is their freedom.

Within the aposentos and moradas of the interior castle, the mystics furnish a number of objects which assume symbolic significance as well. An important furnishing representing both imagination and contemplation is the mirror, whose ambivalent symbolism Cirlot recognizes, since it not only reflects images but "in a way contains and absorbs them" (pp. 211-12). The mirror's reflective properties link it with the natural mirror formed by the spring and, thus, to the Narcissus myth as well as to the locus amoenus of classical literature. As spring or household furnishing, the mirror appears in the works of a number of mystical predecessors of Santa Teresa and San Juan. In the works of Ruysbroeck, St. Bonaventure, and Richard of St. Victor, the mirror reflects the wisdom and presence of God. In the Divina Commedia, it serves as a metaphor for the mind of God. To both Santa Teresa and San Juan, the mirror is a symbol of the soul which reflects God's presence within it. Conversely, to both writers sin and evil desires thwart the reflective qualities of the mirror, thus obscuring or obliterating the image of God which should be represented therein.

The cristalina fuente of San Juan's Cántico espiritual forms a kind of natural mirror in which the Bride longs to see reflected the eyes of her Beloved. The figurative reflection of the Beloved in the "bosques y espesuras / plantadas por la mano del Amado" (CE. IV) prefigures the more explicit reflection the Bride desires in her command to the Beloved: "Descubre tu presencia, / Y máteme tu vista y hermosura" (CE. XI). The "cristalina fuente" of the following strophe serves as a mirror capable of reflecting God's presence in the soul. The Bride's desire to see the "ojos deseados" of the Bridegroom reflected in the spring water is actually a desire to see the Beloved within herself. If, as traditional lore has it, the eyes are mirrors of the soul, the font-mirror would reflect the eyes of both Bride and Beloved joined as one in union. As a mirror image, therefore, the cristalina fuente functions on a number of symbolic levels. It is a natural mirror reflecting whatever faces it. As it reflects the eyes of the Bride, it symbolizes

her soul. Her desire to see the Amado's eyes reflected in the
waters represents her desire for union with him. The multivalent
symbolic meanings associated with mirror, eyes, and spring
culminate in the final strophes of the Cántico where San Juan
connects a number of themes running through the entire poem. The
eyes referred to in strophes XXXI and XXXII recall the "ojos
deseados" of XI, just as the reference to wounding ("te
llagaste") recalls the mutual wound of love suffered by Bride and
Bridegroom at the beginning of the poem and in the Biblical
source. The physical bond of the hair which binds Amado and
amada explicitly symbolizes the soul's captivation in love while
the triple reference to eyes ("mis ojos," "tus ojos," and "Los
míos") coupled with the verbs referring to sight ("Mirástele,"
"mirabas," and "vían") underscore the loving glances shared
between Bride and Bridegroom in union. The hoped-for reflection
of strophe XII culminates in the realization of the Beloved's
presence in the soul symbolized in strophes XXXI-XXXII.[6]

Another furnishing providing a significant symbol of the
ultimate experience is the lecho or tálamo, symbolic of
attainment of the ultimate stages of union, betrothal and
spiritual marriage. San Juan turns to the Biblical source (Cant.
1:15) in order to describe the "lectulus noster floridus."
Combining the epithalamic symbols present in both Canticle and
his own poem, he presents in the commentary a synthesis of the
doctrinal points which the tálamo represents in the mystical
quest:

aquello que me diste, esto es, aquel peso de gloria en
que me predestinaste, ¡oh Esposo mío! en el día de tu
eternidad cuando tuviste por bien de determinar de
criarme, me darás luego allí en el día de mi desposorio
y mis bodas y en el día mío de la alegría de mi
corazón, cuando desatándome de la carne y entrándome en
las subidas cavernas de tu tálamo, transformándome en
ti gloriosamente, bebamos el mosto de las suaves
granadas. (CE. XXXVIII, 9)

Although he enumerates the symbols of mystical union which he has

presented throughout the poem, San Juan also looks ahead to the

"things that lie ahead in glory." In contrast, the lecho

represents not hope but desengaño for Garcilaso, who describes it

as a "duro campo de batalla" in Sonnet XVII. To the mystic it is

the fulfillment of love, while to the Renaissance poet it

symbolizes frustration.

In spite of her many references to betrothal and spiritual

marriage, Santa Teresa mentions neither lecho nor tálamo in her

works. Rather, she chooses the humbler synonym cama to describe

varied aspects of mystical advancement. The life of denial and

sacrifice necessary for spiritual progress is a "cama dura" (Ex.

XI). Conversely, in her own meditations on the Canticle of

Canticles, she exclaims: "¡Oh!, que es un hacer la cama Su

Majestad de rosas y flores para Sí en el alma a quien da este

cuidado" (Med. II, 5). Her emphasis seems to be on God's action

in the soul prior to union, while San Juan's "nuestro lecho

florido" stresses the mutual preparation of both Bride and

Bridegroom. According to Etchegoyen, Santa Teresa's cama

symbolizes "le recueillement ou l'âme s'isole pour recevoir

Dieu."[7]

It is an interpretation which might equally apply to a similar image in Quevedo's poetic rendering of the "Cantar de Cantares de Salomón."[8] When the esposa of his poem explains to her lover that "en ti solo se ve perfección pura, / y ya que sólo remediarme puedes, / cama florida tengo en que te quedes" (vv. 172-74), Quevedo seems to echo the mystic notion that God and soul unite in the "centro del alma." In the concluding strophe of the poem, the bride further pleads that the lover, once united with her, not abandon her but, rather, that he "entra contento, / que es todo incorruptible el aposento" (vv. 175-80). Quevedo's is a faithful rendering of the sense and language of the Biblical source, yet it lacks the emotional impact and urgency of San Juan de la Cruz's Cántico espiritual. While it seems to imitate the source and imagery of the mystic's work, yet it fails to transmit to its reader a similar overriding sense of quest and union present in the mystical poem.

Like Santa Teresa's "cama . . . de rosas y flores," San Juan's description of the litter in the Cántico espiritual (XXIV) recalls the "lectulus floridus" of the Biblical source (Cant. 1:15-16), even as it intimately links this strophe with other parts of the poem and related concepts in all of his mystical imagery. Thus, the "cuevas de leones enlazado" suggest the protection of the soul by virtue and anticipate the "subidas cavernas" of final, transforming union where the mystical lovers are held in the bonds of their mutual love. The royal purple and the allusion to the crown ("coronado") stress the regal nature of the union realized. The crown also recalls the garlands and piñas woven by the lovers from the flower of virtue. "Escudos" are both crown and shield of the soul symbolizing reward and defense since they represent the virtues and gifts of spiritual marriage. As the culmination of the flower imagery in the Cantico, the lecho is the positive response to the violation of human nature by sin alluded to in the preceding strophe ("Donde tu madre fuera violada"). The lecho thus suggests the wedding of divinity to humanity in the person of Christ as well as the concomitant salvation implicit in that union. Incarnation and redemption symbolisms are then subsumed in the mystical union possible between individual soul and God which is the theme of the entire poem, for the virtues and graces of union "se sustentan y florecen y se gozan sólo en la caridad y amor del Rey del cielo" (CE. XXIV, 7).

Interestingly, in his initial reference to the lecho in the commentary, San Juan considers it something less than transforming union. Citing scripture (Cant. 3:1), he admonishes the soul who seeks Christ through the exercise of virtue to set aside "el lecho de sus gustos y deleytes" (CE. III, 2). The true lecho florido is that of transforming union and is not to be confused with the spiritual favors and consolations which may accompany the earlier stages of the mystical way. The flower-strewn marriage bed is also "de paz edificado". In this sense, it recalls the seventh mansion of Santa Teresa's interior castle for both the "séptima morada" and "lecho florido" provide a sanctuary from Satan and his wiles so that the soul resembles a fortress castle except at its very center where spiritual marriage with the Beloved occurs in the bedchamber of the "palacio muy grande y hermoso" (M. VI, 10, iv).

The golden shields of strophe XXIV introduce a wealth of imagery based on jewels, precious stones, and metals also present in the works of both writers. For Santa Teresa and San Juan precious stones and jewels serve principally as touchstones to determine the value of their experiences. Thus, when Santa Teresa compares Christ to a "joya tan preciosa" and divinity to "un muy claro diamante", she not only combines value of the object with the awesome reality it represents, but also narrows the focus of her symbol to ultimate truth. If one of Covarrubias' definitions for joyas current in the mystics' time is added, further layering of meaning occurs. Thus, when he defines jewels as "los arreos que el desposado embía a la desposada" (p. 715) and Santa Teresa, in turn, calls Christ a "joya," she underscores the notion that the ultimate gift received in union is the Bridegroom himself. The virtues or knowledge symbolized by jewels or metals are but aspects of the Amado reflected in the mystic's soul.

While gold serves as a symbol of splendor and worth, diamonds and crystal are most highly prized for their transparency and are related to precious stones as symbols of spirit and intellect conjoined. Both San Juan and Santa Teresa compare the soul to crystal or diamond capable of translucence or refraction of the rays of light passing through it. As San Juan observes, when clean and pure, the mystic, like crystal:

> . . . es embestido de la luz, que, cuántos más grados de luz va recibiendo, tanto más de luz en él se va reconcentrando y tanto más se va el esclareciendo, y puede llegar a tanto por la copiosidad de luz que recibe, que venga él a parecer todo luz y no se divise entre la luz, estando el esclarecido en ella todo lo que puede recebir de ella, que es venir a parecer como ella. (Ll. I, 13)

On the other hand, Santa Teresa remarks on the reverse of the same comparison, noting that the soul in sin covers the crystal with a "paño muy negro". The interior castle, "todo de un diamante u muy claro cristal", may also contain "cosas tan feas . . . como eran mis pecados" (V. XL, 10). The crystal's transparency either absorbs and enhances the light passing through it so as to become virtually one with it, or, conversely, to show clearly the flaws and faults within.

In his commentary on the Cántico espiritual, San Juan equates the crystalline spring with faith. In a play on the word cristalina, he notes the word's evocation of "Cristo su Esposo." In addition, besides the suggestion of baptism implicit in any spring reference, the properties of crystal "en ser pura en las verdades y fuerte y clara, limpia de errores y formas naturales" admirably represent the essential qualities of faith (CE. XII, 3). In a rather tortured effort to allegorize each individual element pertaining to the cristalina fuente, San Juan considers the "semblantes plateados" symbols of the properties and articles which faith puts before the soul, while "las verdades y substancia que en sí contienen son comparadas al oro" (CE. XII, 4). The Bride's desire to see the ojos deseados mirrored in the waters of the spring is much more than the thirst for an intellectual apprehension of the articles of faith. Rather, it is a wish to attain the fulfillment of faith by reflecting within the soul the "image and likeness of God" to which the mystic aspires in union.

In their consideration of gold, jewels, and precious stones, the mystics maintain an essentially positive polarity by equating them with God and his gifts. They thereby emphasize the inestimable value of mystical experience while also laying the basis for another series of images. Thus, just as thieves lust after gold and jewels, so Satan strives to steal these gifts from the mystics. San Juan calls attention to Satan's insidious presence as thief of the soul's treasure in a description which, while scriptural in its source, is still startling in the language it employs. When juxtaposed with Santa Teresa's description of the soul as "tan esmaltada y compuesta de piedras y perlas de virtudes" (Med. VI, 11), San Juan's description of the devil is even more surprising. Recalling the book of Job (41:6-7), he writes: "su cuerpo es como escudos de metal collado, guarnecido con escamas tan apretadas entre sí, que de tal manera se junta una a otra, que no puede entrar el aire por ellas" (CE. XXX, 10). Although the soul clothed in the virtues of spiritual marriage is protected from this enemy, the juxtaposition of Satan clothed in "escudos" with the "escudos" of the "lecho florido" provides a startling contrast. In its own way, it is as effective as Santa Teresa's vision of hell. Since the imagery of gold and jewels has been predominantly positive, the insertion of this negative comparison stands out. It suggests the danger inherent in progress in perfection. Until it reaches the peace and security of spiritual marriage, the soul must beware of the devil's temptations disguised as virtues.

Diamonds, crystal, and gold may symbolize individual virtues or qualities characteristic of the mystic soul just as tesoros and riquezas collectively encompass the wealth of God's creation or the treasure of the graces he dispenses to the soul. While literal riquezas and tesoros are obvious encumbrances to progress, best abandoned or dispersed if the soul wishes to advance, the spiritual treasures of divine wisdom and knowledge hidden in God are accessible to the mystic soul who attains union. In union, the soul is the passive recipient of the riches freely given by the Beloved, for it is God who chooses to "enriquecer las almas por muchos caminos" (M. V, 3, iv).

Nevertheless, as the riquezas and tesoros of consolations and graces mount up in the business of mystical progress, the contemplative must guard against thieves. These are the temptations and distractions which rob the soul of the treasure of prayer. To both writers, thieves usually symbolize obstacles to virtue, but not all robbery need be an obstacle.

Early in the Cántico espiritual, the Bride complains to the absent Bridegroom:

¿Por qué, pues has llagado
Aqueste corazón, no le sanaste?
Y pues me le has robado,
¿Por qué así le dejaste
Y no tomas el robo que robaste?   (CE. IX)

The sense of the passage is metaphorical yet highly charged with amorous, even sexual overtones. The Bride's wounded heart evokes the image of the stag fleeing from the pursuing huntress, an evocation further underscored by repetition of the verb dejaste, and foreshadows the ciervo vulnerado which shares the wound of love. Implicit in the Bride's statement is both the anguish of separation and the idea of her defloration at the hands of her lover. While robo suggests a negative experience, San Juan describes the soul possessed by God "de cuyo amor se siente robado y llagado el corazón" (CE. XI, 2). The Amado's intention is not to deprive the soul of love but, rather, to impel it to greater love. While the Bride's heart is "desaposesiona[do] . . . a su dueño," it is "aposesiona[do] . . . [por] el robador," God (CE. IX, 4). The heart is thus "bien robado" because it will be jointly possessed with God in union. When the thief is God, the end can only be good, so that robo symbolizes the soul's response to the call to union.

Symbolic references to money cast the mystical experience in the literary currency of business. Santa Teresa states the case explicitly by addressing God the Father as a businessman who extends credit to the soul. The graces received cannot be jealously hoarded but must be dispersed. Neither can the nun believe that she has earned consolations from God as her just due. She cannot "poner tasa a quien sin ninguna da sus dones cuando quiere" (V. XXXIX, 9). The business of the soul is to approach union by purging the affections and appetites. Yet, as it nears the unitive state, it is God who is "el principal agente y el mozo de ciego que la ha de guiar por la mano a donde ella [el alma] no sabría ir" (Ll. III, 29), as San Juan explains. Spiritual exercises are the commerce of contemplation, while its wages are love. Beginning prayer is a "gran negoción" which must not be encumbered by the "negocios de mundo . . . porque llegado el Señor del mundo, todo lo echa fuera" (CPe. LIII, 7). In comparisons of souls to debtors and God to creditor, agent, and mozo de ciego, the mystics stress the passive stages of the mystical experience, thereby underscoring the correspondence of the soul with the graces it receives.

Despite the many negative meanings ascribed to worldly negocios, both San Juan and Santa Teresa also utilize the imagery in positive applications. For Santa Teresa the term negocio most often refers to the business of establishing new houses. She distinguishes between worldly concerns and the true negocios of those under her guidance, however, when she explains:

> éstos han de ser vuestros negocios; éstos han de ser vuestros deseos; aquí vuestras lágrimas; éstas vuestras peticiones; no hermanas mías, por negocios acá del mundo, que yo me río y aún me congojo de las cosas que roguemos a Dios por negocios y pleitos por dineros, a los que querría suplicasen a Dios los repisasen todos. (CP. I, 5)

Similarly, San Juan commences his commentary on the Cántico espiritual by urging the would-be mystic to "[dar] de mano a todo

negocio" (CE. I, 1) and continues in the work to equate negocios
with worldly cares. Yet, in the Llama de amor viva he describes
the soul's exercise of acts of love as a "gran negocio". Both
writers' comparisons of prayer, purgation, and union to negocios,
therefore, suggest the active stages of mysticism. Nevertheless,
each also plays on the conceptismo inherent in the word negocio,
when he or she suggests the subtle relationship between God and
the soul.

The mystics' emphasis on negocio (negotium) in attainment of
mystical union is a denial of the otium characteristic of the
classical pastoral mode.[9] Fray Luis de León's "Alma región
luciente," for example, evokes the archetypal figure of the
pastor, who reclines at noon and "con dulce son deleita el santo
oído" (v. 25). So, too, does John Donne's poem, "The Extasie,"
where the poetic lovers recline upon a grassy bank prior to their
exstasis. In Donne's case, the similarity with the archetype
ends, however, when the poem continues. While their bodies "like
sepulchrall statues lay," the lovers' souls "negotiate" above
their recumbent forms.[10] The English metaphysical appears to
echo the mystics' understanding of negocios in his poem. Rather
than the state of repose or even languor which marks the
pastoral, the ecstasy of both Donne's poem and the mystic
experience is a state of activity on a higher plane. Thus, the
mystical negocio and the negotiations of Donne's ecstatic lovers
go beyond the idealized otium of the classical pastoral. At the
same time, the Spanish mystics in their references to negocios

also anticipate Góngora's panegyric of the farmer's life in the
Soledad primera (vv. 819-831), which balances the labor needed to
sustain the rustic life with the rest characteristic of otium.
While Góngora finds inspiration for his work in Virgil's
pastoral, his presentation of the twin concepts shows their
complementary nature. In similar fashion, the negocio of
mystical prayer looks always to the repose of the soul at the
Beloved's breast in spiritual marriage as its ultimate goal.

As diverse as the imagery based on familiar objects and
their concomitant actions is, an underlying unity is also
evident. As Icaza observes:

> . . . there is always in the works of San Juan de la
> Cruz, unity in diversity, progress in variety;
> . . . The kaleidoscope of the secondary symbols is the
> decisive force that hinders any deterioration into
> allegory because it keeps the symbols multivalent.[11]

Although she limits her discussion to San Juan, what she says is
equally true of Santa Teresa. Whether the mystical writer
utilizes buildings, furnishings, or precious stones, a
fundamental cohesion links these images to the others employed.
Castle, palace, mirror, bed, jewel, gold, and gift inexorably
lead the reader to the central figure of the mystical experience,
God. Among the architectural images employed, castle and city
symbolize both defense from distraction and sin as well as haven
in which the mystic finds God. Similarly, morada, palacio, and
aposento evolve from stages on the way to union to the central
chamber of the king. Only casa and cárcel evince negative
meanings derived from traditional symbolism surrounding Platonic

and neo-Platonic attitudes toward sensual man. Nevertheless, the related concept of imprisonment of and by the Beloved remains wholly positive.

Just as city and castle encompass the central room toward which the soul advances, the imagery of precious metals and stones suggests the hidden treasure of God discovered by the soul who proceeds to its profoundest center. Cave and city are but two facets of the same basic concept. Like the furnishings of the castle, the individual metals and stones of the hidden treasure represent aspects of the mystical experience, whether virtues or gifts, which slowly transform the soul into a fitting image of God.

NOTES

[1] J. E. Cirlot, A Dictionary of Symbols, trans. Jack Sage (New York: Philosophical Library, 1962), pp. 38-39. Isidorus, Etymologiae, XV, 2, xiii defines castellum as "castrum antiquii dicebant oppidum loco altissimo situm, quasi casam altam; cuius pluralis numeris castra, diminutivum castellum est." Source studies of Santa Teresa's castle imagery are many and varied. Joseph F. Chorpenning, "The Literary and Theological Method of the Castillo Interior," JHP, 3 (1979), 121-33, summarizes the arguments proposed by such scholars as Morel Fatio, Les Lectures; Hoornaert, Sainte Thérèse; and Etchegoyen, L'Amour divin, who suggest literary sources; Peers and Ricard, "Le Symbolisme du 'Chateau Interieur' chez Sainte Thérèse" in Etudes sur Sainte Thérèse (Paris: Centre de Recherches Hispaniques, Institut d'Etudes Hispaniques, 1968), pp. 20-38, and "Quelques remarques sur les 'Moradas' de Sainte Thérèse," BH, 47 (1945), 187-198, who cite Biblical sources; and Miguel de Unamuno, "Avila de los caballeros" in Por tierras de Portugal y de España (Madrid: Renacimiento, 1911), pp. 173-83; and E. Trueman Dicken, "The Imagery of the Interior Castle and its Implications," Ephemerides Carmeliticae, 21 (1970), 198-218, who believe that the saint had an actual castle in mind. Miguel Asín Palacios, "El símil de los castillos y moradas del alma en la mística islámica y en Santa Teresa," Al-Andalus, 9 (1946), 263-74; and Luce López Baralt,

"Santa Teresa de Jesús y Oriente", believe Santa Teresa is drawing on Islamic sources; while Menéndez Pidal, La lengua de Cristóbal Colón, pp. 129-53; and Cristóbal Cuevas García, "El significante alegórico en el Castillo toroniano," in Letras de Deusto, 24 (1982), 77-97, see the influence of the chivalric novels. Francisco Márquez Villanueva, "El símil del Castillo interior: sentido y génesis," in Actas del congreso internacional teresiano, II (Salamanca: Universidad de Salamanca, 1983), pp. 495-522, suggests a broader range of possible secular sources drawn from Spanish literature.

[2] In Oreste Macrí, ed., La poesía de Fray Luis de León (Salamanca: Anaya, 1970) p. 243, vv. 67 and 70.

[3] Santa Teresa de Jesús, Camino de perfección, ed. José María Aguado, II (Madrid: Espasa-Calpe, 1973), p. 165. The entendimiento is also compared to a mill which grinds uselessly in thought when it should be completely recollected in the prayer of quiet (M. IV, 1, xiii). In contrast, Hugh of St. Victor, Selected Spiritual Writings, trans. Religious of C. S. M. V. (New York: Harper & Row, 1962), p. 124, seems to emphasize the positive work of understanding when he writes: "Wisdom builds herself a house in the heart of man out of reasonable thoughts."

[4] See "De la vida del cielo" vv. 36-40 and "A Felipe Ruíz," vv. 1-5, pp. 247 and 241 respectively in the Macrí edition.

[5] Ramon Llull, Antología de Ramon Llull, I, trans. Ana María

de Saavedra y Francisco de P. Samaranch (Madrid: Dirección General de Relaciones Culturales, 1961), No. 168, p. 109. He also implies the metaphor of body to cárcel in No. 176, p. 111.

[6] The reader familiar with Latin may also be struck by the similarity between the verb adamabas and the Latin word for diamond, adamas. Whether San Juan wished to evoke the diamond-like clarity of the crystalline spring with the use of the word is speculative. The happy accident of the similarity between the two adds another possible layer of meaning to an already rich combination of images.

[7] Etchegoyen, p. 302.

[8] In Obra poética, I, #198, pp. 380-85.

[9] Corominas, Breve diccionario, p. 413, writes: "Tom. del lat. negotium 'ocupación, quehacer', derv. negativo de otium 'reposo'." Thomas G. Rosenmeyer, The Green Cabinet. Theocritus and the European Pastoral Lyric (Berkeley and Los Angeles: University of California Press, 1969), pp. 65-97, summarizes the classical convention of otium.

[10] In The Metaphysical Poets, ed. Helen Gardner (Baltimore: Penguin Books, 1966, p. 75. See also my article "Donne and the Spanish Mystics on Ecstasy," Notre Dame English Journal, 13 (1981), 33.

[11] Icaza, The Stylistic Relationship, p. 76.

Chapter 5

THE BODY: SOCIAL AND PHYSICAL

From imagery based on the wonders of creation to that
derived from inanimate objects the mystics naturally progress to
images which compare stages of mystical advancement to man,
either as social being or as physical entity, because "por la
consideración de que el hombre es un compendio, una cifra, un
sello admirable de lo creado, un simulacro o imagen del universo,
deduce que los tres mundos, generable, celeste e intelectual, se
contienen en él como en un mundo pequeño.[1] In the scale of
being so assiduously examined by medieval scholarship, man is the
pinnacle of creation in the physical universe so that imagery
which looks to the lower orders of creation for effective similes
and metaphors to describe mystical experience naturally turns to
man for equally effective comparisons. As microcosm the physical
body of man subsumes the elements of the greater creation and
thus admirably serves as summary of all other forms of created
being. Yet, just as the individual body is its own mundo
pequeño, so, too, is the social body a reflection of a mundo más
grande or scale of being leading to God as creator. Thus, while
the physical reality of man embodies the soul into whose most

profound center the mystic must proceed, the social reality reflects a scale of perfection to whose heights the mystic aspires to ascend. In the sixteenth-century, the corpus mysticum becomes synonymous with the corpus iuridicum of the Church whose titular head is the Pope, but whose spiritual leader is always Christ. It is to this mystical body with God as head that Santa Teresa and San Juan address themselves and from which they derive their imagery based on the social body.

Social Body

When Santa Teresa addresses God as "emperador . . . Rey . . . [y] Señor sin fin" (CP. XXXVII/XXII, 1) or as "Príncipe mío", she ascribes to societal terms symbolic meanings which indicate the reality to which she aspires, because "as the stars unite with the sun and receive light, so men join with a king and receive honors."[2] The honors desired by the mystic who addresses God in royal terms are the graces of mystical union. At the same time, in describing God in regal terminolooy the mystic not only reflects the microcosmic theory but also the macrocosmic view of which the corpus mysticum is a part. The Canticle of Canticles sets the tone for the comparison when the Bride refers to the Bridegroom as "rex" (Cant. 1:3). To call Christ king and prince is eminently fitting as Fray Luis de León explains in De los nombres de Cristo, because "a quien hizo [Dios] Príncipe de todos los príncipes y solo verdadero Rey entre todos, como cualidad necesaria y preciada la puso."[3]

Santa Teresa's avowed interest in the romances of chivalry,
her predilection for bellicose imagery, and her own dealings with
Philip II concerning the reform may all explain her attraction to
the language of royalty to describe the mystic's relationship to
God. Whatever the source of her inspiration, the fact remains
that she more than San Juan employs regal and courtly imagery in
her works, as in this example where she distinguishes the
heavenly king from his earthly imitators:

> ¡Oh, Rey de gloria y Señor de todos los reyes, como no
> es vuestro reino armado de palillos, pues no tiene
> fin!, ¡cómo no son menester terceros para Vos! Con
> mirar vuestra persona, se ve luego que es sólo El que
> merecéis que os llamen Señor, siqún la Majestad
> mostráis; no es menester gente de acompañamiento ni de
> guarda para que conozcan que sois Rey. Porque acá un
> rey solo mal se conocerá por sí; aunque él más quiera
> ser conocido por rey, no le creerán, que no tiene más
> que los otros, y ansí es razón tenga estas autoridades
> postizas, porque si no las tuviese, no le ternían en
> nada; porque no sale de sí el parecer poderoso, de
> otros le ha de venir la autoridad. (V. XXXVII, 6)

With God as king, those who serve him resemble nobles who wish to
attend their king without thought of recompense. Even as she
emphasizes the individual soul's need to concentrate its energies
on the goal of mystical union, however, Santa Teresa does not
lose sight of the broader struggle for men's souls represented by
the Reformation. Rather, she continually rallies the forces of
the Counter Reformation with a veritable clarion call to arms:
"¡Oh Cristianos!, tiempo es de defender a vuestro Rey y de
acompañarle en tan gran soledad, que son muy pocos los vasallos
que le han quedado y mucha la multitud que acompaña a Lucifer"
(Ex. X).

In addition to being king of creation, God also rules over
and resides in the interior castle of the mystic's soul.
Transforming the popular refrain that where the king is there is
the court, Santa Teresa states that "adonde está Dios, es el
cielo . . . y que adonde está su Majestad, está toda la gloria"
(CP. XLVI/XXVIII, 2). Since she teaches as well that God is
present within, it follows naturally that the mystic will strive
to join the king of creation in the seventh mansion of the
interior castle where he dwells. Each mystic's interior life
thus mirrors the conflicts present in the Church as a whole, not
merely in terms of the currents of reform sweeping through it in
the sixteenth century, but also in the day-to-day practice of the
faith. Those who approach the king in the interior castle
witness "muchas legiones de demonios" pitting "honras y
pretensiones" against the "vasallos" of the senses and powers of
the soul (M. I, 2, xii). Sin is a veritable battlefield on which
the fallen soul commits "traiciones . . . contra su Rey" (Ex.
XIV). The prize offered bv God to the soul in grace is "un
señorío grande . . . señorío de todos los bienes del mundo" (CP.
II, 5), one greater than that offered by any worldly king.
Microcosm and macrocosm thus merge in Santa Teresa's imagery.
The individual mystic caught up in the pursuit of an interior
union mirrors the Church's pursuit of the unity of one faith
serving one God.

In a series of social metaphors, Santa Teresa extends her
comparisons further when she likens the relationship between God

and man to that which exists between king and laborer, servant
and master, or lord and majordomo. As "el que tiene cuydado del
govierno de la casa de un señor,"[4] the mystic is majordomo of
his soul who must account for the spiritual gifts bestowed on him
by the "Señor". The distance which separates soul from God
resembles that which exists between "un bajo labrador" and the
king. While it might seem presumptuous for the soul to converse
"con el príncipe como con un labradorcito u como con una [sic]
pobre," yet the prince it seeks abases himself in humility so
that just such an intimate conversation may occur (CP.
XXXVII/XXII, 4). The mutual interdependence of criado and amo
also reflects the relationship between soul and God; for just as
the servant has the duty to serve his master, so, too, must the
master feed and protect his servant. Although a similar
comparison in San Juan's Subida draws attention to the gulf
separating creature from Creator, in Santa Teresa's hands it
serves a dual purpose. It not only reflects the distance between
God and his creature noted by San Juan, but it also indicates
their mutual responsibilities. While the soul may resemble the
labradora, criado, or mayordomo in relation to God, all of these
positions imply both service on the part of the inferior and
responsibility on the part of the superior. Unlike the human
social order, however, none of them negates the possibility of
union with rey, príncipe, or amo symbolic of God. Although such
a union may appear virtually unattainable, Santa Teresa asserts
that it is precisely to such intimacy that the mystic is called.

Both San Juan and Santa Teresa not only continue the traditional interpretations of esclavo and siervo found in mystical literature, but they also demonstrate a multivalent flexibility of application as well. Thus, while the soul is the willing slave of God according to Santa Teresa, in San Juan's work the roles are reversed. Awed by the enrichment of the soul in union, San Juan remarks that the Bridegroom "se subjecta a[l alma] verdaderamente para la engrandecer, como si El fuesse su siervo y ella fuesse su señor" (CE. XXVII, 2). Such a comparison inevitably recalls the language of courtly love exemplified by the lovestruck shepherds of the pastoral tradition. On the other hand, Santa Teresa implicitly rejects similar comparisons when she wonders at any soul who would speak "con la majestad de Dios como hablaría con su esclavo" (M. I, 1, vii). Rather than a rejection of the familiarity of the mystical lovers present in San Juan's simile, however, Santa Teresa's remark suggests a concern with the casualness and lack of attention which may characterize the conversation between master and slave. She herself may act as "sierva de este Señor y Rey" in combatting "sus esclavos los demonios" (V. XXV, 20), but she does not go so far as to view God as the willing slave of the soul.

Both Santa Teresa and San Juan underscore the intimacy between mystic and God further when they describe certain states of progress in maternal terms. While San Juan likens souls not advancing in prayer to children petulant at not having their own way or Santa Teresa compares points of honor to children's games,

each concentrates references to familial relationships on those
of the nursing child as Santa Teresa does in describing the soul
in the prayer of quiet. In Las moradas, however, she points out
"que si se aparte de los pechos de su madre, ¿qué se quede
esperar de él sino la muerte?" (M. IV, 3, x). The comparison
thus serves to stress both the passivity and the spiritual
infancy of the soul in the prayer of quiet. San Juan takes the
discussion a step further by employing the same simile. If the
soul is content to remain at this stage of progress, seeking
nourishment and consolation at God's figurative breast, "nunca
dejaría de ser pequeñuelo niño, y siempre hablaría de Dios como
pequeñuelo, y sabría de Dios como pequeñuelo" (S. II, 17, vi).
Thus, just as the infant must be weaned from mother's milk if it
would grow, so, too, must the soul leave the security of the
prayer of quiet if it would advance to union. Only by passing
through the nights of sense and spirit can the mystic hope to
achieve a yet greater intimacy with God.

The maternal attributes ascribed to God in the mystics'
descriptions of the prayer of quiet may go unnoticed in part
because attention is focused on the simile of soul to suckling
child which must be weaned from the favors dispensed at its
mother's (God's) breast.[5] As the soul advances, however,
multivalent associations characterize the references to the child
at its mother's breast. In the Cántico espiritual, for example,
the soul in spiritual marriage reclines its "cuello en los dulces
brazos del Amado" and, like the Bride of the Canticle, inquires:

"¿Quién te me diesse, hermano mío, que mamases los pechos de mi madre, de manera que te hallase yo sólo afuera y te besase y ya no me despreciase nadie?" (CE. XXII, 9). San Juan explains that the breast referred to here represents the soul's human nature with its passions and appetites which the Bridegroom "enjugas[e] y apagas[e]" so that it may join him in spiritual marriage.

As the union of spiritual marriage grows more intimate, however, the breast of the Bridegroom is given freely to the Bride. While the intimacy between the mystic lovers grows more profound, it transcends that of all human counterparts. Nevertheless, San Juan focuses on the Amado's breast given freely to the Bride in the intimacy of union, emphasizing the power of its symbolism when he writes:

> Dar el pecho uno a otro es darle su amor y amistad y descubrirle sus secretos como a amigo. Y así, decir el alma que le dio allí su pecho, es decir que allí le comunicó su amor y sus secretos, lo cual hace Dios con el alma en este estado. (CE. XXVII, 4)

What was only suggested in the relationship between soul and God in the prayer of quiet is here made explicit. God embodies both the maternal qualities of the mother giving nourishment to the child and the utter intimacy of the lovers locked in union. From a symbol of dependence from which the soul must be weaned if it would advance, the pechos de la madre now represent the lasting union of spiritual marriage whose favors the soul desires never to lose.

Linked to the simile of mother and child is another symbol of the bond of intimacy enjoyed between soul and God in union, the kiss. In San Juan's commentary on the Cántico espiritual, the beso represents the final stages of union when the author equates spiritual marriage with el beso del alma a Dios" (CE. XXII, 7). In these terms, the beso confirms Perella's observation that "the mystics, unlike ordinary lovers, tend to make of the kiss not merely a preliminary of the love relationship, but love's very terminus."[6] Such is not the case, however, in the works of Santa Teresa, where beso serves much more ambivalent functions. In her own meditations on the Canticle, she initially defines the kiss as "señal de paz y amistad grande entre dos personas" (Med. I, 11). In discussing it, however, she juxtaposes the kiss of the Canticle with that of the world, represented by Judas' kiss of betrayal. The soul that betrays the graces given it in the mystic quest resembles no one so much as the quintessential traitor of the Gospel, who turned the symbol of friendship into a cruel mockery. Rather, the mystic desires but one thing, the "ósculo que pedía la Esposa (M. VII, 3, xiii).

However fitting the kiss may be as a symbol of union, it suffers from at least one defect in communicating to the non-mystic the lasting nature of the experience of mystical union: its transitoriness. For all of its symbolism of intimacy and union, it remains a temporary joining of lovers. Some other symbol must suffice to embody the lasting nature of the final state of union. In the broader context of the mystics' works, the kiss thus points to the symbol of spiritual marriage, "because the Union of Marriage is, as its name implies, no passing, occasionally repeated experience, but an almost continuous one."[7]

That the mystical writer turns to the language of human love for analogies to describe union with the divine Lover is a natural progression. While other symbols convey something of the experience of union of soul and God, none carries the same psychological and emotional power as does spiritual marriage. The immediate source for the comparison is the nuptial language of the Bible. Thus, Christ's union with his spouse, the Church, noted by St. Paul (Eph. 5:23-33), and, more importantly, that of Bride and Bridegroom in the Canticle of Canticles were eagerly seized upon by mystical writers from the time of Origen to provide metaphors for their experiences of union. While the Pauline texts are not as readily extended to mystical interpretations, nevertheless, the long allegorical tradition surrounding the interpretation of the Canticle lays the basis for the mystics' use of it. Although the Spanish mystics adhere to the traditional allegorical interpretation of the Canticle of Canticles, what they bring to their individual commentaries on it as well as to their imagery derived from it is a unique perspective and synthesis.

The predilection of numerous mystics both before and after San Juan and Santa Teresa for imagery based on that of Bride and Bridegroom in the Canticle belies a central fact observed by Montgomery and Underhill. It is not merely the allegorical interpretation of the Biblical source which saw in the Canticle a metaphor for soul and God joined in mystical union which accounts for the mystics' use of imagery based on spiritual marriage. Rather, as both critics assert, the reverse is just as likely: "namely, that the mystic loved the Song of Songs because he there saw reflected, as in a mirror, the most sacred experiences of his soul."[8] Indeed, in seeking adequate analogies to convey some truth concerning the essence of their ineffable experience of union with an infinite God, the mystics could find few better examples of the beauty of pure love, human or divine, than those afforded by the poetic dialogue of Bride and Bridegroom in the Canticle of Canticles. The divine nuptials, which are the end of the mystic's quest, thus "form in some sense a focus of all other mystical symbolisms and of the mystical life itself."[9]

Not only the Canticle of Canticles but also the medieval mystical treatises which utilized the Biblical source as a veritable thesaurus of mystical imagery, offered the Carmelite writers examples of rhetoric suitable to their literary as well as spiritual task. Thus, when Saint Bonaventure likens the embrace of truth to that of Lover embracing Beloved, and Hugh of St. Victor considers God the Bridegroom, and His bride the soul; both writers convert the language of the Canticle to their own mystical uses.[10] The immediate spiritual predecessors of Santa Teresa and San Juan in Spain also place their own individual stamp on the language of love. In his Libro de amigo y Amado, Raimundo Llull at first suggests the relationship of soul with God allegorically presented in the Canticle. Nevertheless, as

Hatzfeld notes: "lo que falta, en las formulaciones aforísticas lulianas de la amistad divina, es la característica fundamental, clásica y católica, de relación entre el alma y Dios. Esta característica es nupcial y lo es radicalmente en la poesía de San Juan."[11] A similar lack of wholly mystical symbolism is evident in De los nombres de Cristo by Fray Luis de León. In the chapter which discusses the title, "Esposo," Fray Luis offers a summary of the significance of the term: "Tres cosas son . . . las que este nombre de Esposo nos da a entender, y las de que nos obliga a tratar: el ayuntamiento y la unidad estrecha que en ella nasce de aquesta unidad; los accidentes, y, como si dixéssemos, los apparatos y circunstancias del desposorio."[12] Although his final reference hints at mystical symbolism, Fray Luis never conveys the sense of transforming union of which spiritual marriage is a symbol. His works speak of aspiration rather than realization of union with the Beloved as he manifests in the concluding verses of "Alma región luciente."

Even in the works of both Carmelite mystics, references to esposa and esposo do not always imply mystical union. When Santa Teresa states that "u somos esposas de tan gran rey, u no" (CP. XIX/XIII,2), she just as readily suggests the role of religious women in the Catholic Church as she does the mystical life. When San Juan urges his readers to "toma[r] a Dios por esposo y amigo con quien [se] ande[n] de continuo" (Dichos LXVII), like Santa Teresa he uses the symbol of the esposo in a non-mystical sense. Nevertheless, in the majority of his works, references to spiritual espousals repeat or extend traditional readings of the Canticle's esposo/esposa that posited as the first spouse of Christ his humanity; the second, the Church; the third, the Blessed Virgin; and the fourth, the soul of the saint.[13] Thus, San Juan's equation of Bridegroom and Bride with Christ and the Church reflects contemporary exegesis in the sixteenth century.

In the works of both authors, the relationship between esposa and divine Esposo mirrors that of earthly lovers bent on eventual marriage. Preceding the consummation of love in marriage are the espousals between potential bride and bridegroom. Desposorio is the prelude to union, when the soul figuratively accepts the Esposo's proposal to proceed to the final mystical state. In Santa Teresa's case, the moment of espousal resembles a virtual proposal of marriage between lovers, as she describes in the Cuentas de conciencia (XXV). When the Esposo offers her his hand then virtually sweeps her off her feet, the event mirrors the marriage proposals of secular letters.

It is in the Moradas that one finds Santa Teresa's most comprehensive description of the nature of spiritual betrothal and marriage. The soul's espousal to God imitates its secular counterpart in the saint's description inasmuch as the couple about to be betrothed "se trata si son conformes y que el uno y el otro se quieran y aun que se vean, para que más se satisfaga el uno del otro." Just so in spiritual betrothal, the soul finds itself in conformity with the will of its Beloved, conscious of what is required of it, and willing to proceed. Nevertheless, even though the soul "bien determinada queda a no tomar otro esposo," the Bridegroom continues to test its resolve (M. VI, 1, i). The wrenching spiritual and physical changes brought about by ecstatic union necessitate the prolonged testing to which the soul finds itself subjected. Returning to the comparison of the poor peasant espoused to the king, Santa Teresa calls attention once again to the gap which separates the would-be lovers. Lest the soul perish at the sight of its divine Lover, therefore, "desposorio . . . debe ser cuando da arrobamientos, que le saca de sus sentidos; porque si estando en ellos se viese tan cerca desta gran Majestad, no era posible, por ventura, quedar con vida" (M. VI, 4, ii). While the Bridegroom effects the desposorio through the medium of rapture in order to spare the soul, the experience of ecstasy as Santa Teresa describes it in her works is in itself a wrenching ordeal.

Although San Juan does not focus on the effects of rapture and ecstasy in the detail present in Santa Teresa's description of desposorio, other similarities between the two authors do exist.[14] Thus, the moment of betrothal in the Cántico espiritual first recalls man's fall and redemption symbolized by the "manzano" beneath which the soul was "reparada / Donde [su] madre fuera violada" (CE. XXIII). The echo of the baptismal bond of desposorio quickly gives way to the deeper bonds of mystical intimacy symbolized by the "lecho florido". In the commentary, San Juan concentrates on the "muchas y grandes comunicaciones y visitas y dones y joyas del Esposo" enjoyed by the Bride (CE. XXII, 3). The esposa of the Cántico also gives her attention wholly to the Esposo, for she "no sabe otra cosa sino amar y andar siempre en deleites de amor con el Esposo" (CE. XXVII, 8). Having passed through the trials and tribulations of purgation, the soul now enjoys "une alternance non hurtée de répos et de mouvement."[15]

Whether the desposorio be marked by peace preceded by a painful period of deprivation or be accomplished in the exalted yet wrenching experience of rapture, both mystics agree that it is not the final state enjoyed by the soul in its quest for a lasting union with the Beloved. Just as it does in the temporal order, desposorio holds out a promise of a permanent union which will only be realized in the consummation of matrimonio espiritual. It is to this end that the soul has been directing all of its energies from the outset. Whether the mystic ventures through the various moradas of Santa Teresa's interior castle in hopes of reaching the innermost wherein dwells the king or pursues the Beloved across the figurative landscape of the soul longing for the repose of the subidas cavernas of San Juan's Cántico, the end desired remains a permanent union symbolized by "el sacramento del matrimonio".[16] Thus, while desposorio marks the illuminative stage, matrimonio espiritual is the culmination of the unitive state.

For Santa Teresa, spiritual marriage occurs in the seventh mansion of the interior castle, a state attained by the soul when

God chooses to place it there. It is distinct from the raptures of betrothal, yet difficult to describe. God manifests himself through the medium of a "vision imaginaria de su sacratísima Humanidad," choosing the moment and circumstances in which to effect the union. In spite of the transformation wrought in the soul by the experience, Santa Teresa stresses that only in heaven can it be assured of a permanent union with the Bridegroom. While in this life the soul must continually remind itself that "de esto sirve este matrimonio espiritual: de que nazcan siempre obras, obras" (M. VII, 4, vi). The test of the validity of all the mystical experiences enjoyed by the soul remains the acts which follow them. A persistent warning echoes through all of Santa Teresa's works to the effect that mystical union is not to be sought in and of itself. If the graces received do not result in good works toward others, then the danger exists that the soul is deceived in what it experiences.

Matrimonio espiritual figures in all three of San Juan's mystical poems either explicitly as in the Cántico espiritual and the Noche oscura or implicitly in the brilliant imagery of the Llama de amor viva. The successive entrances of the Bride in her pursuit of the Amado progressively lead her to the "estado deleitoso del matrimonio espiritual" (CE. XXII, 2), which she has desired since the outset of the poem. She achieves this perfect union when, like the Bride of the Canticle, she reclines in the embrace of the Beloved. The repose of the Bride mirrors the joy of union symbolized by the reunited animals and birds which have served as surrogates of the soul and its divine Lover throughout the entire work. In his final comment of the Cántico, San Juan looks beyond the spiritual marriage "a que Dios le ha querido llegar [al alma] en esta iglesia militante" to that "glorioso matrimonio de la triunfante" which is the beatific vision (CE. XL, 7). The glory which is to come and to which the mystic ultimately aspires remains the magnet which draws the soul inward.

Like the Cántico espiritual, the Noche oscura presents the soul's symbolic journey to union with the Amado. San Juan manifests his powers as a poet when he expresses the essence of transforming union in a three-verse statement remarkable not only for the interplay of sound contained therein but also for its limpid simplicity: "¡Oh noche que juntaste / Amado con amada / Amada en el Amado transformada!" (N. IV, 23-25). While these brief lines capture the soul's complete transformation by love, still, as Spitzer notes, they also stress that "the metaphysical metamorphosis . . . (amada becoming one with el Amado) implies no complimentary transformation (Amado=amada)."[17] Nor does San Juan suggest a total loss of identity on the part of the soul, for transformation cannot imply annihilation to the Christian mystic. What he does capture in sound, however, is a harmonious interchange between the terms of the union ("Amado," "amada," and "transformada") which still retains the identity of the individual elements. Following this ecstatic union is a repetition of the image of the lovers locked in an embrace. In both Cántico and Noche oscura, the language and circumstances of spiritual marriage mirror each other. The longing and eventual fulfillment captured in the mutual search and loving embrace of Bride and Bridegroom transcend those of earthly lovers in part because, as Hatzfeld has noted, "el lugar del encuentro final para el gran abrazo conyugal no se puede determinar topográficamente."[18]

The union symbolized by the Llama de amor viva is at once more sensual and more ethereal than that of the Cántico or the Noche. The series of exclamatory strophes heightens the feeling of ecstatic joy experienced by the soul. Juxtaposed with the specific physical references to wounds, touch, hand, and flame are the non-sensorial "más profundo centro" and the secret dwelling place of the Beloved "en [su] seno." The lingering peace and joy of the Bride experienced in the union thus described looks ahead to eternity, for however much the earthly spiritual marriage may reflect that of eternity, yet it cannot compare with what awaits the soul in heaven.

In the works of both Santa Teresa and San Juan spiritual marriage symbolizes the culmination of the mystic's quest. That it is an aspiration within the grasp of the soul is attested to by the explanations of the state offered by both writers. That it brings with it a concomitant sense of joy and fulfillment as well as a commitment to action on the part of the chosen soul is also evident. In contrast, similar references to esposo and union in the poetry and prose of the Carmelites' contemporary,

Fray Luis de León, show a less certain sense of the possibility of mystical union. In "Alma región luciente," a poem disconcertingly called mystical by a number of literary critics, Fray Luis expresses a longing for a permanent union with the Beloved similar to that intimated by the mystics, but he just as readily emphasizes how difficult such an attainment is. His use of the subjunctive in the final two strophes of the ode underscores the difficulty while calling attention to his longing for such a union.[19]

Amatory poetry in the secular sphere also reflects the anguish experienced by the poet at separation from or loss of the object of his love. The disconsolate Nemoroso of Garcilaso's Egloga I comes to terms with his irreparable loss of Elisa by envisioning reunion with her "en la tercera rueda" (Eg. I, v. 400), just as Quevedo after him contemplates the possibility of joining his beloved after death in "Amor constante más allá de la muerte." Even the possibility of marriage with the women they love holds no promise of unmitigated joy for secular poets, since death or infidelity or fickleness may shred the fabric of the union. The mystic fears no loss of his Beloved save from his own unfaithfulness. Death holds no terror for him because, rather than separation, it assures the lasting union to which he aspires and of which spiritual marriage on earth is but a pale reflection.

While Hatzfeld rightly observes that the topography of the place of mystical union remains non-specific, the mystics

themselves indicate that union occurs "en el centro muy interior
del alma." Santa Teresa's entire Moradas turns on the symbolism
of a combined entrance and ascent to the seventh mansion where
God dwells. Nevertheless, although the soul takes the first
steps on the way to union, it is "su Majestad [que] nos ha de
meter y entrar en el centro de nuestra alma" (M. V, 1, xiii).
Her insistence on the centrality of the place of union is an
implicit affirmation of a Ptolemaic world view which envisions
creation as a series of concentric spheres or ascending steps of
being with God at its center or apex. Trueman Dicken considers
why Santa Teresa chooses the term centro in the Moradas when he
speculates:

> . . . Is it not because this adds something of real
> profundity and significance to her exposition,
> something she was unaware of in her earlier writings?
> She could so easily have done what so many as great or
> almost as great as she have done, and written of
> spiritual progress under the imagery of a journey, the
> ascent of a mountain or the steps of a ladder. But she
> chooses the allegory of penetration to a secret inner
> apartment 'right in the middle.' There is one other
> writer who does so: St. John of the Cross.[20]

In combination with the controlling imagery of the entire work
which revolves around an interior journey to union through the
concentric circles formed by the preliminary mansions of the
spiritual castle, Santa Teresa's use of centro gains added
force. God at the center of the soul's interior castle is not
only its end but also its beginning, its alpha and its omega.

San Juan de la Cruz employs the symbolic center both
directly, as in the Dichos (LXXXIX), but also indirectly as in

the Cántico espiritual and the Noche oscura. Each of these poems
implies a movement inward to the mystic center or upward to the
apex of the spiritual mountain, while the Llama de amor viva
makes explicit reference to "el más profundo centro" and the
"seno" of the soul. The commentary on these verses suggests a
sense of concentricity similar to that which marks Santa Teresa's
Moradas. Nevertheless, San Juan quickly clarifies that the soul
as spirit has neither height nor depth as the physical body does,
so that to speak of more or less profound centers is to describe
the intensity of the experience rather than to suggest a spatial
notion. Even as he summarizes his discussion of centro, he
stresses that the essence of the soul's center remains God. Like
the ameno huerto, the interior bodega, and the tenth rung of the
escala secreta, the más profundo centro expresses in different
terms the same mystical reality.

In their use of centro as a symbol, both Carmelites subsume
a tradition developed in countless Christian and non-Christian
mystical treatises in which "to leave the circumference for the
centre is the equivalent to moving from the exterior to the
interior, from form to contemplation, from multiplicity to unity,
from space to spacelessness, from time to timelessness."[21] In
contrast to Garcilaso's unhappy shepherd who seeks the oblivion
of the "centro de la fuente" (Eg. II, 985) where he may escape
the anguish occasioned by the loss of his beloved, the mystic
joyfully approaches the center where peaceful repose with the
Amado awaits. To both Santa Teresa and San Juan the centro

represents their end and their beginning, the very essence of their experience, God himself, who leads them to transforming union in spiritual marriage. In its very non-specificity, centro is a quintessential symbol of the ineffable mystical union.

Physical Body

Those hierarchical tendencies present in the imagery derived from the social body are also evident in the images based on the physical body which the Spanish mystics employ in their works. Of equal importance is the Neo-Platonist tradition which views man as a composite of physical body and spiritual soul, a composite that is profoundly paradoxical.

> La paradoja es que el hombre se compone de alma y cuerpo; aunque es de origen divino, está sujeto al mal ontológico puesto que en el concepto platónico, la materia es mala porque es un defecto para el espíritu; por este defecto de su naturaleza el hombre siente proclividad al mal moral porque la parte espiritual de su naturaleza puede aceptar como perfecto ningún amor que no sea completamente espiritual, mientras que el cuerpo exige que el amor sea sensual, y por eso, imperfecto. [22]

The mystic's interior journey to union reflects the Plotinian catharsis which calls for sublimation of the sensual appetites if the soul would eventually reach the divine. Nevertheless, the mystics also manifest an ambivalence toward imagery based on the physical body. Thus, man as image not only embodies the apparent Neo-Platonic dichotomy of body and soul but also the microcosmic view expressed by Origen who writes: "Understand that you are another world in miniature and that you are the sun, the moon, and also the stars."[23]

When Santa Teresa and San Juan cast the body or the flesh (cuerpo or carne in their works) in the role of prison or obstacle to the soul's union, they reiterate the Platonic view of man. Such negative connotations for the body set the stage for the penultimate separation of soul from body manifest in the feigned death of mystical ecstasy. The ecstatic flight of the liberated soul suggested in Saint Paul's description of man, "sive in corpore . . . sive extra corpus . . . raptum huiusmodi usque ad tertium caelum" (II Cor. 12:2) and Fray Luis de León's "A Salinas" becomes reality in the mystics' experience where "el espíritu . . . verdaderamente parece sale del cuerpo" (M. VI, 5, vii). The mystic flight makes possible the intimate communication between soul and divine Lover, an experience transcending sensual perception. Nevertheless, the mystic remains in an earthly existence despite his experience of union, so that reintegration of soul and body is the inevitable conclusion of ecstasy.

In the works of both mystics, therefore, it is the sensual appetites of the body which must be eliminated in the advance to union. While his baser instincts prevent his spiritual advancement, man's physical body is not in and of itself an impediment to mystical union. Paradoxically, as the mystic approaches the essential union of soul and God, the language he employs becomes in many respects more sensual. Commenting on San Juan's Noche oscura, for example, Spitzer calls attention to the paradox: "The Catholic saint treats no lesser subject than the ecstatic union, not with a human being but with the divine, in terms that constantly fuse soul and body."[24] Rather than an outright rejection of the physical body, therefore, the mystic describes a purification and veritable spiritualization of it, so much so that the seventeenth-century English metaphysical poet, John Donne, would say of the lovers' bodies in ecstasy: "nor are they drosse to us, but allay" (v. 56). The body thus becomes the medium through which mystics give adequate expression to their ineffable experience of union, an event of earthly existence which yet transcends it.

Just as cuerpo functions as an ambivalent symbol in the works of the Spanish mystics--on the one hand as the flesh which imprisons the soul; on the other, as the necessary bond for the soul in this earthly life--no less is true of specific parts of the body which the Carmelite writers use as figurative representations of different aspects of their mystical experiences. Thus, Hatzfeld remarks that "el símbolo corporal más adecuado para representar la atracción del amor son ojos, por ser los que mejor reflejan el alma humana."[25] Covarrubias' definition of them, which calls "los ojos la parte más preciosa del cuerpo . . . [y] las ventanas adonde el alma suele asomarse, dándonos indicios de sus afectos y pasiones de amor y de odio . . . [y] los mensageros del coraçon y los parleros de lo oculto de nuestros pechos" (p. 835), emphasizes the traditional notions surrounding the symbolic function of the eye as window of the soul.

Unlike Santa Teresa's predominantly colloquial use of eye imagery, San Juan's inclusion of it in the Cántico espiritual is both extensive and subtly tied to the other imagery of the poem. Its importance in the Cántico is initially suggested in the opening strophes which introduce the theme of search on the part of the Bride and an alternating hiding and revealing on the part of the Bridegroom. The Bride's search through the figurative landscape of the soul for the Bridegroom concludes with an almost desperate query addressed to the missing Amado. Following this anguished question is a four-strophe section in which direct references to eyes are made explicit, culminating in the reappearance of the Bridegroom.

In strophe X, the Bride demands of the Amado "Y véante mis ojos, / Pues eres lumbre dellos, / Y solo para ti quiero tenellos," thus making explicit her desire to reunite herself with him, the veritable light of her life. In the commentary, San Juan describes the eyes of the soul's will which desire to "abrirlos sólo a su Dios" (CE. X, 9). The eyes of strophe X, therefore, are those of the soul; the lumbre is God. The succeeding strophe both continues and extends the threads of imagery already established in the poem. The secondary effects of the Bridegroom's passage through the figurative landscape, "mil gracias derramando", no longer suffices. The Bride here desires "cierta presencia afectiva que de si hizo el Amado a el alma", a vision that "no la puede sufrir [el] alma, sino que [tiene] de morir en viéndola" (CE. XI, 4-6). The anticipated death occasioned by a face-to-face meeting with the Bridegroom, however, need not be that of the physical body but, rather, the feigned death of ecstasy.

A subtle shift of focus in eye imagery occurs in strophe XI when the poet refers to the effect of the Bridegroom's glance ("tu vista") directed at the soul. In the following strophe, the shift becomes clearer where the "ojos deseados" refer to those of the Bridegroom. Nevertheless, they also refer to the Bride's, for they are "en [sus] entrañas dibujados." At the same time, however, the spring into which the esposa gazes acts as a natural mirror that reflects the image of the gazer, in this case the soul-Bride. The ambivalence of symbolic meaning attributed to eye references in these strophes reflects the shimmering images which play across the "semblantes plateados" of the "cristalina fuente".

The "Apártalos, Amado / Que voy de vuelo" which opens the next strophe is addressed by the Bride to the Bridegroom. In light of her earlier plea to see the ojos deseados, this contrary demand to take them away "seems strange indeed until it is realized that between the two stanzas the beloved has in fact acceded to the soul's desires: he has granted her the vision of himself, has let her see his eyes, has vouchsafed to her the vision which he has himself."[26] The vision consists of "verdades divinas", but its effect is one of ecstatic flight for the soul. Incapable of sustaining union with the object of her search in the physical body, the Bride is impelled toward an ecstatic union outside the body until restrained by the Bridegroom's counter-command to return.

Significantly, the reappearance of eye imagery occurs only after the soul has properly prepared itself in the intermediate stages of mystical progress. Unlike the precipitous ecstatic flight cut short by the Bridegroom's command to return, in the "interior bodega" the soul drinks deep of knowledge of the Amado in ecstasy. In the aftermath of such intimacy, the soul as Bride rests on the bosom of the Beloved, holding him by the thin thread of "sólo aquel cabello", and wounding him with her loving gaze. Further emphasizing their mutual attraction of love in strophe XXXII, San Juan elaborates on the eye imagery already established. The reflection of each in the eyes of the other recalls the reflection the Bride beheld in the waters of the spring. While the eyes of the earlier strophe were actually those of the soul alone, in this strophe those of both Bride and Bridegroom appear. In his commentary, San Juan explains that "por los ojos del Esposo entiende aquí su divinidad misericordiosa" while those of the Bride represent "las potencias de [su] alma" (CE. XXXII, 3-8). In an interior vision, therefore, the soul gazes on the object of its love, becoming one with it.

In an echo of the Canticle of Canticles (4:9) San Juan indicates that the mystical lovers are bound not only by eye contact but also by "aquel cabello", which ensnares the Bridegroom and binds him to the Bride in love. When San Juan explains in the commentary that the "cabello suyo es su voluntad de ella [el alma] y el amor que tiene al Amado" (CE. XXX, 9), he accentuates the full participation of the soul in the act of union. Unlike ecstasy, where the soul may futilely resist the wrenching separation from the body, the union described here is one of peaceful cooperation. The connecting thread between strophes XXX and XXXI is the "cabello" which binds up the "guirnaldas" made by the lovers as it also binds them together in union. At the same time it is the means whereby the soul ensnares the divine Lover, symbolized by the "águila real" (CE. XXXI, 8). The threads of imagery in the poem thus begin to entertwine.

Although the cabello of the Cántico pertains to the Bride, in the Noche oscura the term refers to the Bridegroom. The shift of emphasis in the two poems reflects a similar shift in its Biblical source. In Canticle 4:9, the strand of hair is that of the Bride which wounds the Bridegroom, while in Canticle 5:11 the locks of hair are those of the Bridegroom likened to palm branches. San Juan follows the strophe dealing with ecstatic union in the Noche oscura (V) with another (VII) which describes a continuing union of soul with Amado in language reminiscent of the Cántico. Both the setting and the details of the strophe recall Canticle 5:11 which enumerates the physical attributes of the Bridegroom and thus parallels the earlier catalogue of the Bride's attributes in Canticle 4:9-16. Paradoxically, the very specific physical details enumerated in both poems create an ethereal, almost unreal, ambience in which the union of the mystical lovers occurs.

In the catalogue of physical attributes which describes the Bride's beauty in the Canticle of Canticles, the strand of hair appears in conjunction with her neck. It is a combination which San Juan repeats in both the Cántico and the Noche oscura. By focusing on a few selected details from the Biblical source, he concentrates the effect of the union between mystic and divine Lover. Thus, in the Cántico, the single lock which seems to float on the neck of the Bride entrances and eventually ensnares the Bridegroom in an embrace of love. In the Noche oscura, on the other hand, it is the Bride who is enthralled by the locks of the Amado. He, in turn, wounds her "en [su] cuello" with a touch of his hand. His explanation in the commentary that "el cuello significa la fortaleza" makes eminent mystical sense while somehow robbing the imagery of its emotional and poetic force.

Nevertheless, the Noche oscura also provides a description of peaceful repose enjoyed by the mystical lovers. In the concluding three strophes of the poem, the poet encapsulates the shared experience of love between the soul and God. Initially, it is the Amado who "quedó dormido" at the breast of the amada and she who stroked his hair. Conversely, it is the Bridegroom who wounds her, so that she "el rostro reclin[ó] sobre el Amado". The utter bliss enjoyed by the soul in this state differs slightly from that of the Bride of the Cántico who in the "interior bodega" received "la sabiduría y secretos y gracias y virtudes y dones de Dios" (CE. XXIV, 3), because the emphasis of the Noche oscura is on the cessation of all activity on the part of the soul save that of loving the Amado.

While the inspiration for San Juan's imagery in the Cántico espiritual and the Noche oscura is primarily the Canticle of Canticles, his poetic language parallels that of Garcilaso's Égloga I. The distressed Nemoroso addresses the missing Elisa in verses 267-276 with a wistful series of questions. Present in the passage are the same physical details--"pecho," "cabello," "cuello," and "ojos"--which San Juan incorporates into his description of the soul's union with the Amado. Although the details present in both poems emphasize the bond of love between the lovers, Nemoroso's pathetic questions underscore his irreparable loss of Elisa through death. San Juan's use of similar language in the context of his mystical poem serves a different purpose, for it calls attention to the unbreakable bond of union between soul and God, transcending the physical bonds intimated by Garcilaso. Ironically, the secular poet's use of present and imperfect tenses emphasizes the sense of loss, because it indicates the gulf which separates what used to be with what is. San Juan's use of preterite and imperfect creates an opposite effect. It holds out the hope of repetition of the experience.

Absent from Santa Teresa's works is the same attention to physical detail based on the human body present in that of San Juan's. While the Canticle of Canticles affords the latter a rich source of poetic language on which to draw when describing the union of the mystical lovers, Santa Teresa's brief commentary on the same Biblical source shows none of her protégé's facility with imagery. Rather, she confines her Meditaciones sobre el Cantar to a few, brief lines, developing only kiss imagery in any detail. In a more familiar vein, however, she draws on other scriptural texts in order to elucidate her observations concerning religious life and mystical advancement. Some of these, such as her reminder that "adonde está su tesoro se va allá el corazón" (M. I, 1, viii), echo the Gospel. Other references which utilize the heart as a symbol recognize in it the power of "un centro, principio y fin de todo movimiento."[27] When both San Juan and Santa Teresa equate the corazón with the will or understanding of the soul, they echo Biblical comparisons. Nevertheless, the dominant symbolism of the heart remains that of the center, "aquel punto encendido del corazón del espíritu" as San Juan describes it (Ll. II, 11).

Such a centrality of purpose and symbolism regarding corazón is most evident in Santa Teresa's description of ecstatic rapture in the Vida. She first likens the absence of the Lord to "una saeta [hincada] en lo más vivo de las entrañas y corazón [del alma]" (V. XXIX, 10). Paradoxically, the moment of union creates a similar effect. Envisioning a cherub armed with a dart, she writes:

> . . . víale en las manos un dardo de oro largo, y al
> fin de el hierro me parecía tener un poco de fuego;
> éste me parecía meter por el corazón algunas veces y
> que me llegava a las entrañas; al sacarle, me parecía

> las llevava consigo y me dejava toda abrasada   en   amor
> grande de Dios.   (V. XXIX, 13)

She   goes   on   to   stipulate that the   experience   "no   es   dolor
corporal, sino espiritual, aunque no deja de participar el cuerpo
algo, y aun harto." Although   Etchegoyen   points   out   that   the
image of the   arrow-pierced   heart   was   virtually   a   cliché   in
sixteenth-century   literature,[28]   Santa   Teresa's   use   of   it
transcends   the conventions of secular literature.   She   achieves
this effect in part through the profoundly personal nature of her
narration in the context of the autobiography.   Her   ability   to
transcend the usual commonplace rendering of it in amatory poetry
is evident in   the   sculpture   and   poetry   it   inspires   in later
generations of artists such as Bernini and Crashaw.

The   figurative   hands   of   the   cherub   who   effects   the
trasverberation are   directed   by   God.   It   is   fitting   as   well as
conventional imagery to speak of   God's   power   in terms of   manos.
In the works of both mystics, references to   mano symbolize   power
and will, for, as Covarrubias later observes: "tener mano,   tener
poder . . . está en mi mano, esta en mi   voluntad" (p.   786). In
each of   San   Juan's   major poems,   therefore,   mano appears at key
moments.   The "mano serena" of the Noche oscura   (VII) wounds the
soul with its touch.   Nevertheless,   it   is   not   specifically   the
hand   of   the Bridegroom, but, rather, that of the   "aire   de   la
almena." In the Cántico espiritual   initial   reference   to   hand
occurs early in the poem when the   Bride addresses the "bosques y
espesuras, / Plantadas por la mano del   Amado" (CE. IV). The hand
of the Bridegroom here   symbolizes   God's   creative power.   After

the Bride's entrance into "el ameno huerto deseado", the Amado betrothes her to himself by the symbolic gift of his hand in a strophe which San Juan explains only cursorily. At the same time, he summarizes the liberality of the Bridegroom evident in the glories of creation through which the soul has passed in the simple gesture of betrothal where the Bride accepts the proffered hand of her lover.

In the Llama de amor viva, the "mano blanda" of God consummates the union with the alma with a touch. A poem which effectively summarizes the essence of a spiritual union thus relies on the language of the senses to convey its message. Both mystics rely on Aristotelian principles regarding the role of the senses in the perception of the world, a principle San Juan enunciates when he claims that "la imaginación no puede fabricar ni imaginar cosas algunas fuera de las que con los sentidos exteriores ha experimentado" (S. II, 12, iv). Nevertheless, he goes on to distinguish these exterior senses from the "sentidos sensitivos interiores, como son memoria, fantasía, imaginativa," by means of which sensuality moves its appetites and longings (CE. XVIII, 7). As Crisógono de Jesus explains "sentido, en la terminología de San Juan de la Cruz, tiene un significado particular. No se refiere a las potencias corporales, que en el lenguaje vulgar y aún en el filosófico llevan ese nombre. Sin excluirlas, implica, además, el orden intelectivo en cuanto discursivo o racional."[29] Whether interior or exterior, San Juan stresses that the senses can be manipulated by the devil in

order to deceive the soul and prevent its progress to union.
Essential to advancement, therefore, is the realization that "la
parte inferior del hombre . . . no es ni puede ser capaz de
conocer ni comprehender a Dios como Dios es" (S. III, 24, ii).
To know God in his essence is, of course, beyond man's capacity
as creature; but to know him in union, insofar as he leads the
soul to it, is within the mystic's grasp.

Even as they call for mortification of the exterior senses
in purgation in order to advance spiritually, the mystics discuss
in sensual terms certain phases of mystical progress. When they
do so, however, both Santa Teresa and San Juan stress that they
are referring to the spiritual senses and not to the corporeal
ones. Santa Teresa may compare the reception of the Eucharist to
seeing Christ enter her "posada . . . con los ojos corporales"
(CP. LXI, 4/XXXIV, 8), yet she sees with the eyes of faith his
presence in the host. Commenting on San Juan's use of the verb
"to see," however, Hatzfeld observes that "it has to be noted
that ver is a mystical word like visión and means 'meet', not
'see' (in the monstrance), as though opposing adoration to
reception of the Eucharist."[30] Santa Teresa, therefore,
combines both meanings of ver in her use of the term in
conjunction with Eucharist. Nevertheless, in strictly mystical
contexts, Hatzfeld's clarification seems to hold.

In the Cántico espiritual, the interplay of sight and search
is more intricately developed. At the outset, the soul searches
for the missing Amado, aware as it does so that "la Esencia

185

divina . . . es ajena de todo ojo mortal y escondida de todo humano entendimiento" (CE. I, 3). While its ultimate quest is the beatific vision, its intermediate one remains union with the Bridegroom whom it pursues. Even as it searches for the Amado, the soul recognizes the power of the vision it requests. When the Bride demands of the Bridegroom: "Descubre tu presencia, / Y máteme tu vista y hermosura", San Juan explains in the commentary that at the moment of spiritual vision, "sería ella [la esposa] arrebatada a la misma hermosura y absorta en la misma hermosura y transformada en la misma hermosura" (CE. XI, 87). At the moment of union, just such a transformation of Amada in Amado occurs, an event most effectively expressed in the Noche oscura. Nevertheless, the commentary on the Cántico explains the transformation as well by likening it to the beatific vision.

Even as they write about interior visions, however, both Santa Teresa and San Juan create an ambience without specific details. Except when she describes her vision of hell or, conversely, the transverberation of her heart, for example, words fail Santa Teresa in trying to explain the higher mystical states in strictly visual terms. San Juan also lacks specificity of visual detail; for, although the Cántico espiritual contains sumptuous descriptions of the interior landscape of the soul, the essence of the ultimate union between Bride and Bridegroom eludes specific definition visually. Similarly, in the Llama de amor viva, the poet relies on imagery which evokes an aura of heat and light, while in the Noche oscura the transformation of amada in

Amado is conveyed through the interplay of sounds in a single strophe devoid of visual effects.

The mystics' hierarchy of senses manifests itself as each is examined in turn. Although a later writer such as Calderón de la Barca establishes hearing as the preeminent sense for understanding the truths of the faith in his autos sacramentales, the Carmelites relegate hearing to a lower order of precedence in their descriptions of mystical advancement. Thus, even though San Juan adheres to the tradition which Calderón carries on in his plays in at least one instance, both he and Santa Teresa usually question the soul's reliance on sight and hearing in interior recollection. Utilizing allusions to the Sirens of classical literature on the one hand (CP. III, 5) or to the prudent serpent of Scripture on the other (S. III, 23, iii), both writers advise their readers to "atapar los oídos" to the distractions of the world. Sight and hearing are too easily led astray. Rather than relying on physical hearing or vision, the mystic soul must open the eyes and ears of the soul, senses symbolic of spiritual understanding.

What the soul perceives by means of its spiritual hearing is a divino silbo enticing it further toward the Bridegroom. To Santa Teresa it is "un silbo tan penetrativo para entenderle el alma, que no le puede dejar de oír" (M. VI, 2, ii), while San Juan describes it as "este divino silbo que entra por el oído del alma [que] no solamente es substancia . . . entendida, sino también descubrimiento de verdades de la divinidad y revelación de secretos suyos ocultos" (CE. XIV-XV, 15). Relying on Scripture to explain further, San Juan cites Job 42:5 then concludes that "luego este oír de el alma es ver con el entendimiento" (CE. XIV-XV, 15). This combination of hearing and sight reflects an earlier combination of hearing and touch, conjoined in the mystic's commentary on the "silbo de los aires amorosos". The interchange of effects among the spiritual senses continues when San Juan links the silbo of this strophe with the "ojos deseados". What the soul was unable to comprehend when confronted with the sight of the desired eyes is now received interiorly as a soft whisper. Nevertheless, the mystic has still not achieved a lasting union with the object of its quest. What the soul receives at this stage of its progress is an understanding, however obscure, of the nature of union with the Amado. At the same time, it begins to perceive "una admirable conveniencia y disposición de la sabiduría en las diferencias de todas sus criaturas y obras." This perception takes a distinctly Pythagorean form of "una armonía de música subidíssima" when the author explains the paradoxical "música callada" and the "soledad sonora." Both are heard by the spiritual senses only.

Serving as counterpoint to the visual imagery which predominates in the Cántico espiritual are the audio effects which San Juan creates throughout the poem to support the unfolding theme of mystical progress. For example, the anguished query with which the poem opens establishes the theme of search. The poet emphasizes the loneliness of the Bride separated from her lover not only through the visual images of wound and absent hart but also by means of the repetitive "e" and "o" sounds, whose assonance conveys aurally the sense of loss experienced by the soul bereft of the Amado. In the middle strophes which follow the reunion of the lovers (CE. XIV-XV), the alliterative "s" and "l" sounds underscore the tranquility and peace enjoyed by the enraptured soul. Finally, in the penultimate strophe sight and sound converge in a series of images which symbolizes the lovers bound in an unbreakable union.

Connected to the sensual details of sight and sound are others which appeal to the remaining senses of smell, taste, and touch. Thus, the flowers and fruits of the mystical garden symbolic of the virtues festooning the soul in union not only delight the eye but emit a fragrant bouquet and satisfy the spiritual palate as well. Appropriately, Santa Teresa's mystical garden, well-tended by the soul and watered by the graces of the "hortelano," produces "flores que [dan] de sí gran olor, para dar recreación a este Señor nuestro" (V. XI, 6). Nevertheless, the fragrance of the flowering virtues also delights the soul itself, as San Juan observes. Both mystics call attention to the mutual gratification of Bride and Bridegroom afforded by the fragrant flowers and unctions of virtue, but San Juan catches the essence of the image in the Llama:

> . . . si ella [el alma] le envía a él [el Amado] sus
> amorosos deseos que le son a El tan olorosos como la
> virgúlica de el humo que sale de las especias
> aromáticas de la mirra y de el incienso (Cant. 3, 6).
> El a ella le envía el olor de sus ungüentos, con que la
> atrae y hace correr hacia El (ibid., 1, 3), que son sus

divinas inspiraciones y toques. (III, 28)

Just as the fragrance of the virtues delights the soul in union, so, too, does the delectability of the Bridegroom's favors entice the soul toward union.

Although the initiate is cautioned to seek the bitter and disagreeable path to union at the outset of his journey, the apogee of the mystic quest marked by ecstasy and ultimately spiritual marriage is couched in the very sensual terms initially discredited in purgation. Thus, the symbolic vine which flourishes in the virtuous soul produces a "vino de dulce sabor" (CE. XVI, 4) as a sign of God's favor. The ecstatic union synthesized in the Llama de amor viva is a "dulce encuentro" likened to a "muerte . . . muy suave y muy dulce" (Ll. I, 30). As the soul advances, it is able to draw out of all that it sees or does "la dulzura de amor que hay" just as the bee is able to extract honey from the plants that it visits (CE. XXVII, 8). San Juan sets as the mystic soul's ultimate goal a lasting union with the Trinity wherein each member would abide with it and the soul would find itself "absorbiéndola el Padre poderosa y fuertemente en el abrazo abisal de su dulzura" (Ll. I, 5). This sweet embrace is a foretaste of heaven.

In their descriptions of the prayer of quiet, Santa Teresa and San Juan both combine references to more than one sense. The reliance of each on the senses of touch, taste, and smell to describe the higher stages of mystical progress subtly underscores the more passive role of the soul in its intimate

union with the Amado. Both clearly emphasize the relative
passivity of the soul in the prayer of quiet when they describe
it in terms of softness. When they advance beyond the prayer of
quiet, it is still the sense of touch which most effectively
conveys the essence of union, for,

> The mystic writer is constantly concerned with the
> apprehension of God, with grasping and holding the
> intangible; and within the unio mystica, the mystic
> believes that he actually does so. Thus, the ideal
> mystic image for God would be one that could
> demonstrate the tangibility of God for the loving
> soul.[31]

Thus, in his commentary on the Llama de amor viva, San Juan
equates the "mano blanda" with God the Father, then goes on to
interpret the "toque" as the Son and the "cauterio" as the Holy
Spirit (Ll. II, 1). Hence, hand, touch, and cautery are one as
the Trinity is one and as mystic and God are one in union. In
the Noche oscura he may distinguish the touch of creatures from
that of God in union, yet he goes on to indicate the effects of
union in terms of the touch of the "mano serena" by extinguishing
all sensual references in the peaceful repose of the final
strophe. Similarly, in the Cántico espiritual there exists a
gradation of the senses culminating in the touch of the "llama
que consume y no da pena" (CE. XXXIX).

Nevertheless, the touch received by the mystic advancing
toward union is not always and unequivocally an experience of
union with the Amado. As the soul experiences the preliminary
touches at the initial stages of mystical progress, it desires
the "divino toque . . . de amor" felt by the Bride of the

Canticle. These "toques de amor," with which Santa Teresa is also familiar, like the "toques sustanciales de divina unión" (N. II, 23, xi), prefigure "'el toque . . . del resplandor de tu gloria y figura de tu sustancia' (Hebr. 1:3), que es tu Unigénito Hijo" (Ll. II, 16). Evident in the gradation of San Juan's interpretation of toque is a hierarchical ordering of the sense, which reflects "an inversion in the traditional (Platonic) hierarchy of the senses which placed sight far above all. In the spiritual senses, sight and hearing are lowest (though not scorned), whereas smell and, even more, taste and touch are the most exalted. . . . And with the sense of touch the kiss was the supreme expression."[32] When San Juan equates the toque with Christ, therefore, he not only touches on the unfathomable depths of mystical union but also foreshadows the glory which is to come in the lasting union of heaven.

By turning to the Canticle of Canticles for inspiration, generations of mystics have found a compendium of terms with which to clothe their apprehensions of an ineffable God. Nevertheless, no less significant in influence is the wealth of secular literature on which the given writer might draw. Thus, not only the sight of the united mystical lovers or the harmonious sound of their song but also the redolence of the pastoral locus amoenus in which they effect their union permeates the treatises of Santa Teresa and San Juan. A divinization of secular symbol thus occurs. Garcilaso's idyllic description of a scene free from worldly cares in his Egloga II (vv. 64-76) captures the nostalgia for lost love made more poignant by the peace and harmony of the setting. The individual details which comprise the description of the locus amoenus, however, are virtually pastoral conventions rather than symbols of some more profound reality. On the other hand, the mystics carry the use of sensual imagery a step further when, like the figurative flowers, fruits, and animals, the sweetness, touch, or fragrance of the mystical experience is transformed into a symbol of the union itself or even of the Amado.

The multifaceted accumulation of meaning evident in the mystics' works is manifest as well in that of later poets, such as Gongora. In Sonnet 3, for example, the poet effects a virtual reversal of the imagery of union. Utilizing the kiss as the controlling image, Góngora transforms the "dulce boca" and "licor sagrado" characteristic of the kiss of lovers to a bitterly disillusioned "veneno armado."[33] By effectively exploiting the conventional appeals to the senses of amatory poetry, Góngora turns them back upon themselves so that the moment of union between the lovers marks no lasting joy but the beginning of desengaño. Thus, while the kiss symbolizes the culmination of the mystic's union with God expressed in tangible terms, it becomes in Góngora's sonnet the beginning of the end of the lovers' union effected by the lesser god, "Amor."

The pain of desengaño intimated by Góngora in the sonnet also reverses the mystics' interpretation of the pain and sorrow associated with their quest for union. Pain of some kind is

inevitably joined to love, for the unequivocal giving of self
requires renunciation of one's own interest with consequently
painful results, just as the inevitable separation of the lovers,
whether mystical or secular, causes poignancy. While the
torments and sorrows occur on the spiritual or psychic plane,
they recall the sense of touch. In both the secular and mystical
spheres, therefore, poet and writer describe the wounds of love
inflicted on them by the beloved or speak of the suffering of
separation.

In each of his major poems, San Juan begins with references
to pain or wounds. The Noche oscura, for example, "begins with a
movement dictated by pain ["con ansias en amores inflamada"] and
by the will to still pain [and] ends with the achievement of
self-forgetfulness free from pain."[34] The "ansias" which
impelled the soul to begin its journey culminate in the wound of
love sustained by it at the conclusion. Nevertheless, it is in
the Cántico espiritual and the Llama de amor viva that San Juan
develops the imagery of wounds in greater detail, imagery which
also appears in Santa Teresa's works. In one sense, the Biblical
basis for the wound of love lies in the Passion of Christ. It
certainly informs the sustaining imagery of San Juan's Pastorcico
sonnet. The Passion also figures predominantly in Teresian
spirituality since it was for her a favorite topic of meditation
as it was for many of her mystical predecessors. Not all
references to heridas, however, concern the grievous wounds
sustained by Christ in his Passion and death.

Santa Teresa may describe the "heridas mortales" of sin, but for the most part the wounds she describes are those received by the soul in union. In spiritual betrothal the soul "siente ser herida sabrosísimamente, mas no atina cómo ni quién la hirió" (M. VI, 2, i). In fact, however, she has already indicated the source of the wound of love in the opening paragraph of the sixth mansions. It is the Bridegroom who touches the soul at its most profound center. The piercing wound of ecstatic union symbolized by the flaming arrow thrust by the cherub through her heart becomes in the Moradas a permanent badge signifying her sustained colloquy with the Esposo. The author captures the essential paradox of the experience when she describes the wound as sabrosa. Petersson remarks that "pain may be a delight, and pleasure may be its cause or its consequence. Here [in the Vida] the simplest, most frequent expression of pleasure-pain is in paradoxes, though pleasure, or benefit, is dominant in the collective effect."[35] The herida de amor of Santa Teresa's Moradas continues the combination of pleasure and pain principles noted by Petersson.

The paradoxical herida is most evident, however, in San Juan's Cántico espiritual whose opening strophe finds the Bride remarking on the wound she has received from her absent lover. In this strophe and in the commentary accompanying it, the poet initiates a consideration of the image which ascribes multilayered meanings to it. On the one hand, it is the esposa who bears the wound, because the Bridegroom "habiéndo[le] herido [a ella]" has fled from her. As the poem progresses, however, it is the Bridegroom himself, symbolized by the stag, who manifests the wound of love. The interchange of wounds between soul and divine Lover thus reflects the interchange of attributes and effects of fauna, flora, and activities evident in the other images of mystical union.

The mystical journey commences in the pain of purgation in which the soul deprives itself of physical and even spiritual pleasures in order to ready itself for union. The consolations in prayer enjoyed in conversion disappear, so that the soul feels abandoned by the God it has slowly come to love. It is this state of longing and loss which San Juan captures in the anguished query of the Bride to the missing Amado, a question wrung from "dolor . . . ansia y gemido . . . del corazón herido ya del amor de Dios" (CE. I, 1). Even as it suffers a sense of loss, the soul also find the "heridas espirituales de amor . . . sabrosísimas y deseables" (CE. I, 19). Like Santa Teresa, San Juan mixes pleasure and pain in the complex quest of soul for union. The soul as Bride pursues God as Bridegroom, therefore, both to alleviate the pain of loss and to deepen the delectable wound of love. San Juan underscores the paradoxical nature of the Bride's action in a further question posed to the missing Bridegroom: "¿Por qué, pues has llagado / Aqueste corazón, no le sanaste?" (CE. IX), followed shortly by the demand that the Amado reveal himself to her so that she might be cured of her "dolencia de amor" (CE. XI). In both the poem and the commentary,

San Juan equates "dolor," "pena," "ansia," and "llaga" with the "herida de amor" which impels the soul onward.

Reunited at last with the Amado at the "cristalina fuente," the soul now observes that he, too, bears a wound of love as the "ciervo vulnerado". Both share the wound, for, as Marlay has pointed out, "God is figured by the wounded stag, but the soul also is, since each is both the pursuer and the pursued."[36] San Juan makes clear the interchange of wounds between the mystical lovers in the commentary. The Bridegroom, ". . . viendo la esposa herida de su amor, él también al gemido della viene herido del amor della; porque en los enamorados la herida de uno es de entrambos" (CE. XIII, 9). Having established an interdependence between soul and God through the medium of the fauna and flora of the Canticle, San Juan now extends the imagery to encompass the effects of love on both parties. If both soul and God are symbolized by the ciervo, then both share as well the "herida de amor." Similarly, if the solitary turtledove symbolizes both mystic and God, then both also share the wound manifest in their love for one another. The Bridegroom "sólo la guía [a la Esposa] a sí mismo, atrayéndola y absorbiéndola en sí" (CE. XXXV, 7). San Juan summarizes the attraction and absorption of soul in God in the penultimate strophe of the poem where both the song of the nightingale and the "llama que consume y no da pena" symbolize transforming union. From the pain of loss to the consummation of the longed for union in the image of the painless flame of love, San Juan brings the converging lines of symbolism together in a single strophe.

Absent from the Llama de amor viva is the sense of anguish on the soul's part which marks the opening verses of the Cántico. The wound inflicted on it by the divine Lover symbolized by the flame touches it "tiernamente". The poet describes the action of love in personal and present terms with his choice of verb ("hieres") even as he disembodies it. The exclamations which open the second verse of the Llama are cries of joy wrenched from the soul, not in agony but in ecstatic union. San Juan's "cauterio suave," "regalada llaga," "mano blanda," and "toque delicado" focus the imagery on the sense of touch, thus elevating it to the pinnacle of mystical expression. The exclamations come from the soul at the climax of its union. The wound of love is an experience which elicits as well the oxymoron of dying life, for Santa Teresa addresses God familiarly when she says to Him "que llegáis [sic] y no ponéis la medicina, herís y no se ve la llaga, matáis dejando con más vida" (Ex. VI, 1). The paradox continues when each mystic observes that only the one who has wounded the soul is capable of curing the wound of love. Santa Teresa awaits the arrival of "el zurujano, que es Dios, a sanaros" (M. III, 2, vi), while San Juan explains in the Cántico that "en las heridas del amor, no puede haber medicina sino de parte del que hirió" (CE. I, 20). Commenting on the herida of the Cántico (XI), Hatzfeld reflects that "ya se sabe que la medicina que se indica en estos versos es el matrimonio místico."[37] Certainly in the context of a continued earthly existence, the mystics seek the "medicine" of spiritual marriage as a remedy for their wounds of love. Nevertheless, in the final analysis, they desire the beatific vision of heaven with its promise of a lasting union for, ultimately, as Merton has noted, "mystical love is a sickness which vision alone can cure."[38] In contrast, the soul suffering the infirmity of faults and imperfections must undergo purgation in which the medicine of grace cures it and enables it to acquire the strength to continue.

Whereas the wound of love is a physical debility turned to positive mystical ends by Santa Teresa and San Juan, some imagery based on bodily deprivation is analogous to different mystical states. Thus, blindness (ceguedad) serves ambivalent symbolic ends when in one instance it describes deprivation of the power of understanding, then in another refers to the excess of light which overwhelms the soul's inner eye with its brilliance. Similarly, dryness (sequedad) implies the aridity in prayer experienced by the mystic at different times in his advance to union, yet thirst for God (sed de amor) suggests the longing for union which marks the final steps to realization of the mystical quest. On the one hand, sequedad describes a spiritual state in which the soul receives little or no consolation in prayer. Equating it to a cold, dry, winter wind, San Juan nevertheless emphasizes its importance to progress, for it will eventually give way to a "sed de amor" satisfied only by union with God.

To Santa Teresa the Gospel account of the Samaritan woman at the well (John 4:1-45) is a fitting analogy for the soul's thirst for union. Some souls may be dissuaded by the difficulty of the task, preferring death from thirst rather than perservering to the quenching waters tasted only after arduous spiritual labor. For those who push on, however, "es sed que se desea tener esta sed (porque entiende el alma su gran valor), y es sed penosísima y que fatiga, trae consigo la mesma satisfacción con que se mata aquella sed" (CP. XXX/XIX, 2). Santa Teresa's fascination with the figure of the Samaritan woman transcends the simple request for the water at the well with its symbolic overtones. In the Meditaciones sobre el Cantar she returns to the same Gospel account citing the Samaritan woman as an example of the perfect fusion of the active and contemplative modes of the religious life. Affected by an "embriaguez divina" because of her conversation with Christ, the woman does not become absorbed in her own joy but, rather, goes to share the message with the townspeople (Med. VII, 5-8). The Samaritan woman thus embodies both the thirst for God and the overflowing generosity which the quenching of that thirst engenders in the mystic joined to God. While the soul need not fear the nearly unquenchable thirst of the early stages of progress, it is still a state which readily leads to rapture, an experience which can have serious physical side effects. Nevertheless, even as the Samaritan woman experienced a divine inebriation which spurred her to action, so, too, may the mystic imitate her. A concomitant result of this sed de amor, however, is the paradoxical life in which the soul longs for permanent union with God even as the body continues its earthly existence. Only in the final stages of union does the mystic soul leave aridity behind, for God brings it to "esta fuente de agua viva y que siente allá el alma y . . . la harta Dios y la quita la sed de las cosas" (CPe. LXXII, 5).

The mystic soul's experience of aridity, then thirst for God, and eventually the satisfying slaking of its thirst with the Bridegroom in union finds parallel expression in terms of hunger and eating. In fact, San Juan combines hunger, thirst, wound, pain, touch, and light in the Noche oscura when he describes the deprivation suffered by the soul in the progressive nights.[39] At the same time, both writers utilize the Biblical account of manna from heaven in order to explain part of the mystic quest. For San Juan, the "manjar del cielo" comes to those souls who have embraced the figurative desert of purgation and consequently turned away from the "manjar de carne". On the other hand, Santa Teresa is overwhelmed by the "diferencia de manjares [que] podemos hacer de El [Dios]," marveling not only at God's manifestation as manna, but also at the diverse forms in which he presents himself to the mystic soul (Med. V, 2). Like San Juan, she also contrasts the food from heaven with the "manjar de puercos," which was the fare of the Gospel Prodigal Son. Both mystics, therefore, establish a clear distinction between heavenly food and earthly sustenance. The mystics go a step further, however, when they distinguish among the varied manjares which God makes available to all souls. The hunger which must impel the mystic onward cannnot be satisfied with creatures. Rather, "for the Christian mystic, Christ is the mediator, and only by feeding on Him can one taste of God."[40] Santa Teresa poses just such a choice for her nuns when she reminds them that the "pan sacratísimo" of the Eucharist is of more lasting sustenance than the "pan de mantenimientos y necesidades corporales" (CP. LX/XXXIV, 2).

Just as sequedad leads to a sed de amor, so, too, does the abstinence of purgation give way to "la hambre y apetito de verle a él [Dios] como es" (CE.VI, 4). The soul's hunger for God may so overwhelm it that "hace desfallecer al alma" (Ll. III, 20) even as its thirst for union nearly undid it. What the soul attains in union is a spiritual satiety or "hartura" which satisfies it much as the quenching drink at the spring did. In fact, the soul's union with the Bridegroom is so complete that it partakes of the Amado himself, for he is a "cena para el alma" (CE.XIV-XV, 29). The meal results in "recreación, hartura y amor" for the soul (CE. XIV-XV, 28). In an earlier passage of the commentary, San Juan combines the varied images of "mansiones," "animales," "manjares," and the dove which returns to the "divina arca del pecho de Dios" in order to emphasize the soul's experience of union (CE.XIV-XV, 3). The mystic thus comes full circle. By rejecting the creatures which were the scraps falling from the Lord's table, the soul has prepared itself to partake of the Creator himself, and, thereby, to be re-created ("recreación"). In spiritual marriage, therefore, the unguents of the Holy Spirit "saborean al alma y la engolosinan más delicadamente de Dios" (Ll. III, 26), thus transforming the negative golosina of purgation to a positive attribute of union.

While not as adept as her gifted protege in turning a phrase, Santa Teresa, nevertheless, echoes his sentiments when she advises her nuns to "considerar la mesa del cielo y el manjar de ella que es Dios" (Aviso XLI). By partaking of the heavenly food, the soul may aspire to sit at the celestial table. Yet Santa Teresa also notes that some eat only sparingly of the manjar which God offers, thus quickly losing its flavor. Only those who ingest a full measure of the proffered food of grace find that it gives life, strength, and "buen sabor". In a more homely passage, she describes the third degree of prayer in the Vida:

> Es un andar como una persona que no tiene necesidad de comer, sino que siente el estómago contento, de manera que no a todo manjar arrostraría, mas no tan harta que, si los ve buenos, deje de comer de buena gana. Ansí no le satisface, ni querría entonces contento del mundo, porque en sí tiene el que le satisface más, mayores, contentos de Dios, deseos de satisfacer su deseo, de gozar más, de estar con El: esto es lo que quiere. (V. XVII, 4)

Her description is at once both graphic and effective. She captures the sense of contentment enjoyed by the soul while also indicating that more remains before it is fully satisfied.

The spiritual satiety of the soul in union which figuratively feeds on the Amado has a parallel in terms of drinking as well. Unlike food imagery, however, inebriation usually describes a state just short of the lasting union of spiritual betrothal and marriage. Initially, inebriation describes the passivity of the soul absorbed in the prayer of quiet where God is "embriagándola [al alma] secretamente en amor infuso" (Ll. III, 50). Both Santa Teresa and San Juan return to the image of the suckling child when they describe the soul enthralled in the Bridegroom's embrace. While Santa Teresa describes the soul "sustentada con aquella leche divina que la va criando su Esposo" (Med. IV, 4), San Juan juxtaposes strophes in the Cántico espiritual which combine entrance into the Bridegroom's winecellar, where the soul drinks deeply of him, with a subsequent allusion to the suckling child. Even as they describe the repose and sustenance of the soul in the Bridegroom's embrace, however, both writers intimate that further states of mystical experience will satisfy it far more than the "embebecimiento sabroso" of the prayer of quiet (M. VI, 2, i). Beyond this intermediate state lies the more violent rapture of ecstatic union symbolized by entry into the figurative winecellar of the symbolic castle.

God places the mystic soul in the bodega "para que allí más sin tasa pueda salir rica." It partakes "conforme a su deseo y se embriague bien, beviendo de todos estos vinos que hay en la despensa de Dios" (Med. VI, 3). The sleep of the faculties which marks the prayer of quiet here gives way to the feigned death of ecstasy. While the source for the image of divine inebriation is ultimately the king's "cellaria" of the Canticle of Canticles (1:3 and 2:4), each mystic interprets the effects of ecstatic union individually.[41] For example, Raimundo Llull states that "el amigo se embriagaba de vino que recordaba, entendía y amaba el amado. Aquel vino empapaba al amado con sus lloros y con las lágrimas de su amigo," (#364), thereby implying at least a modicum of activity on the soul's part. On the other hand, both Carmelites stress the passivity of the soul who is placed in the winecellar by the Bridegroom. In the *Cántico espiritual*, San Juan focuses on the wine tasted by the mystic soul, distinguishing between the "vino nuevo" enjoyed by "nuevos amadores" and the "vino cocido" of proficients. The new wine of the initiates lacks the flavor and smoothness that comes with aging, while the old wine is a "vino del amor ya bien cocido en sustancia" from which the detritus of sense and creature has been removed (CE. XXV, 9-11). Further in the commentary on the Canticle, he returns to the theme of drinking by equating the "bebida del vino adobado" with the "mosto de [las] granadas." Unlike the earlier, less perfect wines tasted by the soul as it advanced, the "mosto de granada" and "vino adobado" savored in the "subidas cavernas" represent the "fruición y deleite de amor, que es bebida del Espíritu Sancto" (CE.XXXVII, 8).[42] Echoing San Juan's distinctions, Santa Teresa likens the different wines dispensed by the king to the variety of "mercedes del Señor, que a uno da poco vino de devoción, a otro más, [y] a otro crece de manera que le comienza a sacar de sí" (Med. VI, 3). To both Carmelites, the quantity and quality of the wine tasted by the soul reflects the different degrees of union achieved by individuals.

Morel underscores the appropriateness of the symbolic drinking by observing that "boire Dieu à cet degré c'est vraiment s'imprégner de lui, non seulement en surface, non pas seulement au fond mais en l'être entier, substance et structure."[43] Thus, San Juan calls attention to the transforming nature of ecstatic union when he describes the effect of the state on the soul which experiences it in terms of the verb beber:

> Porque así como la bebida se difunde y derrama por todos los miembros y venas del cuerpo, así se difunde esta comunicación de Dios sustancialmente en toda el alma, o por mejor decir el alma se transforma en Dios; según la cual transformación bebe el alma de su Dios según la substancia della y según sus potencias espirituales. (CE. XXVI, 5)

When he goes on to describe how each of the powers of the soul in turn imbibes of knowledge, love, and delight in the Amado, he effectively underscores the total absorption of the mystic in loving union with God. It is a comparison found as well in Santa Teresa. Thus, in the Camino de perfección she describes the soul who finds itself engulfed "en esta agua viva" of the Gospel. Her desire to quench her spiritual thirst by imbibing deeply of this living water is as much a desire for transforming union as San Juan's description of the soul drinking of God in the figurative winecellar.

Inebriation is one metaphor for ecstatic experience, but it is by no means the only one utilized by the Spanish Carmelites. Pertinent to the final stages of mystical progress are the experiences of ecstasy, rapture, and flight of the spirit which enthrall the would-be mystic even as they confuse the would-be spectator of the experience. Commenting on the aborted flight of the soul in the Cántico espiritual, for example, San Juan explains that to the bride "lo parecía volaba su alma de las carnes, que es lo que ella deseaba" (CE.XIII, 2). He goes on to explain that the soul's flight from the body makes possible the reception of divine communications which transcend human understanding. During the experience, the body appears lifeless, for "[el vuelo] destruye al cuerpo, y dexa de sentir en él y de tener en él sus acciones, porque las tiene en Dios" (CE. XIII, 6). San Juan's description of the effects of ecstasy reflects that of Saint Thomas Aquinas as propounded in the Summa Theologicae, where he first emphasizes that "man needs to be supernaturally helped to attain this good [ecstasy]" (IIa, IIae, 175, i). Next he explains that

> As long as the state of ecstasy endures, an actual
> turning to images and sense-objects is removed from the
> soul, lest it should impede its elevation to that which
> excels all images, as was said. And so in ecstasy
> there was no need for the soul to be so separated from
> the body as not to be united to it as a kind of form.
> It was needful however that St. Paul's intellect should
> be abstracted from images and the perception of
> sense-objects. (IIa, IIae, 175, ii).

When San Juan also cites Saint Paul in his comments concerning ecstasy, he, too, stresses that whether in the body or out of the body, it is the very extra-sensorial nature of the knowledge infused in the mystic which is essential. Rather than pursuing the subject in detail in the Cántico espiritual, however, San Juan defers to his mentor, advising his readers that "la bienaventurada Teresa de Jesús, nuestra madre, dejó escritas de estas cosas de espíritu admirablemente" (CE. XIII, 7).

Indeed, Santa Teresa devotes considerable attention to distinguishing between the different types of rapture or ecstasy which may overcome the soul. The degrees which the saint discerns are summarized by Dicken:

> Briefly, the saint distinguishes five main types of trance or rapture, and maintains her classification with a fair degree of consistency in each of the three works in which she expounds her teaching on this topic extensively and systematically, namely in the Life, Relation V and the Mansions. The five categories are: arrobamiento (trance); arrebatamiento (rapture); ímpetu (transport); vuelo de espíritu (flight of the spirit); and herida (wound, spiritual wound). Other terms which occur are either synonymous with one or other of these, or describe a variation of one of the main categories, e. g., rapto (ravishment); levantamiento (exaltation); impulso (impulse); suspensión (suspension); éstasis, éxtasis (ecstasy).
> It must be said at once that all these phenomena are essentially of the same order of experience, differing from one another only in the mode of their effect on the soul and in other non-essential ways.[44]

In the Cuentas de conciencia, she compares "arrobamiento" and "arrebatamiento," finding that in the first the soul "va poco a poco muriéndose a estas cosas esteriores y perdiendo los sentidos y viviendo a Dios." The second, however, "viene con sola una noticia que Su Majestad da en lo más íntimo del alma, con velocidad" (Cuentas LIV, 8). On the other hand, flight of the spirit, "es un no sé qué como se llama, que sube de lo más íntimo del alma" (LIV, 9). In all of the types which she explains, Santa Teresa emphasizes that genuine ecstasy comes from God, while counterfeit experience is of dubious origin and even greater harm. Applying the Gospel dictum that "by their fruits you shall known them," the saint rejects all extraordinary mystical experience which does not lead to an increase in charity.

Similar to the metaphoric inebriation and the ecstatic experience, the images of sueño and muerte also convey a sense of otherworldliness in describing the mystic experience. San Juan de la Cruz describes his "sueño espiritual" when he writes of the soul's rest at the breast of the Amado. Sueño here refers to a state akin to rapture in which the soul is absorbed in loving the Bridegroom. Even as sleep is a feigned death, so, too, is ecstasy an apparent death of the body which enables the soul to soar to union. The mystic longs to "morir de amor" yet, conversely, "no se acaba de morir" (CE. VIII, 2). The paradox of dying life occurs in both mystics' similar glosses of the traditional estribillo, "Vivo sin vivir en mí." At the same time, San Juan and Santa Teresa echo Saint Bernard who describes the "death of angels . . . [which] is that ecstasy which alone, or in a special manner, is called contemplation,"[45] even as they anticipate the lovers of John Donne's "The Extasie" who "like sepulchrall statues lay; / All day."[46] The death of ecstasy arises from "muy excesivo gozo y deleite" (M. VI, 11, xi). As San Juan explains in the Cántico, the sight of God, which the soul glimpses however indirectly in ecstatic union, causes the mystic to long for the actual death of the body that the beauty of God may be savored eternally. To attain that joyous death, the soul willingly accepts "mil acervísimas muertes" of temporal and spiritual sacrifice. Thus, the actual death of the body becomes a welcome event to the lover of God even as it remains a loathsome fear to the sinner.

To arrive at such joyous acceptance of the physical death of the body, the mystic has first endured the mortification of senses and spirit which are a necessary prelude to union, for "para entrar en esta divina unión ha de morir todo lo que vive en el alma" (S. I, 11, viii). Just as the "muerte corporal y natural" makes possible entry into eternal life, so, does "mortificación de todos los vicios y apetitos" lead to the "vida espiritual perfecta" (Ll. II, 32). Both San Juan and Santa Teresa echo the Pauline admonition to put off the old man and to put on the new in Christ (Eph. 4:22-24). Each, in fact, plays on the twin paradoxes of loss and pain, death and life, to describe the necessity of purgation if the soul would progress.

San Juan's commentary on and translation of Saint Paul's epistle combines the concept of death with that of desnudez, another image of deprivation which the mystic develops in detail. For San Juan, the state of desnudez is the sine qua non of advancement to union. It is, finally, the complete abandonment of the will, even the self, to God so that the mystic's will may be God's and his self realized completely in union. Stressing the essential necessity of desnudez to advancement, he likens it to a passage of the Canticle of Canticles (5:7) where "'(el) desnudar el manto a la Esposa y llegarla de noche'" is the prelude to donning the "nuevo manto que pretendía del desposorio" (N. II, 24, iv). Stripped of all attachment to creatures and to its own will, the soul is able to see in them the hand of the Amado "mil gracias derramando". Ultimately, only when the soul finds itself "desnuda y purgada de las imperfecciones . . . así del sentido como del espíritu" can it rejoice in the new springtime "en libertad y anchura y alegría de espíritu, en la cual siente la dulce voz de el Esposo, que es su dulce filomena" (CE. XXXIX, 8). Once again, San Juan deftly connects the imagery of emptying characteristic of purgation with the fulfillment of union in which the wealth of sensual detail belies the spiritual abnegation which preceded it.

Once stripped of spiritual and sensible favors, the soul will find that "la vestirá Dios de su pureza, gusto y voluntad" (Dichos XCVII). Both San Juan and Santa Teresa play on the donning and doffing of clothes to signify the spiritual transformation which takes place in mystical progress. It is when both mystics utilize the term disfraz, however, that the ambivalent, even paradoxical, nature of clothes imagery is most apparent. According to Covarrubias, disfraz "es el hábito y vestido que un hombre toma para dissimularse y poder ir con más libertad. Disfrazarse: Dissimularse. Disfraçado, el que se dissimula" (p. 477). It is a definition which San Juan anticipates when he explains that "disfrazarse no es otra cosa que disimularse y encubrirse debajo de otro traje y figura que de suyo tenía ahora" (N. II, 21, ii). In a conventional sense, therefore, it is a term easily applied by both Santa Teresa and

San Juan to Satan, who figuratively cloaks himself in clothing which deceives the soul. Even as they evoke the image of the evangelical wolf in sheep's clothing, however, both mystics also and unequivocally turn disfraz to wholly positive ends.

In a lengthy commentary on the second strophe of the Noche, San Juan details the meaning of the soul's going out "a escuras y segura / por la secreta escala, disfrazada". In the Subida, he explains that disfrazada means that the soul wears "el traje y vestido y término natural mudado en divino, subiendo por fe" (S. II, 1, i). In the Noche, he offers a more detailed and, at times, forced explanation of the disfraz donned by the soul. In order to approach union the soul puts on "el traje de estas tres virtudes," which are the theological virtues of faith, hope, and charity. Specifying further, San Juan remarks that the disfraz consists of an interior, white tunic symbolic of faith; a green "almilla" or waistcoat with military connotations symbolic of hope; and, finally, a purple toga representative of charity (N. II, 21, iii, vi, x). He stresses the allegorical nature of these garments by explaining further how each in turn protects the soul from the attacks of the three principal enemies of spiritual advancement: the world, the flesh, and the devil. What is intriguing about the Spanish mystic's use of the term disfraz to symbolize the state of the soul clothed in virtue, however, is the apparent reversal of the definition he himself offered in the same book. If "disfrazarse" is "disimularse," then there exists a contradiction, for it would seem that the soul in ecstatic union has no reason to dissimulate its true feelings. Rather, it would wish to demonstrate clearly its love of the Bridegroom. In his extended commentary, San Juan tries to explain that the soul dons the symbolic clothing of the virtues for two important reasons: "para debajo de aquella forma o traje mostrar de fuera la voluntad y pretensión que en el corazón tiene para ganar la gracia y voluntad de quien bien quiere; ahora también para encubrir[se] de sus émulos, Y ansí po[de]r hacer mejor su hecho" (N. II, 21, ii). Hence, the soul both masks its own shortcomings from its enemies even as it demonstrates the deepest longings of its heart to be one with God. It is, therefore, a disfraz a lo divino quite unlike that of the escudero of the Lazarillo de Tormes, who "iba por la calle con razonable vestido," ineffectually deceiving himself, his servant, and, eventually, the authorities of his sorry state.

The mystics ultimately aspire to exchange the "vestiduras y traje del mundo" for the "vestid[ura] de esperanza de vida eterna" (N. II, 21, vi). Thus clothed they will resemble the Bride of the Canticles who wears "vestiduras de bodas" befitting her station. The graces and gifts which comprise the bridal clothing fittingly adorn the soul for its spiritual marriage to the Bridegroom, a union foreshadowed in the bridal regalia described by Ezechiel (16:5-14). Unlike the detailed description of the vestments of the theological virtues presented in the Noche oscura, San Juan's references to the clothing of spiritual marriage is less specific. He calls it a "vestidura de preciosa variedad" (CE.XXX, 6) or ties it to the imagery of flowers and garlands. As another facet of the complex combining and restating of the central truth surrounding mystical union, clothes imagery thus subtly interconnects with seemingly disparate terms such as flowers and light in order to underscore the essential message. All creation reflects the Creator so that union with him encompasses a virtual divinization of creature as well. The force which gives impetus to the Spanish mystics' imagery insofar as it encompasses social relationships is, of course, love. For the Christian mystic who believes in a personal God, the goal of union necessarily employs language which parallels that of human passion and love. Whether the imagery employed reflects that of the Old Testament Canticle of Canticles or the New Testament Gospels, whether the relationship described be based on respect and duty between master and servant or reflect the intimacy of bride and bridegroom, the essential underpinning remains love. Nevertheless, as all mystical writers acknowledge, the experience of union remains at heart ineffable, so that the language of human love can be but a pale reflection of the divine experience. The social and physical body of man thus falls short of adequately expressing the nature of the glory which is to come and which, in a special way, the mystic claims to have experienced while still in this earthly existence.

Chapter 5

NOTES

[1] Morales Borrero, La geometría mística, p. 47.

[2] George P. Conger, Theories of Macrocosmos and Microcosmos in the History of Philosophy (New York: Columbia University Press, 1922), p. 49.

[3] Fray Luis de León, Obras completas castellanas, I, ed. Félix García, O. S. A. (Madrid: BAC, 1977), p. 577.

[4] Covarrubias, p. 780.

[5] Helmut Hatzfeld, "Los elementos constituyentes de la poesía mística" in Actas del Primer Congreso Internacional de Hispanistas (Oxford: Oxford University Press, 1964), p. 323.

[6] Nicolas J. Perella, The Kiss Sacred and Profane (Berkeley and Los Angeles: University of California Press, 1969), p. 40.

[7] Peers, Studies I, pp. 151-2. See also my article entitled "The Mystical Kiss and the Canticle of Canticles: Three Interpretations," American Benedictine Review, 33 (1982), 302-311, for a comparison of the mystics' use of kiss symbolism with that of St. Bernard of Clairvaux.

[8] Underhill, Mysticism, p. 137. James A. Montgomery, "The Song of Songs in Early and Mediaeval Christian Use," in The Song of Songs: A Symposium, ed. W. H. Schoff (Philadelphia: Commercial

Museum, 1924), pp. 29-30, asserts that "the Song has by no means been the cause and origin of this mystic and often erotic expression of spiritual longings and relations. That spiritual passion is germane to every religion of mystical character and found its voice within the Church without regard to the canonical book."

[9] Ewer, p. 179.

[10] Saint Bonaventure, The Enkindling of Love also called the Triple Way, ed. William I. Joffe (Paterson, N. J.: St. Anthony Guild Press, 1956), p. 70. Hugh of St. Victor, The Divine Love. The Two Treatises De Laude Caritatis and De Amore Sponsi ad Sponsam, trans. a Religious of C. S. M. V. (London: A. R. Mowbray & Co., 1956), p. 26.

[11] Hatzfeld, "Los elementos constituyentes," p. 31.

[12] De los nombres de Cristo (Madrid: Espasa-Calpe, 1957), p. 219.

[13] A. Robert, Le Cantique des Cantiques (Paris: J. Gabalda, 1963), pp. 46-47.

[14] With reference to rapture and ecstasy, San Juan directs his readers to Santa Teresa's works where she "dejó escritas de estas cosas de espíritu admirablemente" (CE. XIII, 7).

[15] Georges Morel, Le Sens de l'existence selon saint Jean de la Croix, II (Paris: Aubier, 1960), p. 128.

216

[16] San Juan makes clear in the _argumento_ of the Cántico _espiritual_ (1) that he wishes to describe the soul's progress through the stages of the mystical life until "llega a el último estado de perfección, que es matrimonio espiritual."

[17] Leo Spitzer, "Three Poems on Ecstasy (John Donne, Saint John of the Cross, Richard Wagner)," in A Method of Interpreting Literature (New York: Russell and Russell, 1967), p. 35.

[18] Hatzfeld, "Los elementos," p. 322.

[19] See my article "'Alma región luciente' of Fray Luis de León," REH, 15 (1981), 425-441.

[20] Dicken, "The Imagery of the Interior Castle," p. 213.

[21] Cirlot, p. 40.

[22] Alexander A. Parker, "Metáfora y símbolo en la interpretación de Calderón," in Frank Pierce and Cyril A. Jones, eds., Actas del Primer Congreso Internacional de Hispanistas (Oxford: Dolphin Book Co., for the international Association of Hispanists, 1964), pp. 56-7.

[23] Cited in Cirlot, p. 196.

[24] Spitzer, "Three poems," p. 21.

[25] Helmut Hatzfeld, "La estilización del amor divino en Dante, San Juan de la Cruz, Pascal y Angelus Silesius," in Estudios literarios sobre mística española (Madrid: Gredos, 1968), p. 405.

[26] E. W. Trueman Dicken, The Crucible of Love (New York: Sheed and Ward, 1963), pp. 439-40.

[27] Covarrubias, p. 355.

[28] Etchegoyen, p. 243.

[29] Crisógono de Jesús, San Juan de la Cruz, el hombre, II, pp. 127-28.

[30] Hatzfeld, "Two Types," p. 446.

[31] James C. Franklin, Mystical Transformations (Rutherford, N. J.: Farleigh Dickinson University Press, 1978), p. 29.

[32] Perella. p. 39.

[33] Poems of Góngora, p. 88.

[34] Spitzer, "Three Poems," p. 25.

[35] Robert T. Petersson, The Art of Ecstasy. Teresa, Bernini, and Crashaw (New York: Atheneum, 1970), p. 33.

[36] Marlay p. 366. McInnis, "Eucharistic and Conjugal Symbolism," p. 130, states that "the scenes of consummation in John's poem become scenes of consumption through a dependence upon Eucharistic imagery."

[37] Hatzfeld, "La estilización," p. 391.

[38] Merton, The Ascent, p. 299.

[39] Morel, Le Sens, III, pp. 81-2, writes "Que l'idée de nourriture et de boisson apparaisse ainsi aux commencements de la nuit est d'importance capitale: dans la vie naturelle le stade buccal où le nourrisson se montre normalement absorbant et possessif est premier; le sevrage est la transition au stade ultérieur. Il en est de même sous mode absolument original dans la vie veritable: de même que l'aliment est moyen premier pour la substance humaine corporelle de se développer et renouveler, de même il devient symbole fondamental d'une expérience mystique dont l'un des sense est assimilation."

[40] Roland H. Bainton, "Man, God and the Church in the Age of the Renaissance," in The Renaissance: A Symposium (New York: The Metropolitan Museum of Art, 1962), repr. The Renaissance (New York: 1953), p. 87.

[41] López Baralt, San Juan de la Cruz y el Islam, pp. 231-234, shows parallels between San Juan's references to wine and those of the Sufi mystics.

[42] McInnis, "Eucharistic and Conjugal Symbolism," p. 133, believes that "the draught of spiced wine becomes the Bridegroom himself of whom the bride drinks directly, in an adaptation of the Eucharist to the mystical union of the soul and God.

[43] Morel, Le Sens, III, p. 130.

[44] Dicken, Crucible, p. 396.

[45] St. Bernard of Clairvaux, On the Song of Songs. Sermones in Cantica Canticorum, trans. and ed. A Religious of C. S. M. V. (London: A. R. Mowbray and Co.; New York: Morehouse-Gorman, 1952), pp. 163-64.

[46] Gardner, ed., The Metaphysical Poets, p. 75.

Chapter 6

FAMILIAR ACTIVITIES

With the comparison of the soul to a wounded deer, to a fortress capable of repelling the enemies of sin and distraction, or to a king leading his troops, the mystics establish the basis for a series of images derived from familiar activities associated with the animate creatures who inhabit their mystical landscape. At the same time, activities derived from social aspects of sixteenth-century life also inform their works. Among those which Santa Teresa and San Juan consider are warfare, hunting, games, travel, and the fine arts, such as sculpting, painting, and music. While warfare, hunting, and travel suggest activity outside the figurative walls of the castle, gaming and the fine arts, like the riches and treasures of the cave or the intricacies of government, are located within. As they elaborate on the comparisons available to them, however, both writers continue to stress the interiority of the mystical quest.

Warfare

Presenting the spiritual life as a kind of warfare between the soul and its enemies, both external and internal, is hardly unique to San Juan and Santa Teresa. Neither is the related symbolism which pits the soul in amorous conflict with its divine Lover. Rather, both comparisons have antecedents in Scripture, ascetical literature, and secular prose and poetry which precede the works of the Spanish Carmelites. In ascetical works, warfare symbolizes man's search for an "inner unity in his actions, in his thoughts and also between his actions and his thoughts."[1] Such bellicose imagery inspires St. Paul in his mandate to the Christians of Ephesus (6:11). Similarly, writers more contemporary with the Carmelites also rely heavily on the symbolism of spiritual warfare. Erasmus begins his Enquiridión by citing Job 7:1, then devotes the first three chapters of the work to a discussion of why "toda la vida de los mortales no es aquí sino una perpetua guerra."[2] One of Santa Teresa's favorite books, Osuna's Tercer abecedario, devotes the greater part of two tratados to similar imagery, while San Ignacio de Loyola's Ejercicios espirituales reflect the author's own military background. Although far from an exhaustive list of sources which influence the mystics directly or indirectly, each of these works indicates the widespread reliance on the comparison of spiritual progress to warfare. Even as the mystics perpetuate much of the ascetical symbolism associated with spiritual warfare, they also extend its meaning by endowing it with an unmistakably mystical stamp.

The soul's symbolic fortification against enemies who would combat its efforts to achieve its mystical goal provides the basis for the imagery of spiritual warfare. Although San Juan believes its surest defense lies in the acquisition of virtues which serve "como fuertes escudos contra los vicios" (CE. XXIV, 9), nevertheless, it inevitably meets enemies who impede its progress. Only after purgation does the soul find itself "en cierto refugio, donde se ve estar más alejada de el enemigo" (N. II, 23, iv). In summing up the imagery of spiritual combat, Santa Teresa describes the soul:

> . . . como uno que está en una batalla: sabe que si le vencen, no le perdonarán la vida; y que ya que no muera en la batalla, ha de morir después--es averiguado, a mi parecer, que peleará con mucho más ánimo y no temerá tanto los golpes, porque lleva delante lo que le importa la vitoria. (CP. XXXIX/XXIII, 5)

It comes as no surprise, therefore, that the opening lines of her Camino de perfección are "as vigorous as a declaration of war," for "the style itself is military in its precision."[3] Certainly the religious upheavals of Reformation Europe were a major consideration of hers, evidenced not only in the Camino, but also in her other works. The historical reality of religious wars being fought on actual battlefields so soon after Spain's own struggles in the Reconquista coupled with her avid reading of libros de caballería as a child undoubtedly contribute to her predilection for battle imagery. At the same time, however, both she and San Juan tap other sources of warfare imagery present in secular and religious literature throughout the ages.

The soul's chief enemies are the powers of darkness and the passions of men or, as Covarrubias defines enemigo:

"absolutamente se toma por el demonio, por ser enemigo universal del linage humano y nuestro adversario" (p. 518). Both definitions stress the exterior and interior nature of spiritual progress. As countless spiritual and religious writers before and after him, therefore, San Juan reduces the principal enemies of the soul to the world, the flesh, and the devil, all of which "hacen guerra y dificultan el camino" (CE. III, 6). In utilizing the tripartite notion of temptation, San Juan casts the enemies of spiritual advancement in familiar, even trite terms. Nevertheless, where he provides an objective recounting of the traditional enemies of the soul, Santa Teresa creates a more effective image by elaborating on the concept of warfare. She goes beyond the general terms to the personification of evil, Satan or Lucifer. For her the contending armies arrayed against each other in spiritual combat are headed respectively by Christ, "el capitán de amor" (CPv. VI, 9) and Satan. All Christians are called to take up the effective weapons of virtue in order to defend their King, Christ. While a multitude accompanies Lucifer, only "muy pocos vasallos" follow Christ. By designating both Christ and Satan captains of their respective armies, Santa Teresa underscores the deadly serious nature of the spiritual conflict facing all Christians. Under the command of their "infernal capitán" sinners turn from God, disdaining to join the army of Christ, the "great Captain of the Wars [who] brings power and leadership" in battle. [4] Only with God's grace can souls overcome the temptations facing them and advance in virtue, guided by "los capitanes de este castillo" who are Christ's representatives on earth.

While Christ captains the army of God, those called to the mystical life are lieutenants expected to fight a different sort of war from that of the ordinary foot soldier:

> . . . Un pobre soldado vase su paso a paso, y si se asconde [sic] alguna vez para no entrar adonde ve el mayor tropel, no le echan de ver ni pierde honra ni vida. El alferez, aunque no pelea, lleva la bandera, y aunque le hagan pedazos no la ha de dejar de las manos. Tienen todos los ojos en el. ¿Pensáis que da poco trabajo al que el rey da estos oficios? Por un poquito de más honra, se obligan a padecer mucho más; y si tantito les sienten flaqueza, todo va perdido. (CP. XXIX/XVIII, 3-4)

Santa Teresa thus carries the traditional notion of spiritual warfare a step further by pointing out the special role which the mystic fills in the cosmic battle of good and evil. While all Christians are called to the arms of Christ, only some receive the additional duty and privilege of being his standard-bearers in prayer. The soldiers who pursue mystical prayer are "más contentos cuando hay querra", because only through war with the exterior enemies of temptation and distraction and the interior ones of faults and failings can they win the spoils of mystical union. By elaborating on the idea of spiritual combat Santa Teresa lifts the image from the ascetical notion of combatting sin in one's personal life to the mystical plane of carrying the standard of the king and eventually joining him in union.

While the mystics convert the imagery of warfare from its ascetical sense to that of a quest for union, they reflect however palely the language of chivalric romance. Santa Teresa acknowledges in the Vida her own surreptitious reading of the pot-boiling libros de caballería, an admission not reflected in San Juan's works. Nevertheless, both writers describe the highly individualized adventure of the mystic quest in terms evocative of some of the chivalresque vocabulary found in secular letters. Since both forms of literature trace their roots to the mysteries, some similarity may be discerned between mystic and grail quester. Ramon Llull consciously utilizes the chivalric mode in the composition of his Blanquerna, a novel which includes the longer, more clearly mystical, Libro del amigo y Amado. Both Catalán Franciscan and Castilian Carmelite suggest that their quest is for mystical union. In this sense, the goal is a personal one on the part of soul aided by God to attain an extraordinary state not essential to salvation. In contrast, Lope de Vega transforms the chivalvic mode more particularly to mankind's salvation when he integrates aspects of the genre into the composition of his Auto de la puente del mundo. Equating Christ with the prototypical chivalric hero, Amadís de Gaula, the playwright pits the Caballero de la Cruz and his Doce Pares against the Príncipe de las tinieblas and his powers of darkness. What is of interest to Lope is not the individual salvation of a single soul so much as that of all mankind. Warfare symbolism in general and resonances of the grail quest in particular, therefore, speak to broader religious and mystical concerns. Ostensibly more individual in the focus of their imagery, nevertheless, the mystics never entirely lose sight of their broader responsibilities within their religious community.

Although some battle imagery occurs in the Canticle of Canticles, San Juan includes very little in his poetic rendering of the Biblical source. Only at the conclusion of the Cántico espiritual (XL) does he turn from the essentially pastoral ambience in which most of the poem is set in order to insert a strophe which lends a jarring note to the tone of peaceful repose which envelops the united lovers. While the references to Aminadab suggest his chariots (Cant. 6:11) and those to cerco and caballería strongly imply war, San Juan's emphasis in this strophe is on peace. Aminadab is not present; the siege is over; the cavalry looks for water rather than for the enemy. By interposing three bellicose images so evocative of the clamor of war, San Juan underscores in paradoxical fashion the peace enjoyed by the soul. The repose of the mystical lovers is doubly quiet and peaceful, just as the battlefield takes on an eerie silence when the battle ceases. The poet also suggests the price exacted for the peace of mystical union by suggesting the spiritual conflict necessary to attain the goal.

The commentary attempts to explain the strophe allegorically and thereby reduce to simple terms the multivalent meanings present in the poem. San Juan considers Aminadab the devil, ever at war with the soul, disturbing it "con la innumerable munición de su artillería" in order to prevent its entrance into the fortress of interior recollection (CE. XL, 3). The siege refers to the passions and appetites of the soul which now lie vanquished, while the cavalry are the corporeal senses. Through the conversion of the cave where the soul enjoys union into a fortress which has resisted the siege engines of Satan's temptations and the persistent distractions which come through the senses, San Juan extends the predominantly pastoral imagery of the Cántico to include that of the familiar castle-fortress-palace. An interconnection suggested by the bodegas and cuevas de leones enlazados is here made quietly explicit by the poet.

San Juan's designation of Aminadab as the devil is a novel interpretation of a fairly obscure Biblical figure. Fray Luis de León, for example, discerns no correspondence between Aminadab and Satan in his commentary on the Canticle, nor do most Biblical commentators. Cassiodorus, in fact, considers him a prefiguration of Christ, not Satan. Besides viewing Aminadab as a symbol of evil, San Juan also converts the chariots (quadrigas) of the Canticle to cavalry (caballería) cresting a hill in search of water. All of these changes convert a vague reference in the Vulgate to a more specifically military image in the poem which is interpreted allegorically in the commentary as a symbol of malevolence conquered in the peace of mystical union.

By deliberately equating Aminadab with Satan, San Juan accomplishes a number of effects. Like Santa Teresa, he personifies the principal enemy of the soul and juxtaposes him with the passions and appetites which all lie vanquished by the union of _Amado_ and _Amada_. With Santa Teresa, he implies that in union peace reigns in the mystic's soul although war may rage without. Finally, he unconsciously emphasizes an essentially ascetic view of warfare symbolism. For San Juan the struggle is envisioned as a battle against impediments to union, whether these be outside forces or the interior faults of the individual. He does not perceive God as an adversary to be overcome or one with whom the soul does battle. At the same time, although he converts Aminadab's charioteers to cavalrymen, he describes Satan's principal armament as "munición de . . . artillería" (_CE_. XL, 3) with which he batters the fortress of the soul. The reference to siege explains, in part, the association of artillery and the fortress-soul. On another level, however, San Juan also anticipates an association which Covarrubias explains later in his dictionary: "se llamó artillería por el arte diabólica de su invención" (p. 154). San Juan thus combines in a single strophe a number of military images (chariots which are absent, a siege which has ended, artillery which is silent, cavalry at ease) all vanquished by the fortress-soul totally at peace in a unitive embrace with the _Amado_.

Even though Santa Teresa remarks that "todas las armas con que se podía defender le parece que las ve en manos de su contrario" (_M_. VI, 1, x), the soul is still able to achieve victory because God is on its side. Enumerating the arms available to the Christian to combat the wiles of its enemy enjoys a long tradition in religious and otherwise secular literature. Juan Ruiz intercalates the lengthy section entitled "Armas con las que todo buen cristiano debe armarse para vencer al mundo, al demonio y a la carne" into the _Libro de buen amor_ as a virtual tour de force which juxtaposes the seven deadly sins with the seven sacraments, the corporal works of mercy, the gifts of the Holy Spirit, and the virtues. The archpriest summarizes with mathematical precision his schema of the Christian life. In contrast, the mystics presuppose acquisition of the rudiments of virtuous living on the part of any aspiring to union. The military accoutrements present on their spiritual battlefields, therefore, are far less schematized than their medieval countryman's. Nevertheless, the mystic's arms suggest that the warfare is far from one-sided. A book of meditation is "como una compañía u escudo" which deflects the blows of distracting thoughts (V. IV, 9). The mystic defends the spoils of prayer "con la espada en la mano de la consideración" (_Med._ II, 14). The banners of religious houses bear the _armas_ of poverty while the mystic dedicated to pursuing union is like an "alcaide de esta fortaleza" of the soul who ascends to its highest tower bearing God's flag. The rapidity with which a soul may experience rapture resembles "la presteza que sale la pelota de un arcabuz cuando le ponen el fuego" (_M._ VI, 5, ix). Significantly, only one weapon is placed in the hands of God or of his envoy.

Traditionally, the arrow or dart is the weapon of Eros or Cupid who wounds the unsuspecting lover; yet it also signifies the light of supreme power and, when "balanced against the symbol of the 'mystic centre' . . . such as the heart" symbolizes conjunction."[5] To Richard of St. Victor the fiery dart is the weapon of the divine Lover which causes an ecstatic rapture in the mystic wounded by it, a mystical transformation of Origen's "loveworthy spear of [God's] knowledge."[6] For the Carmelite mystics, therefore, the saetas or flechas de amor are the Amado's symbolic weapons used to wound the soul "en lo más vivo de las entrañas y corazón" (V. XXIX, 10). Santa Teresa relates the transverberation of her soul by describing an angelic Cupid wielding a burning "dardo de oro," which he proceeds to "meter por el corazón algunas veces y que me llegava a las entrañas." As a result the saint "toda abrasava en amor grande de Dios" (V. XXIX, 13). Bernini's sculpture inspired by this passage in the Vida captures both the passionate eroticism latent in the incident as well as the mystical rapture which the saint claims to have experienced. San Juan employs an example analogous to that of his mentor when he explains one level of the cauterio de amor inflicted on the soul by God. The soul inflamed by God's love believes itself to be "embesti[da] en ella un serafín con una flecha o dardo enarbolado encendidísimo en fuego de amor, traspasando a esta alma que ya está encendida como ascua, o, por mejor decir, como llama" (Ll. II, 9). In the case of both writers the arrow or dart causes an increase in mystical passion. It becomes the instrument of ecstatic union, transporting the soul touched by it to a higher level of love for God. At the same time, the _saeta_ or _dardo_ subsumes the related imagery of fire and wound present in other contexts of the mystics' works.

Just as San Juan compresses a number of symbolic meanings in his single war reference in the _Cántico_, Santa Teresa also uses the weapons of war effectively in her extended comparisons of mystical advancement to spiritual warfare. Some of the similes, such as rapture compared to a musket shot or a book of spiritual reading to a shield, are effective on more than one level. The rapidity of the shot corresponds to the rapidity and unexpectedness of rapture. The unusual choice of a military comparison of force, speed, and startling sound fixes the concept more firmly in the reader's mind than another, less hackneyed phrase might. Assigning artillery to the armament of the devil is a particularly apt symbol of the power of this enemy to batter the soul. Santa Teresa's facility in making these unusual yet effective comparisons lends her works a refreshing quality which expresses doctrine in highly readable prose.

Her mystical language inspires not only the Italian sculptor but the English metaphysical poet, Richard Crashaw, as well.[7] He casts much of his "Hymn to the Name and Honor of the Admirable Saint Teresa" in the bellicose vocabulary found in the _Vida_. Initially touched by the saint's childhood adventure in seeking martyrdom at the hands of the Moors, Crashaw next turns to the "milder martyrdom" (v. 68) of the mystic way. What awaits her is a "death more mystical and high" (v. 76). God's

. . . is the dart must make the death
Whose stroke shall taste thy hallowed breath;
A dart thrice dipped in that rich flame
Which writes thy spouse's radiant name
Upon the roof of heav'n, . . . (vv. 79-83)

Crashaw transforms Santa Teresa's bellicose imagery to his own ends by fixing on the dying life metaphor of mystical union. This "milder martyrdom" eventually achieved by the saint comes about because of the dart or arrow. It is the means whereby the Spanish Carmelite eventually wins the heavenly crown of eternal union with the divine Lover, for her mystical martyrdom is a prelude to eternal life. It also inspires others to follow her example, so that in eternity she will behold "thousands of crowned souls" (v. 165), a veritable army of her religious community who "must learn in life to die like thee" (v. 182).

The cosmic strife of the mystics' warfare imagery stands in sharp contrast to the cosmic harmony which marks their elemental imagery. Since combat tends to characterize the purgative state more than the others, both writers juxtapose the soul still struggling with imperfection with the contending forces of creation. Even in strife they make possible the reality of an ordered world. It is a paradox present in both the macrocosm and the microcosm as Gracián later explains in El Criticón.[8] For the mystics the strife is an interior one altogether in which the soul struggles with its own failings. As such it is characteristic of purgation and partly of illumination. When transforming union is finally achieved, however, harmony reigns both within and without.

As the soul passes from the ascetical and purgative practices necessary to "dominarse a sí mismo," it enters a new stage of spiritual warfare in which the adversary is no longer its own base instincts or Satan, but, rather, God. Santa Teresa develops the rather bizarre notion of the soul at war with God in convincing fashion. Especially in her discussion of ecstasy and rapture, she considers the mystic's initial resistance to the onslaught of this state "una pelea grande". The soul feels as if it has struggled with a giant and lost, for the Lover sweeps it into ecstatic experience despite its attempts to resist. At the illuminative stage of mystical experience, therefore, spiritual combat becomes a "guerra de amor" between the soul and God.

> Pues, Señor, comenzada esta batalla, a quién ha de ir
> a combatir, sino a quien se ha hecho señor de esta
> fortaleza adonde moraven--que es lo más superior de el
> alma--y echádolas fuera a ellas, para que tornen a
> conquistar a su conquistador, y ya cansadas de haverse
> visto sin El, presto se dan por vencidas y se emplean
> perdiendo todas sus fuerzas y pelean mejor, y, en
> dándose por vencidas, vencen a su vencedor? (Ex. XVI)

What begins as a sometimes frightening spiritual struggle in the ascetical and purgative practices necessary for advancement becomes a complex symbol as the mystics consider the later stages of the mystical experience. Initially the soul contends with its own failings or the temptations of Satan. Its loyalty waivers as it first seems to join the multitudes which follow the devil's banner but finally opts for service in the ranks of the "Great Captain of the wars." As it grows in virtue and prayer, the would-be mystic soul rises from the ranks to which all Christians are called to serve as <u>alferez</u>, carrying the King's banner to the highest tower of the spiritual fortress. Along the way, the soul, fearing the unknown, feebly resists the Lover's attempts to take it outside the body in ecstatic union. Only when this final resistance is overcome can the soul achieve spiritual marriage, joining the King in the <u>septima</u> <u>morada</u> where peace reigns. The mystics transform a fairly straightforward symbol of ascetic practice into a complex one which attempts to represent the countervailing struggles present in mystical progress.

Games

Reducing the scope of spiritual warfare to a more manageable size, Santa Teresa compares the soul's advancement in prayer to a chess game. In this stylized battle, it is necessary to arrange the board correctly: "Pues cree quien no sabe concertar las piezas en el juego del ajedrez, que sabrá mal jugar; y si no sabe dar jaque, no sabrá dar mate" (<u>CPe</u>. XXIV, 1). The basics of the game must be mastered in order to checkmate "este rey divino". The same complexity present in the larger context of spiritual warfare appears in chess imagery. Noting the major role played by the queen in the outcome of the game, Santa Teresa may have fixed on this aspect in order to explain advancement in prayer. The preparation and training necessary on the part of the soul still depend on God's grace because "no se da [mate] este rey sino a quien se le da del todo" (<u>CPe</u>. XXIV, 4). What begins with the soul's activity concludes with God's, for the object of the

mystical chess game is to capture the King, who, in this
spiritual context, allows himself to be taken.

Other games provide passing images utilized by both writers
sparingly, yet, at times, effectivoly. Santa Teresa's comparison
of the trials visited on the soul by temptation to a game of jai
alai in which "andan los demonios como jugando a la pelota con el
alma" (V. XXX, 11)[9] provides a refreshing counterpoint to the
military image of the soul battered by the artillery of its
enemies. Nevertheless, advancement in prayer is no child's
game. Rather, as San Juan points out, the soul aflame with love
happily exercises itself in "las artes y juegos de amor" (Ll. I,
8). Like spiritual warfare, games cast mystical experience in
competitive terms with difficulties to be overcome in order to
achieve the desired victory. The nature of the goal awaiting the
mystic makes the contest both arduous and desirable.

What may seem on the surface rather frivolous comparisons on
the mystics' part for the serious business of mystical progress,
actually have a logical basis in the nature of both game and
ritual. In his study of the play-element in culture, Johann
Huizinga draws an analogy between the chessboard and the temple
or magic circle, places set aside for the orderly activity of
play and worship. Citing a passage in Plato (Laws VII, 76), he
observes that "the Platonic identification of play and holiness
does not defile the latter by calling it play, rather it exalts
the concept of play to the highest region of the spirit."[10]
Santa Teresa and San Juan conceive of the mystical experience in

gaming terms which harmonize with the Platonic notion that
Huizinga cites. The mystic does become God's plaything just as
God allows himself to be taken in the mystical chess match. The
freedom, the non-materiality, the boundaries of spiritual time
and place, and the orderly progression of the mystical game
reflect the characteristics which Huizinga observes in all games
(pp. 13-14).

Frank Warnke broadens the scope of Huizinga's work when he
applies it to Baroque poetry in Europe. Not just specific
references to games but also the play on words and concepts in
metaphysical and conceptista poetry are for him examples of "a
kind of serious jocularity, expressed in witty metaphor, pun, and
elaborate formalism, with the final effect of achieving a
breakthrough into a kind of solemn lightheartedness, the result
of a transcendence of or liberation from the mundane and
secular."[11] In this sense, the glosses by both Santa Teresa and
San Juan on the popular song, "Vivo sin vivir en mí," play on the
dying life experienced by the mystic longing for eternity yet
confined to an earthly existence. Warnke offers the example of
Lope de Vega's sonnet, "Pastor, que con tus silbos amorosos," to
demonstrate the serious jocularity he discerns in divine poetry
at play. The same observation may apply to San Juan's a lo
divino version of "Un pastorcico." The mystic's poem contains
both the agonistic mode as well as the play element discerned by
the critic, for it plays on the concepts of pastoral love poetry
and the crucifixion when the forgotten pastorcico willingly dies

while embracing the tree of the cross.[12]

The end desired by the mystic in the game as in spiritual warfare is victory over his enemies and the "santa paz" which accompanies it. Throughout the passage to union, the soul may experience fleeting moments of peace. Thus, San Juan discerns a certain peace following the "guerra de la oscura noche" of purgation when the soul once controls its appetites and passions (N. II, 24, ii). Santa Teresa warns against the "paz que da el mundo" (Med. III, 7) as well as the false peace of the devil, who tries to deceive the soul by retreating temporarily "para hacerle después mucho mayor guerra" (M. V, 2, ix). The mystic distinguishes between true and false peace only by studying the effects which result. Satan cannot give the soul peace which "provoca a alabanzas de Dios" (M. VI, 6, x), but only a false imitation which comes from settling for some temporal good rather than looking to the ultimate goal of prayer.

The soul achieves another intermediate plane of peace in the illuminative stage where it begins to enjoy "gran suavidad de paz y amigabilidad amorosa con Dios" (N. II, 7, iv). Once having passed through the purgative war with its passions and appetites, the soul seeks and enjoys a peace which comes with the quieting of "todas las potencias" in the prayer of quiet. The final and unshakeable peace awaiting the mystic in the temporal world is that realized in spiritual marriage where, as San Juan notes, the tres principales enemigos lie completely vanquished. The only peace which surpasses that of spiritual marriage is the "paz perpetua" enjoyed by the church triumphant "en perfección de amor". As in so much of their imagery, therefore, the spiritual warfare and gaming which San Juan and Santa Teresa utilize admit of multiple meanings and ambivalent polarity. While spiritual warfare is a struggle, sometimes a frightening one, it is essential if the soul wishes to reach union. The foes vary; loyalties waiver. With victory comes peace, but it must be the paz which God gives and not the false peace of complacency and pride.

Hunting

Although not as extensive an image in the mystics' store of figurative language, hunting does occur in passing but significant fashion in at least two of San Juan's works and tangentially in Santa Teresa's. Both authors perpetuate a tradition with origins in the lyrics of Gil Vicente and the cancioneros as well as the cultured works of the Spanish Renaissance poets. Although Edith Rogers believes that the hunt serves primarily as the scene, the circumstance, the atmosphere and not as the subject of traditional ballads, Dámaso Alonso's review of possible sources for San Juan's "Tras de un amoroso lance" implies a contrary view. The poems he cites all cast the love-hunt in terms of pursuit and capture of the maiden by the caballero. [13]

The opening strophes of the Cántico espiritual certainly suggest the hunt, yet the roles of pursuer and pursued are curiously inverted. It is the Bride who hunts the Lover, symbolized by the _ciervo_, who flees from the huntress after wounding her. This is not the satiric inversion present in Juan Ruiz's _serranas_, but, rather, a complex relationship between hunter and hunted which points to the union actualized in the _subidas_ _cavernas_. God searches out the soul so that it may, in turn, search for him. The "flechas" which wound both Bride and Lover and the "zaga de [su] huella" which leads the soul to the winecellar of interior contemplation underscore the interdependence of the principals in the mystical love-hunt.

In the works of Santa Teresa, virtually no direct references to hunting appear, yet the comparison of the soul to a small bird seized by a bird of prey representing God suggests the art of falconry. In addition, some measure of hunting analogies exists in the saint's description of her transverberation in the _Vida_ as well as in the poem, "Vivo sin vivir en mí." Since it is God who wounds the soul through his surrogate angel with the "dardo de amor" and God, who as the "águila caudalosa" seizes the humbler bird representative of the soul, Santa Teresa casts her hunting allusions in terms of the soul pursued by divine Lover. In contrast, when San Juan employs the imagery of falconry, he makes some intriguing alterations. His lyric, "Tras de un amoroso lance," centers almost completely on a hunting image. The soul, symbolized in this work by a falcon, flies "tan alto, tan alto / Que le [dio] a la caza alcance." Although dazzled by the brilliance of its quarry, the soul pursues it in a "lance divino" spurred on by love. Paradox accompanies the falcon's flight as it does the mystic's ascent through a lowering by humility:

> Cuanto más alto llegaba
> De este lance tan subido,
> Tanto más bajo y rendido
> Y abatido me hallaba. (vv. 21-24)

The poet calls attention to the successful capture of the desired prey through the repetition of the estribillo, "le di a la caza alcance," thus effectively combining progress and hunting imagery in a single, short poem. [14]

Nevertheless, San Juan's symbol of the "lance divino" reverses the roles established by Santa Teresa's águila caudalosa comparison; for, in his case, it is the soul who pursues its divine prey as a bird on the wing. At the same time, he subsumes the royal origins of falconry as Covarrubias later indicates in his explanation that "caça de altanería [es] sólo para los príncipes y grandes señores" (p. 258). In the Cántico espiritual, San Juan provides the answer to how the soul is able to assume the royal prerogative as falcon and falconer. The ability of the low-flying bird of the soul to capture the divine bird of the heights is possible only because "el águila real muy subida . . . se viene a lo bajo, queriendo ser presa" (CE. XXXI, 7). Thus, in his longer poem San Juan also likens God to the eagle which allows itself to be captured by a much humbler bird.

For mystic and poet alike, hunting and falconry are effective symbols on more than one level since they incorporate diverse aspects of mystical and poetic experience into a single activity. The royal nature of both the pursuit and the divine prey, the exaltation of flight and snaring of the lover, the alternating soaring and swooping, the suggestion of ascent toward blinding light, and the cooperation of God in making the capture possible cast falconry on a higher plane in the hands of the Carmelite mystics. At the same time, the love hunt subsumes the more extensive fauna and flora imagery of symbolic animals and landscape as well as the images of progress and warfare. Finally, both hunting and falconry underscore the ambivalent activity of pursuer and pursued in the mystical love-hunt.

Travel

That life itself is a journey from birth to the unknown which lies beyond death with pauses, reversals, and digressions along the way is a theme common in literature. Spiritual writers turn the journey of life from mere passage through space to "an expression of the urgent desire for discovery and change that underlies the actual movement and experience of travelling."[15] The journey for the spiritual man, therefore, is evolutionary, movement in which change occurs as he nears his goal. For the individual called to the mystical quest, the "journey to God is complete when he attains knowledge of Him [in] 'Illumination'." Once this journey to God is complete, the mystic next travels in God in the unitive state, aspiring to attain the spiritual city, the innermost mansion, the highest sphere, or the most profound center of his soul where that union with the Amado will be realized.[16]

The basis of the comparison of spiritual life to a journey appears in the Gospel admonition, "si quis vult me sequi, deneget semetipsum, et tollat crucem suam, et sequatur me" (Mark 8:34). The mystics simply build on the premise, conceiving their progress toward union with God as a long, hard journey towards a known and definite goal or state. Even when represented as an outward journey, however, the internal nature of the desired goal never fully disappears. Such is certainly the case in Santa Teresa's conception of the mystical journey as entrance into and progress through the interior castle of the soul. So, too, is the ascetical and mystical progress envisioned by San Juan de la Cruz in the Subida al monte Carmelo. Representation of the journey to union in the works of both writers is twofold. On the one hand, it is seen as progress on a symbolically horizontal plane to the center of the soul where union with God as Bridegroom occurs. On the other hand, it is also represented as ascent of a steep mountain to the "cumbre". While both kinds of progress may seem "almost matter of fact rather than symbolic to any one who admits the reality of any kind of spiritual progress,"[17] both Santa Teresa and San Juan bring to the imagery of travel the same variety and elaboration present in all of their figurative language.

In addition to the Gospel admonition to leave all in order to follow Christ, other scriptural and religious sources exist for the mystics' inclusion of the road as the principal course to

be travelled in order to attain union. Fray Luis de León reviews
the various scriptural meanings for camino in De los nombres de
Cristo before settling on that inspired by Christ's own words:
"Ego sum via, veritas et vita. Nomo venit ad Patrem, nisi per
me" (Mark 8:34). Santa Teresa takes her cue from this Biblical
passage also by reminding her readers that Christ is the road
which "han de ir los que le siguen si no se quieren perder" (V.
XI, 6). The road to God is a "camino real", a sure route along
which have passed the saints impelled by both love, which
quickened their steps, and fear, which guided them with care.

Facing the Christian of every walk of life, therefore, is
the choice of two roads to follow: "de virtud y relisión y falta
de relisión" (V. VII, 5). It is a choice offered implicitly in
the Gospel invitation "si quis vult me sequi". Danger lies in
walking "con el hilo de la gente" while one finds security by
advancing alone along the road to God (V. XXXV, 14). As San Juan
observes, only by leaving the road of worldliness can the soul
advance toward God. In paradoxical terms he describes progress
on the road of the spirit by means of a series of contradictions:

> Por tanto, en este camino, el [dejar su camino es
> entrar en camino o, por mejor decir el] pasar al
> término y dejar su modo es entrar en [el términol que
> no tiene modo, que es Dios; . . . De donde el venir
> aquí es salir (de aquí y de allí), saliendo de sí muy
> lejos de ese bajo para esto, sobre todo alto. (S. II,
> 4, v)

Like the gate which allows entry into the interior castle, the
road on which the initiate begins his journey to God is prayer.
Nevertheless, not all travel the same route, for just as there

are many mansions left unvisited by Santa Teresa en Las moradas, so there are many roads in prayer enjoyed by some and not by others. Santa Teresa thus reiterates a basic tenet that finds its scriptural foundation in Christ's statement that "in domo Patris mei mansiones multae sunt" (John 14:2). The approaches to God in prayer are varied; the goal is unchangeable.

Even though the road of contemplation may appear open to any who would choose to travel it, it is, in fact, a camino espiritual to which God leads very few. Rather, discursive prayer is the "via ordinaria," in which the soul relies on its imagination and senses to reach its destination. Since spiritual directors are more likely to find this way comprehensible, they are tempted to keep charges there who might otherwise be called to the contemplative way. As San Juan describes it, contemplation is "tan diferente camino," one traveled in darkness and aridity where the powers of the soul lie quiet because "ya Dios es el que obra en el ánima" (N. I, 9, vii). Beyond the purgation of senses and spirit lies the "via iluminativa" of infused contemplation.

Recalling the words of the prophet Baruch (3:23), San Juan stresses the blindness of the understanding as it passes through the nights of sense and spirit toward God. In a certain sense, he believes that the soul travels into unknown territory when it enters the stage of contemplation known as the noche pasiva del alma. In an extended simile, he explains the journey into the unknown:

> Así como el caminante, que, para ir a nuevas tierras no
> sabidas, va por nuevos caminos no sabidos ni
> experimentados, que [camina no] guiado por lo que sabía
> antes, sino en dudas y por el dicho de otros, ya claro
> está que éste no podría venir a nuevas tierras ni saber
> más de lo que antes sabía, si no fuera por caminos
> nuevos nunca sabidos, y dejados los que sabía , . . Así
> de la misma manera, cuando el alma va aprovechando más,
> va a escuras y no sabiendo. (N. II, 16, viii)

In contrast, Santa Teresa advises her readers to follow the
example of the saints by serving others. She does not wish to
"ir por camino no andado, que nos perderemos al mejor tiempo" (M.
VII, 4, xii). Although she admits that the soul advances to God
by means of his "secretos caminos", she also suggests that the
mystic must follow the example of those who have already
traversed these roads. Her dependence on other mystical works
may explain this suggestion in part. On the other hand, although
San Juan does not specifically exclude reliance on the experience
of other mystics, his emphasis seems to be on the psychological
aspect of the dark night of the senses. For each mystic, passage
through the dark night is travel into an unknown territory,
because, even though others may have preceded him, each person
makes the passage in a uniquely individual way. Thus, the
passage is into unknown territory on an individual basis, while a
shared experience on the collective level.

Just as serpents and cosas ponzoñosas fill the moat as
deterrents to those who wish to enter the interior castle, so the
condition of the road may discourage some from beginning or
continuing the mystical journey. In a passage which recalls both
the Gospel and the image of the castle, San Juan describes the

gate as narrow and the road strait which leads to union (S. II, 7, ii). For San Juan the constricted path to union is made so by the requisite negation which he deems essential to the dark night. In a reversal of the traditional image of the strait and narrow path to God, however, Santa Teresa proposes a counter-example: "ni se como 'es estrecho el camino que lleva a Vos.' Camino real veo que es, que no senda; camino que quien de verdad se pone en él, va más seguro" (V. XXXV, 13). To her the senda is the route of temptation where the physical characteristics of a narrow, mountain path continually threaten the traveler with danger:

> Senda llamo yo y ruín senda y angosto camino el que de una parte está un valle muy hondo adonde caer y de la otra un despeñadero; no se han descuidado cuando se despeñan y se hacen pedazos. El que os ama de verdad, Bien mío, siguro va por ancho camino y real. (V. XXXV, 13-14)[18]

Santa Teresa's description of the road to union as an ancho camino y real contrasts directly with San Juan's condemnation of those who flee the narrow road to virtue "buscando el ancho de su consuelo," which only leads to perdition (Ll. II, 27), even as it echoes Laredo's allusion to "the broad, level and most joyful road of quiet contemplation."[19]

Apparently influenced by the Gospel passage on which he comments, San Juan maintains the traditional notion of the road to God as the strait and narrow path. Santa Teresa reflects a different tradition when she reverses the terms of the comparison. While San Juan's symbol is in keeping with the via

negativa which characterizes his mystical doctrine, Santa
Teresa's suggests a less rigid and less ascetical view of the
mystical experience. Her flexibility of description is in
keeping with the goal she seeks, for only a royal road should
lead to the majesty of God. Furthermore, San Juan stresses the
temptations to be overcome while Santa Teresa suggests the graces
to be received. Further descriptions of the road by both writers
emphasize these distinctions. Thus, while both authors presume
the soul's proper disposition for a successful journey, Santa
Teresa continually repeats the fact that it is ultimately God and
not the soul who chooses those called to contemplative prayer.
The contradictory descriptions of the road to God simply continue
the underlying paradox of the entire mystical experience: that
is, that the trials and difficulties encountered in progressing
to union count as little once the goal is reached. What was
barrancoso y áspero seems suave to the soul in union.

Santa Teresa and San Juan diverge further in their
respective descriptions of the via purgativa. To San Juan the
night of the senses corresponds to the narrow gate and the night
of the spirit to the strait road, both made "tan estrecho[s].
oscuro[s] y terrible[s]" because few travel them (N. I, 11, iv).
Santa Teresa, however, wonders at those who fear to "ponerse en
el camino de la perfección." Guided by the Sun of Justice, souls
need not fear traveling by night. To San Juan, therefore, it is
imperative that the soul travel "el camino tan estrecho, oscuro y
terrible"; to Santa Teresa no road lit by the Sun of Justice is

ever truly dark. Although Santa Teresa implies that the journey on the road to perfection is not as harrowing as San Juan's, both authors agree that the surest road to follow is that of the cross, an assertion based on St. Mark's Gospel admonition (8:34). Many who have begun the road never finish, precisely because they fail to "abrazar a la cruz".

While the ascetical practices implied by the cross are the visible difficulties confronting the mystic, other, subtler obstacles also impede his progress. San Juan's rejection of "bienes temporales y deleytes corporales . . . consuelos y deleytes espirituales" which he finds symbolized in the flowers and beasts along the Bride's path (CE. III, 5) all represent impediments to progress. In his commentary he enumerates them in fairly dry, theological fashion. In contrast, Santa Teresa provides a much more graphic, even poetic description of the "mil caídas y tropiezos" facing the soul which strays from the true road to union. Those seeking spiritual gifts and consolations resemble the traveler who meets with a serious mishap:

> . . . pareciéndonos vamos siguros, damos con nosotros
> en un hoyo que no podemos salir de el que (aunque no
> sea de conocido pecado mortal para llevarnos al
> infierno todas veces) es que nos jarreta las piernas
> para no andar este camino de que comencé a tratar--que
> no se me ha olvidado--. Ya véis como ha de andar uno,
> metido en una gran hoya; allí se le acaba la vida (y
> harto hará si no ahonda hacia bajo para ir al
> infierno), mas nunca medra. Ya que esto no es, ni
> aprovecha a sí ni a los otros; antes daña, porque como
> se está el hoyo hecho, muchos que van por el camino
> pueden caer en él. Si sale y le atapa con tierra no
> hace daño a sí ni a los otros. (CP. LXVI/XXXVIII, 4)

For Santa Teresa, "la santa andariega," the vicissitudes of

travel in sixteenth-century Spain were a familiar experience. Turning them to spiritual ends was as natural as describing the various methods for watering the convent garden. Although San Juan's designation of Satan as the source of impediments to progress and the theological virtues as the surest protection from his wiles is theologically sound, it lacks the vividness of Santa Teresa's description of the many pitfalls and potholes scarring the camino espiritual.

While their use of the road as a symbol for mystical progress is quite similar, San Juan and Santa Teresa do differ in some of the symbolic meanings they attribute to it. San Juan maintains a traditional interpretation of the road to heaven as the strait and narrow path of self-denial and advancement in virtue. The soul achieves mystical union by passing through the dark nights of sense and spirit on the via purgativa. While not completely rejecting this tradition, Santa Teresa repeats a reversal of the traditional symbol when she calls the way to God "camino real . . . y no senda". Rather than suggesting the ease with which the soul travels this camino, Santa Teresa indicates God's generosity in affording souls the means to come to him. Although it is still a camino de la cruz for those who love God, the way is sure and the road seems wide. By thus expanding the symbolic meanings of camino and senda in the mystical context, Santa Teresa continues the multivalence which both mystics apply to the symbols they employ.

Fine Arts

Distinct from warfare, gaming, and hunting as activities of sixteenth-century life, nevertheless, the fine arts of painting, sculpture, and music also serve the mystics as appropriate metaphors for their experience. San Juan especially manifests a fascination with the fine arts, a fact due, perhaps, in part to his early training in the plastic arts. Painting and sculpture are particularly apt activities for mystical progress since the soul, like the empty canvas or rough-cut wood, through the arduous work of purgation, slowly transforms itself into a thing of beauty, an image of the Creator.

In an evocation of scholastic theology, San Juan likens the soul to "una tabla rasa y lisa" on which nothing is painted (S. I, 3, iii). As the mystic advances in virtue he sets himself the task of sketching "cierto dibujo de amor." The sketch slowly approximates the figure of Christ as the soul conforms its will to his. Like all craftsmen devoted to perfecting their art, the soul turns all of its faculties to the task of creating God's image within. From blank canvas, through first tentative strokes, to final masterpiece the soul, through the practice of virtue, conforms more perfectly to the will of God and thus creates within itself the divine image and likeness.

The ambivalence characteristic of much mystical imagery recurs in that of painting and sculpture. Thus, just as the roles of pursuer and pursued blur in the mystical love-hunt, so, too, those of painter and portrait undergo a similar reversal. Initially, the soul as craftsman fashions itself into a suitable work of art which, through the embellishment of virtue, slowly reflects the Creator. In union, however, the soul is itself the work of art painted, not by its own hand, but by God's. Through the correspondence essential to love, "emparejan tan en uno los amantes, que se transfiguran el uno en el otro" (CE. XI, 12). While the strophe from the Cántico on which he comments in this passage anticipates the ultimate union of the lovers, the transformation of Bride into image of the Bridegroom is best exemplified in the Noche oscura (V). Through a series of stylistic and phonetic devices the poet draws the lovers together in the space of two verses in a lexical and poetic union which transfigures one into the other more effectively than a thousand word-pictures.

Unlike San Juan, Santa Teresa evinces no similar interest in comparing the soul to a work of art. She does acknowledge some understanding of the plastic arts, however, in a sort of backhanded way. Cautioning her nuns against a desire for visions, she also points out that some confessors may be over-zealous in their condemnation of them. She cites the advice given her by "un gran letrado," who pointed out "que el demonio es gran pintor, y si le mostrase muy al vivo una imagen del Señor, que no le pesaría, para con ella avivar la devoción y hacer a el demonio querra con sus mesmas maldades" (M. VI, 9, xiii). Calderón also elaborates on the painter-painting simile in his auto sacramental, "El pintor de su deshonra," when he first presents God as the Pintor who creates humanity as "Bella imagen, en quien ya / obra de [su] mano diestra, / en [ella] la beldad se muestra" (p. 834).[20]

Although Calderón does not suggest the mystical bride understood by Santa Teresa or San Juan, he echoes at least some of their language. As the _auto_ continues, Lucero successfully tempts Naturaleza, leading the painter to describe himself as "pintor de su deshonra" in creating fallen mankind (p. 839). Nevertheless, just as the devil of Santa Teresa's work is too clever by half; so, too, Calderón's Lucero, in assuming the role of painter, spells out his eventual defeat (p. 842). His attempt to maintain control of humanity leads him to create the work of the crucifixion which will redeem mankind. Calderón's work looks to the sweep of salvation history rather than the individual experience of a single soul and God, yet it is also in harmony with the mystics' multivalent approach to painting.

In his study of mysticism and the fine arts in the Baroque, Emilio Orozco credits Santa Teresa with a painter's appreciation of the mystical life when he cites her "plásticas y realistas visiones en las que lo concreto y tangible, lo perceptible por los sentidos, es siempre fundamental."[21] Perhaps the best example of the Teresian attention to detailed description of her mystical experiences is that of the transverberation of her heart in the _Vida_. Its actual, plastic recreation by Bernini in the sculpture for the Coronaro chapel testifies to the vibrancy of the saint's description that inspired it. Except in this indirect manner, however, Santa Teresa does not utilize painting and sculpture as San Juan does. On the other hand, he, like she, warns his readers against the bad advice sometimes proffered by inexperienced spiritual directors.

Although the impediments to creating a suitable work of art may lie in the lack of talent on the part of the painter, San Juan also warns of the delicate painting which can be ruined by "una tosca mano con bajos y toscos colores." The soul adorned by the figurative hand of the Holy Spirit must be guided by an informed spiritual director, for "sería . . . mayor y más notable y de más lástima que si borrase muchos rostros de pinturas común" (Ll. III, 42). It is incumbent upon the spiritual director to preserve and, if possible, to enhance the mystical portrait both God and soul have labored to create. To do so, the confessor must be aware of his talents and his shortcomings. Thus, in a series of comparisons based on the arts, San Juan advises spiritual counselors to recognize their abilities:

> No cualquiera que sabe desbastar el madero sabe entallar la imagen, ni cualquiera que sabe entallar sabe perfilarla y pulirla, y no cualquiera que sabe pulirla sabrá pintarla, ni cualquiera que sabe pintarla sabrá poner la última mano y perfección; porque cada uno de estos no puede en la imagen hacer más de lo que sabe, y si quisiere pasar adelante sería echalla a perder. (Ll. III, 57)

Each of the necessary operations enumerated in the citation corresponds to a stage of advancement in prayer. The soul has passed through the trials of purgation "por fuego y martillo" (Ll. II, 26) in order to fashion itself into a worthy work of art. At the point of loving contemplation no inexperienced spiritual director should disrupt the delicate state of the soul by "martillar y macear . . . como herrero" (Ll. III, 43).

Just as painting and sculpture unite Bride and Bridegroom in a single work of art, so, too, the union of soul with God is also symbolized by la música callada and the amenas liras of San Juan's Cántico espiritual. Music fittingly symbolizes union since it requires an amalgamation of diverse elements in order to create a harmonious whole. The traditional acceptance of a cosmic harmony governing the universe was a commonplace of the sixteenth century, deriving from the ancient Greeks. Plato's Timaeus proposes such a world view, one accepted by Fray Luis de León, who readily incorporates it into his poetic cosmovision. It is equally discernible in the works of Fray Luis's contemporaries, San Juan de la Cruz and Santa Teresa de Jesús.

San Juan's Cántico espiritual suggests the role of music as a symbol of harmony explicitly in the title and implicitly in the references to it which recur throughout the poem. The first direct reference to music in the poem occurs in the two-strophe catalogue of nature which follows the reunion of the Bride and Bridegroom at the spring. The double oxymoron of "la música callada, / la soledad sonora" (CE. XIV) foreshadows the ineffability of the transcendent mystical experience. As Maio explains: "just as silent music involves two contraries (non-sound and sound), so does nature and supernature involve two contraries (non-being and being). The soul is aware of supernatural music only when the natural faculties are silent."[22] San Juan's reference also suggests the conception of music proposed by Cassiodorus and Boethius. Both philosophers regard music as a science engaged in for its speculative interests. As Tatarkiewioz explains: "this leads to the paradoxical conclusion that, if music is a mathematical science, sound is not essential."[23] The highest form of music, therefore, is la música callada, which symbolizes the source of all harmony, God. By association, it also suggests the cosmic harmony of the spheres unheard by man on earth, yet essential to the working of creation.

Following the third catalogue of nature and prior to the entrance of the mystical lovers into the ameno huerto, San Juan inserts his second direct reference to music. The "amenas liras" and "canto de sirenas" quiet the faculties and passions of the soul enabling the Bride to approach union. The description of the liras in the commentary subtly links the appeals to sound, touch, and smell through the use of synesthesia, for the "amenas liras" bring the soul "suavidad" while the "canto de sirenas es tan sabroso y deleitoso" (CE. XX-XXI, 16). Music, garden, and senses are thus joined by both proximity and effect in the poem.

San Juan further extends the conjunction of the three groups of imagery in his final references to song in the Cántico. The penultimate strophe of the poem offers yet another catalogue of nature, albeit an abbreviated one, which recalls earlier events in the poem at the consummation of the lovers' union in spiritual marriage. The "canto de la dulce Filomena" not only suggests the references to music in the poem but also links these references to the equally complex fauna imagery. Rather than diverse images, therefore, fauna, flora, senses, spheres, and music are, in fact, facets of the harmonious whole of creation. The transforming union of Bride and divine Lover results in "un júbilo de Dios grande, como un cantar nuevo" (Ll. II, 36), an anticipation of "el cantar nuevo de la vida gloriosa" (CE. XXXIX, 10) which awaits in paradise.

The chorus of individual songs sung by souls in praise of the Creator results in "una concordancia del amor" which blends with the cosmic harmony of the spheres of creation, a concept explicitly developed in Fray Luis de León's poem, "A Francisco Salinas." In analyzing Fray Luis's poem, Alonso explains the Pythagorean comparison of cosmic order to the playing of a zither or harp: "cada cuerpo celeste es como una cuerda; cada uno, como cada cuerda, emite un sonido diferente; todos consuenan en la universal sinfonía."[24] Recalling the Apocalypse (14:2), San Juan envisions a similar symphony in which the "muchos citaredos que citarizaban en sus cítaras" symbolize the different gifts which each soul receives: "así cada uno canta su alabanza diferentemente y todas en una concordancia de amor así como música" (CE. XIV-XV, 26). The microcosm of each individual soul creates its own music by harmonizing its rational and sensual portions (CE. XVI, 10), thereby reflecting the greater harmony of all creation praising the Creator, for "la armonía del alma concuerda con la del universo y tiernamente le responde mezclándose y confundiéndose sus sonidos."[25]

Although Santa Teresa almost completely ignores the fine arts as images, she does make passing reference to music in two of her works, demonstrating in the proceso a rudimentary notion of harmony and dissonance. Denigrating those with an inordinate interest in their own reputations, she writes: "por poco que sea el punto de honra es como en el canto de órgano, que un punto u compás que se yerre, disuena toda la música" (V. XXXI, 21). Similarly, she observes that the religious who engages in vocal prayer without the necessary recollection "mala música hará". In their use of music imagery as in all of their images and symbols, both San Juan and Santa Teresa reflect:

> un sentimiento cósmico que sea una síntesis armónica de impresión estética pasiva, de verdad en toda su transcendencia y elevación y de amor sereno y justo a la naturaleza; faltando una de estas tres cualidades, o aminorada una de ellas, el sentimiento cósmico no será perfecto.[26]

Like the imagery based on society, creation, or familiar objects, that derived from the diverse activities of sixteenth-century life reveals a complexity of development and significance in the works of the Spanish Carmelite mystics. Drawing on a long tradition in secular and religious literature, Santa Teresa and San Juan perpetuate ascetical notions of spiritual warfare and hunting even as they extend the possibilities of both activities in order to deal with the complex alternation of roles of soul and divine Lover. While warfare encompasses the imagery of fortress and castle, hunting subsumes that of fauna and flora. Both assume the societal structures of sixteenth-century Spain for complete understanding. The mystics achieve a layering effect in which otherwise straightforward images enjoy a complexity of multivalent possibilities through association with other equally complex images.

A similar multivalence of meaning and application characterizes travel and the fine arts, activities in the mystics' works not as fully developed as those of warfare and hunting. Painting and sculpture afford graphic metaphors for the transformation of soul into "image and likeness of God," even as they suggest the limited call to mystical union. Soul and God engage in a mutual act of re-creation in which the Bride becomes a worthy reflection of her Lover's art. Music serves the dual function of symbolizing the interior harmony of the soul as microcosm in which union is possible and the greater harmony of the macrocosm whose existence praises the Creator. Through union the mystic weds these two chords "en el más profundo centro de su alma," thus harmonizing the diverse notes of the varied images of his or her works into a spiritual canticle of praise.

Chapter 6

NOTES

[1] Cirlot, pp. 363-64. López Baralt, San Juan de la Cruz y el Islam, pp. 271-277 and 361-362, suggests possible Islamic sources for San Juan's use of spiritual combat.

[2] Desiderius Erasmus, El Enquiridión o manual del caballero cristiano, ed. Dámaso Alonso (Madrid: C. S. I. C., 1971), p. 111.

[3] Hoornaert, Saint Teresa, pp. 226-27.

[4] Ewer, p. 67.

[5] Cirlot, p. 19.

[6] Origen, The Song of Songs. Commentary and Homilies Ancient Christian Writers 26, trans. R. P. Lawson, eds. Johannes Quaten and Joseph Plumpe (Westminster, Md.: The Newman Press; London: Longman's Green & Co., 1957), p. 198. Richard of St. Victor, Selected Writings on Contemplation, trans. Clare Kirchberger (London: Faber & Faber, 1957), p. 215.

[7] In The Metaphysical Poets, ed. Helen Gardner, pp. 208-213. Petersson, The Art of Ecstasy, provides a thorough study of the relationship between the Vida, Bernini's work, and Crashaw's poem.

[8] Baltasar Gracián, El Criticón, 8th ed. (Madrid: Espasa-Calpe, 1943), Pt. I, Crisi 3, pp. 28-9.

[9] Mario Praz, _Studies_ _in_ _Seventeenth_ _Century_ _Imagery_, I (London: The Warburg Institute University of London, 1939), p. 13, suggests an emblem from Solorzano Pereira's _Emblemata_ as a possible source for this image.

[10] Johann Huizinga, _Homo_ _Ludens_ (Boston: Beacon Press, 1950), pp. 18-19 and 20.

[11] Frank J. Warnke, _Versions_ _of_ _Baroque_ (New Haven and London: Yale University Press, 1972), p. 97.

[12] José Manuel Blecua, "Los antecedentes del poema 'Pastorcico' de San Juan de la Cruz" in _Sobre_ _poesía_ _de_ _la_ _edad_ _de_ _oro_ (Madrid: Gredos, 1970), pp. 96-99, first indicates a possible secular source for San Juan's poem. Terence O'Reilly, "The Literary and Devotional Context of the 'Pastorcico'," _FMLS_, 18 (1982), 364, contrasts San Juan's shepherd with that of its secular manifestation; as does Joaquín Gimeno Casalduero, "El pastorcico de San Juan y el pastorcillo de las Redondillas," _HR_, 47 (1979), 77-85.

[13] See Edith Rogers, "The Hunt in the Romancero and Other Traditional Ballads," _HR_, 42 (1974), 133, and Dámaso Alonso, "La caza de amor es de altanería. Sobre precedentes de una poesía de San Juan de la Cruz," _BRAE_, 26 (1947), 63-79.

[14] John G. Cummins, "'Aqueste lance divino': San Juan's Falconry Images," in Salvador Bacarisse, et al., eds., _What's_ _Past_ _is_ _Prologue:_ _A_ _Collection_ _of_ _Essays_ _in_ _Honour_ _of_ _L._ _J._

<u>Woodward</u> (Edinburgh: Scottish Academic Press, 1984), 28-32, analyses San Juan's use of falconry in this poem and contrasts it with Alonso's interpretation in <u>La poesía de San Juan de la Cruz</u>, p. 236.

[15] Cirlot, pp. 165-65.

[16] Underhill, pp. 130-31.

[17] Ewer, p. 57.

[18] Luis Maldonado Arenas, <u>Experiencia religiosa y lenguaje en santa Teresa</u> (Madrid: PPC, 1982), p. 26, says of this passage that "está claro que el camino es ahora el símbolo de un vivir según la voluntad de Dios, un seguir la perfección, un marchar, un avanzar hacia Dios a traves de la fe e, implícitamente, a través de la oración como actitud de fe."

[19] Bernadino de Laredo, <u>The Ascent of Mount Sion; Being the Third Book of the Treatise of That Name</u>, trans. E. Allison Peers (London: Faber & Faber, 1952), pp. 70-1.

[20] Pedro Calderón de la Barca, <u>Obras completas</u>, III, <u>Autos sacramentales</u> (Madrid: Aguilar, 1967), p. 834.

[21] Emilio Orozco, <u>Mística, plástica y barroco</u> (Madrid: Cupsa, 1977), p. 38.

[22] Eugene A. Maio, <u>St. John of the Cross: the Imagery of Eros</u> (Madrid: Playor, 1973), p. 104.

[23] Wladvslaw Tatarkiewicz, History of Aesthetics, II, Medieval Aesthetics, ed. C. Barrett (Mouton, The Hague; Paris: Polish Scientific Publishers, 1970), pp. 74-5.

[24] Poesía española, 5th ed., p. 180. Earlier in the same analysis Alonso discerns "un movimiento ascensional" (p. 176) in this poem.

[25] Alonso, Poesía española, p. 181.

[26] Emeterio de Jesús María, O. C. D., "La poesía sanjuanista en la evolución del sentimiento cósmico," El Monte Carmelo, 43 (1942), 479.

Chapter 7

ELEMENTS

A world view conceptualized in the great chain of being or
in the concentric spheres of the Ptolemaic universe ascribes to
the four elements of earth, air, water, and fire a uniquely dual
role. They are at once "aquello último en que todas las cosas
pueden venir a resolverse, y de donde tomaron principio" as
Covarrubias explains (p. 502). As such they pertain to both the
source of the material world as the essential building blocks of
all matter and conversely form the ultimate end of matter as
well. Similarly, they constitute both the essence of the
microcosm, which is man, while also distinguishing the spheres of
the macrocosm as envisioned in ancient and medieval cosmology.
The interdependence of the elements and consequent harmony of the
cosmic vision attained in such a world view finds succinct
expression in El Criticón of Baltasar Gracián, who explains:

> El agua necesita de la tierra que la sustente; la
> tierra del agua que la fecunde; el aire se aumenta del
> agua, y del aire se ceba y alienta el fuego. Todo está
> así ponderado y compasado para la unión de las partes,
> y ellas en orden a la conservación de todo el
> Universo. (Pt. I, Crisi 3)[1]

In the same passage, Gracián summarizes the great chain of being, beginning with the elements and ascending to the Christian terminus in God. The author concludes his resume of creation by observing that "de esta suerte, con tan maravillosa desposición y concierto, está todo ordenado, ayudándose las unas criaturas a las otras; para su aumento y conservación." Such an interdependence of function by the elements echoes Isidore's description of them in the Etymologiae (XIII, 3, ii). Both Gracián and Covarrubias thus continue into the seventeenth century a weltanschauung already beginning to crumble before the onslaught of Copernican astronomical theory.

While neither Santa Teresa nor San Juan de la Cruz imposes a hierarchical ordering of imagery based exclusively on a Ptolemaic conception of the universe, nevertheless, both do indicate a perception of a universe described in these terms. Thus, when San Juan explains the symbolic significance of the bosques in the Cántico espiritual, he does so in terms which reflect such a traditional world view and which will be echoed by his literary successors:

> Llama bosques a los elementos, que son tierra, agua, ayre y fuego, porque así como amenísimos bosques están poblados de espesas criaturas, a las cuales aquí llama espesuras por el grande número y mucha diferencia que hay dellas en cada elemento. En la tierra inumerables variedades de animales y plantas; en el agua inumerables diferencias de peces; y en el aire mucha diversidad de aves; y el elemento de fuego que concurre con todos para la animación y conservación dellos; y así cada suerte de animales vive en su elemento y está locada y plantada en él como en su bosque y región donde nace y se cría; y a la verdad, así lo mandó dios en la creación dellos, mandando a la tierra que produxese las plantas y los animales, y a la mar y agua los peces, y a el aire hizo morada de las aves. (CE. IV, 2)

San Juan's ordered universe, in which each creature as well as each element looks to its divine alpha and omega for sustenance and significance, continues a western understanding of the four elements "from pre-Socratic days onwards as the 'Cardinal Points' of material existence, and, by a close parallel, also of spiritual life."[2] For the mystic, the dividing line between the two worlds--matter and spirit--is easily traversed, as he makes clear when he likens the purity and simplicity of the elements to the goal of the spirit to "estar sencillo, puro y desnudo de todas maneras de afecciones naturales" (N. II, 9, i). The combination of the spiritual realities experienced in mystical union with the essential matter of the universe thus finds its highest expression in the elemental imagery employed not only by San Juan de la Cruz and Santa Teresa but by their literary successors as well.

As envisioned in the Ptolemaic cosmology, the four elements of earth, water, air, and fire constitute the first two spheres of the universe. Radiating from these in concentric circles are the remaining spheres made up of the planets and stars and culminating in the Christian view in the eleventh, or Empyrean, where God resides. With earth as the starting point, the ancients fixed on the interplay of the nature of each of the elements to explain not only the exterior world but also the interior world of man's nature. Thus, the cold, dry element of earth shared the first sphere with the cold, wet element of water. Both are found in the first sphere, in part, because of their perceived heaviness. In the second ring is the warm, yet damp element of air; while above this is found the hot, dry element of fire. First Isidore, later San Juan in his explanation of the significance of the bosques, and then Gracián in his description of the elements touch on the mutual interdependence of these four. In the works of Santa Teresa and San Juan, elemental imagery reflects some of these ancient notions concerning the universe. Nevertheless, at the same time, both mystical writers individualize the symbolic meaning of each of the elements to varying degrees and thereby alter, however imperceptibly, the conception of the universe which they transmit to subsequent generations.

Earth

As noted above, first among the elements as well as the spheres is earth, described by Isidore as "in media mundi regione posita [est], omnibus partibus caeli in modum centri aequali intervallo consistens" and later by Covarrubias as "elementum frigidum et siccum."[3] Interestingly, however, neither of the Carmelite writers focuses on the qualities of earth described by the ancients. Rather, each mystic considers a number of symbolic meanings for tierra most of which are drawn from tradition. Thus, when Santa Teresa says of Christ that he is "en la tierra y vestido de ella," she echoes a familiar figurative notion of man's body as clay. San Juan carries the analogy a step further when he equates "la hermosura y todas las demás partes naturales" with earth, then concludes "que de ahí vienen y a la tierra vuelven" (S. III, 21, ii). Santa Teresa reverses the symbolism somewhat in her famous garden passage in the Vida. In the extended simile, the soul rather than the body is symbolized by "tierra" which must be cultivated and watered if the mystical garden is to flourish. While the soul may be "esta miserable tierra" (V. XIV, 11), nevertheless, it has the potential of nurturing an abundance of mystical favors if the "hortolano" so disposes it.

Evident in the mystics' use of the term tierra is the variety of connotations the word suggests in Spanish. Equally obvious, however, is a multivalent application which suits each author's needs. While no innovative use of tierra in their mystical lexicon occurs, nevertheless, both writers are intriguing in what they omit from the symbolism. Save for San Juan's detailed explanation of the bosques, neither mystic considers tierra in terms of the Ptolemaic cosmology except in the most general way. Nor do they discuss tierra in terms of the elemental qualities ascribed to it by either their literary forebears or successors. Considering the importance of other elemental imagery in the works of both writers, it is an interesting omission.

If one broadens the focus of earth imagery to encompass specific geographic features of topography, further complication occurs. In a religious order which proudly traces its lineage to the prophet Elias and his solitary life in the deserts of the

Holy Land, it comes as no surprise to find references to
desiertos in the works of the Carmelite mystics. Once again,
however, the desert as a symbol of solitude and recollection is a
virtual convention in religious literature of the period. The
attraction of San Juan and Santa Teresa to desierto can thus be
ascribed to both the historical roots of their order as well as
to the tradition of solitude which inspired the formation of the
first communities of monks. On a deeper level, however, the
desert also appeals to the ascetical and purgative urges which
initiate the mystic quest. It is, as Cirlot explains, "in a way
a negative landscape, . . . the 'realm of abstraction' located
outside the sphere of existence, susceptible only to things
transcendent" (p. 79). It is also, of course, the realm of the
sun, the preeminent symbol of the deity. Despite the potential
for an extended application of mystical significance which
desierto thus offers each author, however, neither develops the
image beyond the conventional uses already mentioned. In Santa
Teresa's case this may be explained by noting her decided
preference for water imagery. San Juan's case is more perplexing
considering his more ascetical bent and predilection for images
of light and fire to describe union.

In a related series of images based on the topography of his
mystical landscape, however, San Juan focuses on the heights
ascended in mystical union. "That one who looks to Carmel as his
home should think of the spiritual life as the metaphorical
climbing of a mountain is almost inevitable." Indeed, when faced

with a work whose title specifically refers to ascent, such as the Subida al monte Carmelo, we "expect its teaching to be unfolded in terms of an extended allegory, in which the soul will appear as a climber, overcoming the hardships of the mountain until he arrives triumphantly at the summit."[4] The reader considering the elaborate diagram depicting the mount which appears as the frontispiece to most editions of the Subida,[5] as well as San Juan's stated intention in the argumento to describe "el modo de subir hasta la cumbre del monte, que es el alto estado de la perfección que aquí llamamos unión del alma con Dios" (S. Argum.) finds further reason to expect development of this image in the work.

The image of ascent appears in a number of works by both San Juan and Santa Teresa. To each writer, the initial ascents of the lower peaks of self-control and prayer are necessary preludes to the final assault on the mountain of perfection. Obstacles to advancement are as varied as the lack of competent guides or simply a lack of sufficient grace. For those called to the heights of union, the summit offers a sense of sovereign freedom to the soul.

Since movement toward God takes the soul along the road of prayer, camino symbolizes contemplation. In the same way, the mountain stands for the contemplative prayer which leads the soul through the mystical states preparatory to transforming union. Nevertheless, camino and monte also symbolize Christ, for he is the means, both by example and by grace, through which the mystic may approach the Father. The mystics, therefore, subsume not only the scriptural and patristic ascriptions of mountain to Christ but also Fray Luis de León's De los nombres de Cristo, where the monte is Christ. All urge their readers to ascend to the cumbre. When Santa Teresa observes that God wishes souls to "subir a las Moradas que deseamos" (M. IV, 1, vii) so that they may eventually ascend to "su cámara", she extends the symbolic possibilities of ascent in order to encompass the castle, mansions, and rooms.

The extension of the symbol to include other meanings predates Santa Teresa's implied connection. To the Fathers of the Church, Christ is the heavenly Jerusalem, a city set on a mountaintop, a comparison echoed later by Laredo. Since it was common practice to situate the castle on a peak, the interrelation of ascent of a mountain with the other symbols developed by both writers becomes clearer. Similarly, as Giamatti points out, the Christian earthly paradise as well as the Christian garden is invariably associated with the mountaintop.[6] Hence, to ascend the mountain in the mystical quest is to approach a synthesis of virtually all of the symbolism developed in the mystics' works. Castle, city, garden, and mountain are one, as are cueva, bodega, and caverna. The mystical journey is an ascent to God through a paradoxical descent into the core of the soul's being. The mystic penetrates the darkness of Plato's cave by journeying inward to the brilliant light "en el más profundo centro."

Even as the heights symbolize both God and union to the mystics, so, too, do the depths. In San Juan's Cántico, the soul finally achieves union in "las subidas / Cavernas de la piedra" (CE. XXXVII), an image encompassing both height and depth. Anticipating the final scene of union in the cavernas, however, are the cuevas de leones. San Juan transforms a passing reference in his Biblical source (Cant. 4:8) to an intriguing application in his poem. Where the Canticle calls on the Bride to come forth "de cubilibus leonum, de montibus pardorum," San Juan presents the "lecho florido" of the reunited lovers "de cuevas de leones enlazado" (CE. XXIV). He equates the lions' dens with "las virtudes que posee el alma en este estado de unión con Dios," virtues which strengthen the soul and make it less vulnerable to attack (CE. XXIV, 4). His use of the metaphoric cuevas goes further when it juxtaposes the power, strength, and royalty of the lion with the otherwise amorous yet regal setting of the lecho. While the threats to the soul's peaceful repose have been stilled in union, the reality of the struggle to attain that state is never far from the mind of the poet. At the same time, the position of this strophe between those which indicate the Bride's successive entrances, first "en el ameno huerto deseado" (CE. XXII), then "en la interior bodega" (CE. XXVI), subliminally sets the stage through association for the ultimate entrance into "las subidas / cavernas de la piedra" (CE. XXXVII) of union.

In the final entrance of the Cántico espiritual, bride and

Bridegroom ascend to "las subidas / Cavernas de la piedra" in order to taste the joys of a lasting union. Calling the "piedra" a symbol of Christ and the "subidas cavernas" emblems of the mysteries revealed in union (CE. XXXVII, 3), San Juan goes on to tie the symbolism to that developed earlier in the poem. When he compares the entrance into the caverns to that of the Bride's into the "bodega", he not only recalls the inebriation of ecstatic union but also the soul's repose at the breast of the Beloved. At the same time, he underscores that this final entrance leads the soul to "la consumación de amor de Dios" (CE. XXXVIII, 2). Transforming union in love with the Amado has impelled the Bride to pursue her quest from the outset. She realizes her goal in the "subidas cavernas de la piedra."

Reappearing in the Llama de amor viva in a context similar to that of the Cántico espiritual, the "profundas cavernas del sentido" are also associated with diverse strands of imagery which serve to elaborate San Juan's mystical message. In his commentary on the verse, he equates the caverns with the three powers of the soul: memory, understanding, and will, which, once purged in the dark nights of sense and spirit, are now illuminated by the splendor of a limitless God. In fact, as Hatzfeld points out, he goes so far as to personify the cavernas "con estómago (!), hambre y sed, ansiedades y deseos. Tienen ojos . . . que estaban ciegos con nubes y cataratas."[7]

While Hatzfeld ascribes these apparently bizarre associations to the mystic's desire to explain his message to spiritual persons by utilizing any means available, the extent of San Juan's imaginative combinations serves to tie this passage to other symbols developed elsewhere in his works. Thus, the description of the caverns in terms of hunger and thirst recall the symbolic hunger and thirst experienced by the soul in the initial stages of purgation, just as the reference to "la iluminación y purificación del alma" (Ll. III, 18) in the same passage anticipates light imagery. As he goes on to explain each caverna in turn, San Juan extends the interrelationship of imagery even further. If the first cavern is the soul's understanding, then "su vacío es sed de Dios, y ésta es tan grande cuando él está dispuesto, que la compara David a la del ciervo." The waters it thirsts for are the wisdom of God. Similarly, if the second cavern is the will, the emptiness it experiences is a hunger for God and the perfection of its love. Finally, if the third caverna represents the memory, its emptiness is the "deshacimiento y derretimiento de el alma por la posesión de Dios" (Ll. III, 21). As the commentary continues, San Juan also associates the cavernas with spiritual betrothal and marriage, the palace and marriage bed of the king as well as the jewels, unguents, and other spices associated with these royal appurtenances (25), the search of the Bride and Bridegroom for each other (28), and with the flame which illumines the interior of the soul in union. That is, he incorporates virtually the entire spectrum of his mystical language in explaining the significance of the cuevas and later the cavernas. In doing so, he inextricably ties the seemingly disparate threads of imagery into a virtual knot of symbolism, each part essential to the composition of the whole.

Air

From the mystical depths of the subidas cavernas to the second sphere of the Ptolemaic cosmology is not as great a leap as might be suspected on the part of San Juan and, to a lesser extent, Santa Teresa. Air, "aquel espacio que ay entre el elemento del fuego y el de la tierra" as Covarrubias defines it (p. 59), has also elicited a number of symbolic connotations in its literary history. Christian exegesis most often equates air and wind with the Holy Ghost, the life-giving spirit of Genesis (1:2), while classical tradition includes it as an essential part of the locus amoenus. Cirlot summarizes the symbolic qualities of air when he explains that:

> Air is essentially related to three sets of ideas: the creative breath of life, and, hence, speech; the stormy wind, connected in many mythologies with the idea of creation; and, finally, space as a medium for movement and for the emergence of the life-processes. Light, flight, lightness, as well as scent and smell, are all related to the symbolism of air. (p. 6)

As will be apparent in the consideration of the mystic's references to air and its related imagery, many of these traditional applications obtain.

In his initial references to air, however, San Juan foregoes much of traditional symbolism, choosing instead to combine the image of air with an even more dominant image in his works, darkness. When he describes the effect of worldly desires on the soul's ability to receive enlightenment from God, he equates it with the inability that "tiene el aire tenebroso para recebir la [ilustración] del sol" (S. I, 8, ii). While aire has a negative connotation in this context, in a later passage of the same work, San Juan remarks that God spoke to the patriarchs in darkness, and, specifically, to Job "en el aire tenebroso" (S. II, 9, iii). Whether he associates negative symbolic value to the aire as he does when describing the vanity of worldly things, or, conversely, he assigns a positive sense in describing the medium of God's communication with man, in the Subida al monte Carmelo San Juan utilizes images of air which have no reference directly either to the wind of love or to the Holy Spirit.

Such a reversal of symbolism does not mark the Cántico espiritual, however, a work which presents a sustained development of the symbol of air and wind in both traditional terms of Christian exegesis and the classic locus amoenus as well as in the uniquely mystical terms at the heart of the work. In the associations which he makes either implicitly or explicitly in the Cántico, San Juan reveals the tissue of imagery which forms the poetic message of his work. Implicit in the vuelo, ciervo vulnerado, and cristalina fuente are a wealth of associations to the love hunt, the wound of love, and the fauna of the Cántico's spiritual landscape. For example, his reference to the "espíritu de amor que causa . . . este vuelo" (CE. XIII, 11) clearly refers to the Holy Spirit. Nevertheless, he goes beyond the conventional bounds of the comparison which equates the Holy Spirit with the air or wind by overlaying his commentary with Trinitarian theology. The Holy Spirit is the active spiration of the love of the Father for the Son in the Trinity. The mystic soul thus shares in the life of the Trinity when God communicates with it through the love generated by the ecstatic experience. Further elaborating on the "aire de tu vuelo," San Juan points out that air, which can refresh the soul and cool the passions of love, acts in paradoxical fashion, "porque tiene tal propriedad este fuego de amor, que el aire con que toma fresco y refrigerio es más fuego de amor" (CE. XIII, 12).

The "silbo de los aires amorosos" of the next strophe continues the association of air with the Holy Spirit, for the whisper is a breath, a breeze, and a quiet communicator of knowledge. Hence, it both touches, even carresses, the Bride as it communicates through her sense of hearing an understanding of the love she experiences. By combining the suggestion of a light air or breeze represented in the silbo with the aires amorosos which both refresh and enliven the Bride's love, San Juan not only assumes two of the symbolic characteristics of air later noted by Cirlot but also establishes a subtle transition to the next form that the element will take in the poem. When the Bride addresses the winds which sweep the poetic landscape of the soul, she banishes the "Cierzo muerto" even as she invites the "Austro" to "aspirar por [su] huerto" (CE. XVII). On the one hand, the strophe is a clear evocation of the Scriptural source where the

sponsa addresses a similar command to the winds (Cant. 4:16-5:1).
On the other hand, it continues the association of warm, fecund
breezes with the classical topos of the locus amoenus which also
underlies San Juan's poetic landscape.

The killing north wind dries and scatters the flowers of the
garden while the milder south wind brings rains which nourish the
soil and allow the garden to flourish. San Juan and Fray Luis de
León offer similar interpretations of the winds and their effect
in the spiritual garden even though the Agustinian writer
attributes the action of addressing the wind to the Bridegroom
rather than to the Bride.[8] San Juan's commentary on the strophe
is brief, yet it does explain the symbolism of both winds. The
cierzo represents spiritual dryness or "sequedad," which withers
the budding flowers of virtue and affective exercises. In
contrast, the austro denotes the Holy Spirit who engenders love
in the soul, represented by the garden. The Bride desires the
life-giving austro to "aspirar por [su] huerto." When the author
calls attention to the use of "por" instead of "en," noting that
the latter implies an infusion of divine graces while the former
merely asks that the Esposo set in motion the virtues and
perfections already implanted in it, he reflects the sense of
Fray Luis' interpretation of the Scriptural passage even though
he alters the speaker. At the same time, he underscores the
interconnection of image and symbol throughout the poem, because
present in the associations are the garden, flowers, fruit trees,
birds, and ciervo, which figure so prominently in the unfolding

mystical message. Present as well in the commentary is the anticipatory nature of this reunion of Bride and Bridegroom evident in both the petitioning nature of the Bride's commands to the winds and the future tense of pacerá. The positive response of the Austro to the Bride's request sets the stage for the ultimate union of spiritual marriage.

What is only potential in the dismissal of the cierzo and invitation to the austro becomes actualized in the penultimate strophe of the Cántico where the Bride envisions the effects wrought on the mystical lovers locked in the embrace of union. Combined in the strophe are the nightingale's song, the grove, night, flame, and the "aspirar del aire." What God offers the soul in spiritual marriage is no less than a share in the life of the Trinity, an awesome gift of love and a fitting culmination of the air imagery present in the poem as a whole.

Continuing the interconnection of imagery manifest in his works, San Juan explains the significance of the "resplandores" of the "lámparas de fuego" which illuminate the "profundas cavernas del sentido". Like the "toque delicado" and the "silbo de los aires amorosos" of the Cántico (XIII), the "resplandores" represent the amorous communications transmitted by God to the soul in union. With the knowledge received in union, the soul glows with an interior heat and light so that it resembles "el aire que está dentro de la llama, encendido y transformado en la llama, porque la llama no es otra cosa que aire inflamado" (Ll. III, 9). The sharing of elemental qualities between air and flame in the interior <u>cavernas</u> of the soul blurs the distinguishing characteristics of each, yet, the "resplandores" are neither air nor flame exclusively but, rather, a joining of the two. Even as they are inextricably bound in union, therefore, each still maintains its identity as does the mystic in union with God.

In the commentary, San Juan goes on to equate the "llama" with the Holy Spirit and the air with the soul. By inflaming the air, the Holy Spirit enables the soul to approach its goal of an eternal life with God. Concluding the discussion, he relies on the Ptolemaic cosmology to explain that

> así como la llama todos los movimientos y llamaradas
> que hace con el aire inflamado son a fin de llevarle
> consigo al centro de su esfera, y todos aquellos
> movimientos que hace es porfiar por llevarlo más a sí,
> mas como porque el aire está en su propia esfera, no le
> lleva. (<u>Ll</u>. III, 10)

Only in eternity can the soul (<u>aire</u>) finally achieve its ultimate goal of a permanent life in Christ. From the "aire tenebroso" of the <u>Subida</u>, San Juan comes full circle, so that, once again the soul, symbolized by the air, is both the medium and object of God's communication and transformation by love.

Water

Sharing the first sphere of earth in the ancient cosmology is the element of water, a substance of such symbolic power that it appears in virtually the entire spectrum of religious and secular literature in some form. Cirlot touches on the universal appeal of water as a symbol when he explains that "the waters, in

short, symbolize the universal congress of potentialities, the
fons et origo, which precedes all form and all creation." He
goes on to call attention to its transitional place among the
other three elements and, hence, its mediating symbolism between
life and death (p. 365). Isidore goes so far as to claim that
"aquarum elementum ceteris omnibus imperat," a belief which
Covarrubias echoes in his dictionary.[9] From the moment in
Genesis when the "Spiritus Dei ferebatur super aquas" (Gen. 1:2)
until the "fluvium aquae vitae" of the Apocalypse (22:1-2), water
figures prominently as a symbol of both life and death in
Scripture. To all writers whether sacred or profane, however,
water "est vraiment l'élément transitoire. Il est la
métamorphose ontologique essentielle entre le feu et la
terre."[10]

For the mystical writer both water and fire represent
powerful, elemental images ideal for expressing the ineffable in
its most essential forms. As Alonso remarks:

> La mística de todas las épocas ha gustado de utilizar
> para sus símbolos los elementos más puros, que la
> Naturaleza puede ofrecer. Entre estos, el agua ocupa
> uno de los primeros lugares, por la constancia de su
> empleo místico, por la variedad y matices de su
> simbolización.[11]

When applied to water imagery in the works of Santa Teresa and
San Juan, Alonso's observations concerning the element's appeal
seem to hold, for each writer utilizes it in a variety of ways.
Be it Santa Teresa's references the fourfold method of watering
the spiritual garden of the soul or San Juan's description of the

Bride gazing into the crystalline waters of the Cántico's spring, water figures often and importantly in the mystical lexicon of the Carmelite writers.

In the Camino de perfección, Santa Teresa enumerates three properties of water which she interprets symbolically in mystical terms. The first property "es que enfría" (XXXI, 1/XIX, 3); the second that it "limpia cosas no limpias" (XXXI, 4/XIX, 6); and the third, that it quenches one's thirst (XXXI, 5/XIX, 8). While considering each of these properties, Santa Teresa incorporates related information in order to tie the physical qualities of water to her mystical concerns. Thus, water's ability to cool passion places it in juxtaposition with its elemental contrary, fire. Nevertheless, the author explains that at times water may actually cause the fire to blaze even more. She interprets the anomaly symbolically when she equates the tar present in the water with imperfection and the fire with God's love which purges the soul of the detritus of sin and consequently increases its ability to love. While the water that originates in the earth cannot quench such a fire, the "agua celestial" is compatible with it since both elements "no son contrarios sino de una tierra" (CP. XXXI, 3/XIX, 4). In an apparent reversal, however, the saint contrasts the "agua viva . . . celestial . . . clara" of a spring with "el agua corriendo por la tierra" (CP. XXXI, 4/XIX, 6). The first suggests the purity of well water, similar to that promised the Samaritan woman, while the second may contain impurities. Santa Teresa urges her readers to imbibe the "agua viva" of grace and prayer, not only because it can slake their spiritual thirst, but also because it cleanses and refreshes the soul. It offers the soul, therefore, all three properties of water as the author enumerated them. Only God can offer the soul this living water to drink since he himself is "esta agua viva". The soul is incapable of advancing on the road of perfection "sin gota de esta agua," because it will invariably die of thirst before reaching its destination.

Her repeated exhortations in the Camino to drink the living water draw attention to the burning desire which fires the mystic's passion to achieve union. To describe the ultimate absorption of soul in God, she chooses an even more effective simile when she likens God's indwelling in the soul to "una esponja que embeve el agua en sí" (Cuentas XLIX). The analogy underscores God's dual role as both source and end of the living waters which impel and sustain the mystic. The soul seeks the agua viva in order to slake its thirst for God. Therefore, for Santa Teresa "el agua representa el elemento vital en el cual el alma vive, obra y se va acercando a su esposo."[12] Nowhere is this vivifying quality of water made more manifest than in the saint's extended digression concerning the fourfold method of watering the garden of the soul which occupies fully a quarter of the Vida.

As noted previously, the four ways of watering the garden-soul is undoubtedly Santa Teresa's most famous comparison, yet she states that she did not originate the simile but, rather, that she had "leído u oído esta comparación" previously (V. XI, 6). What is certain is that water becomes a key symbol in her works to represent prayer and the grace to engage in it. In comparing the soul to a garden, she postulates four ways to water it in order to make it flourish. First, one can draw water from a well by hand, an arduous and time-consuming approach. The second method posits a noria or winch which facilitates the labor expended. Thirdly, a river or brook passing through the garden provides even better irrigation with virtually no work. Finally, God may water the garden with rain, thus eliminating all labor by the gardener. After presenting this summary of the fourfold method Santa Teresa turns to an explanation of each stage in terms of mystical progress. She employs stylistic devices characteristic of all of her works when she presents digressions, ellipses, adumbrations, and personal reminiscences which "offer an almost circular presentation of doctrinal terms around which the 'charla' (chat) [is] developed in an almost inexhaustible imagery."[13]

The first water naturally corresponds to the initial stage of purgation in which beginners expend a great deal of energy in recollection in order to irrigate the garden-soul with prayer (agua). She emphasizes both the active participation of the mystic soul at this initial stage and God's role in its progress. With great difficulty the soul draws water "para regar estas flores," but it is God who determines the capacity of the well. At times he chooses to dry it up, so that the soul can sustain the flowers only with its own tears. As long as it shows its willingness to work the garden and God chooses to assist it, the flowers and plants will continue to grow "con dar agua" or, conversely, "sin ella" (V. XI, 3).

In the second stage of mystical progress, Santa Teresa credits God with providing the gardener with "un torno y arcaduces" so that more water may be drawn with less work and, consequently, the soul may experience more rest from continuous labor. She names this method the prayer of quiet. This higher level of prayer is one of "grandes bienes y mercedes" where the soul can bask in the "gustos de la gloria" it has now received (V. XIV, 4). In contrast to the tears of the first water, those of the second come from God and "van con gozo". While provision for additional grace symbolized by the pump to draw more water with less labor conveys the sense of the decreasing activity of the soul in the prayer of quiet, the second water of the Vida is not as effective an analogy for this stage of mystical progress as a different one utilized in the Moradas.

In the fourth mansion, Santa Teresa visualizes "dos fuentes con dos pilas que se hinchen de agua," then goes on to distinguish between the way in which the two basins fill. One is fed by a system of "arcaduces y artificio," while the other fills silently from below (M. IV, 2, ii-iii). The former she likens to meditation, while the second represents the prayer of quiet. In terms of describing the passivity of the soul in the prayer of quiet, the basin silently fed from a hidden source is far more effective than the earlier comparison in the Vida. As she points out in explaining the comparison in the Moradas, use of the arcaduces better describes the soul engaged in discursive prayer.

The third level of prayer resembles "un agua corriente de río o de fuente," which waters the garden with considerably less labor but greater efficiency. As the soul becomes increasingly more passive, God's activity in mystical progress grows, a development Santa Teresa notes by pointing out that "quiere el Señor aquí ayudar a el hortolano de manera que casi El es el hortolano y el que lo hace todo" (V. XVI, 1). Further underscoring the passivity of the soul, she goes on to describe it virtually engulfed in its love for God. While her allusion to a sort of divine inebriation at this stage suggests ecstatic union, it is not clear to many scholars exactly what the third water represents in terms of traditional divisions of mystical progress. There is no comparable stage described in the Moradas, a later work in which the author presents a surer grasp of her understanding of the steps in mystical prayer. When juxtaposed with San Juan's references to rivers, the ambivalence of the symbol as later noted bv Cirlot becomes clear.

Whereas Santa Teresa's use of the río in the Vida suggests "fertility and the progressive irrigation of the soil," San Juan's references to the running water reflects "the irreversible passage of time and, in consequence . . . a sense of loss and oblivion."[14] It is precisely such a sense of mutability and loss which San Juan describes in terms of running water in the Cántico (XIX, 1), an allusion which recalls the Egloga I of Garcilaso where Salicio laments his lost love beside the "agua clara con sonido" (v. 51) which rushes past. Like the "ríos sonorosos" of San Juan's poem, the flowing waters of Garcilaso's work represent loss and change. In another reference in the Cántico espiritual, San Juan reverses the polarity of running water when he enumerates the properties of the "ríos sonorosos:"

> Los ríos tienen tres propriedades. La primera que todo lo que encuentran lo envisten y anegan. La segunda, que hinchen todos los bajos y vacíos que hallan delante. La tercera, que tienen tal sonido que todo otro sonido privan y ocupan. Y porque en esta comunicación de Dios que vamos diciendo siente el alma en él estas tres propiedades muy sabrosamente, dice que su Amado es los ríos sonorosos. (CE. XIV-XV, 9)

Although each of the properties he lists has the potential for negative effects in the soul, each, in fact, signals advancement wherein the mystic is first cleansed and then filled with God's grace and love.

The three properties of the river noted by San Juan in the Cántico when juxtaposed with Santa Teresa's three properties of water outlined in the Camino offer an intriguing distinction between each writer's view of the mystic way. Santa Teresa emphasizes positive aspects of refreshment, cleansing, and quenching while San Juan suggests a necessary emptying as a prerequisite to the inundating or obliterating effect of the "ríos sonorosos." In terms of their overall approach to the mystical life as well as the imagery that describes it, a similar polarity is evident. The nadas of San Juan's frontispiece for the Subida as well as the dominant imagery of night underscore the asceticism of his message, of the need to deprive the soul systematically and completely of sensual and spiritual dependence before union is possible. In contrast, Santa Teresa approaches the problem from the opposite direction. Hers is a call to embrace all in order to be filled completely by the Bridegroom in spiritual marriage. The garden of the soul assuredly must be weeded, but the principal activity thereafter is to fill it with all that bespeaks the Creator.

Santa Teresa's final method of watering the garden of the soul surrenders all activity to God who allows rain to soak the earth. Again, the symbol is not unique to the Carmelite author as Ewer explains:

> The Rain watering the thirsty earth that the gardens and fields may flourish is a commoner idea, one that has penetrated deeply into ordinary religious devotion. Vide hymns which plead for 'Showers of Blessings,' and the common symbol of 'dryness' for the lack of 'sensible consolations' in one's devotions. The odd fact, however, is that in spite of the availability of the 'Showers of Blessings' concept, and in spite of the Scriptural authority for thinking of the Lord as coming to the heart as rain upon the thirsty ground, nevertheless the presence of 'sensible consolations' which is of course the opposite of 'dryness' is commonly symbolized as 'sweetness.'[15]

In the Vida, however, the author does not juxtapose sweetness as the symbolic antidote to dryness. Rather, she reiterates a number of those water images already described in earlier stages of the fourfold method. The soul in union is moved to tears similar to those it shed in the prayer of union, yet distinct from those of purgation. She goes a step further, however, when she ascribes the origin of her tears to God, then contrasts them with the "agua de tan mal pozo" which she herself produces (V. XIX, 6). Tears thus given by God have the power to clarify the well water. Such a startling reversal of the symbolic water of prayer which heretofore has filled the garden's well actually underscores the soul's dependence on God as it advances toward union even as it combines two disparate water images.

When Santa Teresa describes the physical effects wrought in the soul in the fourth level of prayer, the state most closely resembles ecstatic union. Not only the initial description of the soul "muerta . . . a el mundo" (V. XVIII, 1), whose memory and understanding are inebriated "de aquel vino divino", but also the depiction of the well-turned earth of the garden in which "el agua se embeve tanto que casi nunca se seca" (V. XIX, 3) serve to cast the fourth water in the imagery associated with ecstasy. Furthermore, the details of her personal experience of the fourth water also suggest ecstatic union.

At the time she composed the Vida, the saint had not attained the level of prayer she was later to designate spiritual marriage. In the fourth water, therefore, she speaks in terms of ecstatic union as the culmination of the mystical experience. Only when she came to write the Moradas had her own mystical life achieved its apogee in spiritual marriage, so that the societal analogy replaces that of water as the dominant symbol of the seventh mansion. Nevertheless, at least one allusion to water does appear in the later work in a context reminiscent of the language of the Vida.

Likening the soul in the seventh mansion to "el árbol que está cabe las corrientes de las aguas" (M. VII, 2, xiii). Santa Teresa both recalls the extended metaphor of the Vida while also completing an analogy which opened the Moradas. In the first mansion, the soul is a tree planted near "esta fuente de vida," the source of all the waters which nourish it and the antithesis of a spring producing "negrísima agua de mal olor" (M. I, 2, ii). Her dual springs separate the sources of the soul's propensity for either cupidity or charity.

Not only in the Moradas, but in all of her mystical writings, Santa Teresa's numerous allusions to the fuente constitute a symbol equally as persuasive as the fourfold method of watering the garden of the soul in describing mystical prayer. Both the Biblical connotations associated with the image as well as the spring's function as defined by Isidore and Covarrubias make it a multivalent symbol of grace, prayer, and ultimately God. Especially in the Camino de perfección, she casts the mystical journey in terms of progress toward "esta fuente de vida". When the journey is complete the soul finds itself engulfed in God who allows it to drink from the fount of living water that is unitive prayer. Her scriptural source for the allusion is the Gospel account of the Samaritan woman who encounters Christ at the well (John 4). Her fascination with the Samaritan woman's conversation leads her to explain that she was "muy aficionada a aquel evangelio [y] . . . desde muy niña lo era y suplicava muchas veces a el Señor me diese aquel agua" (V. XXX, 19). Indeed, she cites the passage in virtually all of her mystical works as a compelling example of the mystic's goal in prayer. In doing so, she joins the symbolism of journey to that of water and inebriation, for throughout the Camino de perfección and the Meditaciones the road leads the mystic to the fount of living water where she may imbibe deeply of God just as the Samaritan woman "iva . . . con aquella borrachez divina dando gritos por las calles" (Med. VII, 6). The agua viva represents not only unitive prayer on earth but the eternal union of heaven as well for Santa Teresa, since the mystic's thirst for union with God can only truly be quenched in eternity.

While Santa Teresa relies on a single, dominant Biblical source for explaining the "fuente de aguas vivas" in her works, San Juan manifests his broader understanding of Scripture and traditional poetry in his own allusions to water. In the lyrical "Cantar de la alma que se huelga de conoscer a Dios por fee," the poet makes the spring the central image of his poem. More familiarly known by the refrain which is repeated throughout the poem, Aunque es de noche refers at length to "la fonte, que mana y corre" (v. 1), that San Juan describes as "aquella eterna fonte," "ascondida," fathomless, unfordable; yet life-giving, clear, beautiful, and bountiful. It is a spring, not simply of faith, but of the Creator himself, limpid yet mysterious, hidden, ultimately, "en este vivo pan por darnos vida" (vv. 27-28).

While related to the Cántico's fuente as both a symbol of faith and vitality, the "fonte que mana y corre" also differs from it. The unfathomable depths of the fonte epitomize the Creator who both sustains his creatures even as he remains mysterious to them. Although they may partake of him in the Eucharist, they can never truly plumb the depths of the Trinity. Such an intimate knowledge of the Creator eludes the mystic as well, yet the personal intimacy of the divine Lover enjoyed by the soul in mystical union is a foretaste of the beatific vision of heaven. Whereas the fuente of the Cántico first functions as a mirror in which the Bride wishes to see reflected the eyes of her missing Amado, the fonte of Aunque es de noche invites contemplation of its depths rather than mirroring the image of the soul reflected in the waters of faith. While no less personal in his description of the fonte, as evidenced by the use of first person throughout the poem, San Juan manifests his wonder at the mysteries of faith as well as his intellectual grasp of those aspects of faith attainable through reason. He clearly distinguishes between what he knows and what he does not know by repeating the phrases "sé yo" and "no . . . sé." He knows of the existence of the spring, its course, its effects in nature, its depth, its luminosity, its capacity and omnipotence, and finally, its hidden presence in the Eucharist. What he does not know and cannot know is the spring's origin, "pues no le tiene." The spring of Aunque es de noche is not just faith but God himself in his manifold works and power, who, for the

Catholic poet, resides in man's company in the Eucharist. Hence, this poem deals with the truths of Catholicism accessible to all the faithful, first through the waters of baptism and then continuously in the consecrated host reserved in the tabernacle.

The crystalline spring of the Cántico espiritual also evokes both traditional poetry, where the fuente serves as "el lugar donde se encuentran los amantes,"[16] as well as the psalms (41:2), where the stag seeks refreshment in its waters. When San Juan explains the symbolism of the refrigerio sought by his mystical lovers at the spring, he deftly overlays Biblical and folkloric motifs in a single reference. Combined with eye imagery, that of the water of the cristalina fuente makes of it a symbol fraught with complex and interrelated threads of association and meaning.

Such a layering of meaning characterizes the entire Cántico espiritual so profoundly yet subtly that it makes subsequent attempts at similar interconnection appear less intricate in comparison. Gracián may draw analogous threads of imagery together in El Criticón when Andrenio explains:

> --No me podía sacar . . . volviendo al agua de mirar su alegre transparencia, aquel su continuo movimiento, hidrópica la vista de los líquidos cristales. --Dicen que los ojos (ponderó Critilo) se componen de los dos humores acuo y cristalino, y ésta es la causa por qué gustan tanto de mirar las aguas, de suerte que sin cansarse, estará embebido un hombre todo un día, viéndolas brillar, caer y correr. (Pt. I, Crisi 3, p. 28)

Even as the water, eyes, and crystal recall the associations in San Juan's Cántico, however, the three are complementary substances as Critilo points out. Nevertheless, when Andrenio observes that contemplation of the harmony of the water environment reminds him of the harmony of the universe, Critilo counters with a contrary notion asserting that "todo este Universo se compone de contrarios y se concierta de desconciertos." What San Juan intimates in the development of his imagery, Gracián makes clear. Although Gracián proposes a moral overview of creation, San Juan has gone a step further in suggesting a higher plane of reality and relationship available to the mystic soul. His poetry and prose, therefore, manifest a complex interrelationship of symbolism more suggested than clearly stated.

The cristalina fuente is but the first of the water references found in the Cántico espiritual; for not just the stag and deer search for refreshment in the mystical setting of the poem but the other symbolic animals also seek consolation at the water's edge. The tórtola declines to drink while separated from its mate, yet gladly imbibes the water of high contemplation when reunited with the Amado. What the Bride searched for at the outset is fulfilled at the conclusion. Not only in the lasting nature of the refrigerio enjoyed by the united mystical lovers, but also in the subtle repetition of related imagery, San Juan underscores the sense of completeness. The singular nature of the union achieved between soul and God results in a profound interchange of love and activity, an effect San Juan accentuates by applying to the soul imagery which has heretofore pertained essentially to the _Amado_. Addressing the soul familiarly, he explains the characteristics of lasting union:

> . . . Y darte a tu Señor Dios descanso siempre, y llenará de resplandores tu alma, y librará tus huesos, y serás como un huerto de regadío y como una fuente de aguas, cuyas aguas no faltarán. Edificarse han en ti las soledades de los siglos y los principios y fundamentos de una generación y de otra generación. (_CE_. XXXVI, 2)

The soul will truly be one with its Lover in mystical union when it becomes, in effect, a garden and a "fonte que mana y corre."

Whether its source is a spring, well, or river, fresh water almost always enjoys wholly positive applications in the mystics' works since it ultimately quenches their spiritual thirst in union. As Santa Teresa notes in her explanation concerning the properties of water, however, slaking thirst is but one of them. Another equally important function is putting out fires. Nevertheless, since Fire also symbolizes the soul's love for God, when fully ablaze it cannot be quenched by earthly waters. It begins as a spark of prayer, a "centellica que comienza el Señor a encender en el alma del verdadero amor suyo." Nourished carefully at the outset so that the water of earthly concerns does not snuff it out, it may eventually begin "a encender el gran fuego que echa llamas de sí" (_V_. XV, 4). When the water is from heaven in the form of additional graces of prayer, then there is even less cause for concern since the fire and water are no longer contrary elements, "sino de una tierra." As complements, each element takes on the characteristics of the other, creating a paradoxical situation in which "el agua le enciende [al fuego] más y ayuda a sustentar, y el fuego ayuda a el agua a enfríar" (CPe. XXXI, 3).

Where Osuna chooses to describe conversion in terms of the interplay between water and fire in the Abecedario, Santa Teresa goes a step further by suggesting the union of spiritual marriage. In doing so, she anticipates Bachelard's assertion that "toute combinaison des éléments materiels est, pour l'inconscient, un mariage."[17]

In San Juan's case, the combination of fire and water takes the form of an extended simile in the Noche oscura and the Llama where the author compares the gradual transformation of the soul by mystical experience to a green log thrown on a fire. It is a comparison he first introduces in the Subida where he compares the impediment to transforming union of a single, slight imperfection to a log "[que] no se transforma en el fuego por un sólo grado de calor" (S. I, 11, vi). Elaborating on the analogy further in a later passage of the same work, he again cites the need for the proper degrees of heat if the log would be ignited. Employing any of the other elements to ignite the wood is useless, for only heat can bring it to flames. He develops the comparison in still greater detail in the commentary on the Noche oscura where he first enumerates the physical changes apparent in a green log placed on a fire:

> porque el fuego material, en aplicándose al madero, lo primero que hace es comenzarle a secar, echándole la humedad fuera y haciéndole llorar el agua que en sí tiene; luego le va poniendo negro, oscuro y feo aun de mal olor y, yéndole secando poco a poco, le va sacando a luz y echando afuera todos los accidentes feos y

oscuros que tiene contrarios al fuego, y, finalmente,
comenzándole a inflamar por de fuera y calentarle,
viene a transformarle en sí y ponerle hermoso como el
mismo fuego. (N. II, 10, i)[18]

It is apparent in the commentary that the water converted into
smoke by the fire refers not to virtue but to the passions which
impede the soul's progress. As the fire takes hold, it disperses
these impediments, drying and blackening the log in the process.
Eventually, it enters more deeply into the very core of the wood
"disponiendo a lo más interior para poseerlo". Having passed
through these purgative stages, the soul next, "con ansias, en
amores inflamada," continues its journey through the nights of
sense and spirit to illumination and finally to union.

While the simile does not appear in the Cántico espiritual,
San Juan does return to it in the Llama de amor viva. In the
Llama, the wood is completely transformed into and consumed by
the fire until it, too, gives off sparks and flames, which
represent the acts of love performed by the soul through the
graces of the Holy Spirit. The log consumed by the fire has
passed from purgation to union and become one with the fire of
love. In his extended comparison, therefore, San Juan combines
the traditional symbolism of the tree as an image of man with the
transforming nature of fire which purges and alters that which it
consumes; eventually making it one with itself. While the mystic
soul may be symbolized by the carefully cultivated tree which
eventually bears fruit, it may also be represented by the same
tree hewn into logs and placed in the fire of God's cleansing
fire of love.

As the fire enters more deeply into the center of the log, it dissipates whatever moisture may remain therein. In similar fashion but at a higher level of mystical experience, San Juan describes the "lámparas de fuego" of the Llama where the fire combines with the living waters "de manera que estas lámparas de fuego son aguas del espíritu como las que vinieron sobre los Apóstoles (Act, 2,3)" (Ll. III, 8). San Juan intertwines Trinitarian concepts into the fabric of his commentary, for he goes on to explain that the communication achieved by the soul at this stage of its progress is both fire and water: water because the Holy Spirit is hidden in the interior reaches of the soul, yet fire as well because it inflames the soul in love of God. Rather than contrary forces at work in the soul, fire and water ultimately complement each other in the ecstatic union described here by the mystic.

Fire

The fourth, final, and highest element of the Ptolemaic universe, fire "era symbolo de la natura divina."[19] As Langer describes it, it is "a natural symbol of life and passion, though it is the one element in which nothing can actually live. Its mobility and flare, its heat and color, make it an irresistible symbol of all that is living, feeling, and active."[20] Like water it is formless, ever-changing, elusive yet highly visible and felt, transforming and regenerating, free and fluid. In virtually all religions, it assumes a central symbolic place in ritual and art. In Christianity it is a paradoxical symbol of both divinity and eternal punishment, of purgation and illumination, of destruction and rebirth. To Bachelard it is "preeminently the connecting link for all symbols [because] it unites matter and spirit, vice and virtue."[21] For the Spanish mystics as well it is an element fraught with multivalent symbolic possibilities.

In deference to the symbolic use of fire in both Biblical exegesis and devotional literature, San Juan and Santa Teresa equate it, on the one hand, with God or, on the other, with either the passions or the "fuego eterno" of hell. At the same time, in an apparent rejection of traditional symbolism, San Juan also warns "los que imaginan a Dios debajo de algunas figuras destas [criaturas, o como un gran fuego o resplandor . . . harto lejos van dél" (S. II, 12, v). He then explains that any limitation of the deity leads to error as surely as does reliance on visions, so the mystic must systematically strip himself of sensible aids in order to advance. Neither author denies the efficacy of fire imagery in their works, however, since both utilize it in its various manifestations in order to describe the levels of mystical progress and union.

The divine fire begins as a spark which has the power to ignite a conflagration. Both Santa Teresa and San Juan describe the centella in similar terms: she to warn those who approach the fire of God's love that "una centellica que salte la abrasará toda" (CP. LXII/XXXV, 1), and he to observe that "a veces esta

divina centella deja al alma abrasándose y quemándose en amor"
(CE. XXV, 8). In the Noche oscura, San Juan pictures the soul at
the start of its mystical journey, "con ansias, en amores
inflamada" guided only by the light "que en el corazón ardía".
Through virtually the entire commentary of the Subida, he
describes the cleansing fires of purgation, citing Biblical
examples at length to support his exegesis. It is an
interpretation he carries over to the Noche commentary, expanding
the potential of the fire in the process to include both sense
and spirit. In the first of the dark nights, it is a dark fire,
felt but not seen. The author juxtaposes the spiritual "fuego
amoroso, tenebroso [de] esta vida" with the exceedingly more
painful "fuego tenebroso, material [de] la otra vida" (N. II, 12,
i). The latter is a remorselessly severe fire while the former
is a loving one which purges the soul of impurity so that it may
eventually be illumined by God's grace.

Once purified by fire, the mystic next turns his will wholly
to loving God. He is both inflamed and illumined by the fire of
love in preparation for the climax of his experience. What the
soul aspires to is "otra inflamación de otro amor mejor, que es
el de su Esposo" (S. I, 14, ii). The mystic looks to the guiding
light that "en el corazón ardía" to impel him further to union.
Although San Juan's commentary on the Noche concludes abruptly
before the author can explain fully the last six strophes of the
poem, he does suggest the level of ardor required by the mystic
in his detailed outline of the ten rungs of the "secreta escala"

of strophe II. At the outset, the soul languishes with love then searches unceasingly for the Bridegroom. The third rung of the secret ladder requires the soul to "obrar y la pone [al alma] calor para no faltar," so that the time and effort it expends seem brief in retrospect "por el incendio de amor en que ya va ardiendo" (N. II, 19, iii). In the Cántico the reunited lovers briefly enjoy the "aire" and "fresco" of the "otero" only to discover "que el aire con que toma fresco y refrigerio es más fuego de amor, porque en el amante el amor es llama que arde con apetito de arder más, según hace la llama del fuego natural" (CE. XIII, 12). As at the fourth rung of the ladder, the mystic learns to suffer tirelessly, so that he may be inflamed and burn with desire for God in order to ascend higher. In this life, the ninth rung represents the state of the perfect where "hace arder al alma con suavidad" (N. II, 20, iv), an image which Surgy equates with spiritual marriage "realisé sur ce double plan. Le Saint-Esprit, vive flamme d'amour, après avoir purifié totalement l'âme dans le creuset de la nuit, la fait maintenant bruler d'un amour suave."[22] All that the mystic can aspire to beyond this level is the beatific vision of heaven, which equals the tenth and final rung of the ladder.

Both mystics successfully utilize fire in conventional poetic terms to convey a sense of passionate love, just as generations of writers before and since have done. In the works of Santa Teresa and, even more so, in those of San Juan, therefore, the symbolic flame of love assumes meaning

transcending prior poetic and mystical applications. At the same
time, San Juan incorporates the traditions of both religious and
secular literature in transforming the symbol of the flame to his
own ends.

Santa Teresa employs the flame as a mystical symbol in her
works, but she avoids the sustained development of it
characteristic of her colleague's work. Passing allusions to the
Bible or to the flames of hell are conventional uses of the
image. In one extended simile she likens the effects of ecstatic
union to the flame, remarking that "el alma alguna vez sale de sí
mesma a manera de un fuego que está ardiendo y hecho llama."
Nevertheless, "esta llama sube muy arriba del fuego, mas no por
eso es cosa diferente, si no la mesma llama que está en el fuego"
(V. XVIII, 2). In contradistinction to the sulphurous fires she
describes in her terrifying vision of hell, the ecstatic flame is
one which offers the soul both pleasure as well as pain. The
pain of the ecstatic mystical lover is at once physical and
spiritual. While the saint enumerates the physical changes
characteristic of ecstasy in her Cuentas (LIV, 7-14), there
exists as well the pain of separation from the object of its love
that the soul feels afterwards. The fleeting nature of ecstatic
union in contrast to the more peaceful and lasting bond achieved
in spiritual marriage makes the pain endured at this intermediate
state exquisite yet ultimately bearable if the mystic
perserveres.

Santa Teresa's equation of the soul with the mariposa opens

other avenues of flame symbolism. What initially attracts the author to the moth as a mystical symbol is the transformation it undergoes in its passage through the various stages of worm, larva, and, finally, beautiful moth. She does not ignore the other aspect of the moth's nature, however, for she fixes on its fatal attraction to the flame as well. Nevertheless, for the soul turned mariposa, death in the flame of God's love represents fulfillment rather than destruction. Manifest in the mystics' use of both the mariposa-flame image and later of the flame in isolation, are preeminent examples of the fusion of imagery throughout their works.

What each mystic aspires to is the "llama que consume y no da pena" introduced by San Juan in the Cántico espiritual and developed more fully as the "llama de amor viva" in the poem and commentary of the same name. As he does with virtually the entire symbolism of the Cántico, San Juan interrelates concepts throughout the work, so that his reference in the penultimate strophe of the poem to the llama has been foreshadowed from the outset, and, thereby, conveys a multivalent mystical import. From the beginning of the commentary, the author describes the amorous wounds suffered by the Bride in her first encounter with the Amado as "unos encendidos toques de amor que, a manera de saeta de fuego, hieren y traspasan el alma," so that "parece consumirse en aquella llama" (CE. I, 17). Lida has already pointed out the Virgilian overtones of San Juan's use of the ciervo vulnerado in the opening strophes of the Cántico and its association with the "huida, flecha [y] llama," yet San Juan does not stop with these comparisons.

In its next appearance in the poem, fire assumes the form of "lumbre . . . de [los] ojos" of the Bride. Although he focuses in the commentary on the imagery of light suggested by the allusion, San Juan also reflects Bembo's speech in Book IV of The Courtier where the knight "notices that his eyes seize upon her image and carry it to her heart." The lady returns his gaze and "those lively spirits which shine forth from her eyes continue to add fresh fuel to the fire."[23] To San Juan, God is "lumbre sobrenatural de los ojos del alma, sin la cual está en tinieblas, llamale ella aquí por afición lumbre de sus ojos, al modo que el amante suele llamar al que ama lumbre de sus ojos, para mostrar la afición que le tiene" (CE. X, 8). In combining the suggestion of flame with the symbol of eyes, the author establishes the basis for connecting the imagery of both more firmly and more clearly in his next reference to them in the commentary.

When the lovers reunite beside the crystalline spring, eye imagery reappears and is tied to elemental images in the process. As a result of the reflection on the spring's surface, the soul commences an ecstatic flight cut short by the Amado's command to return and to cool its passion. San Juan discerns a dual function in the "aire de tu vuelo" of the strophe. On the one hand, it is a cooling breeze which dampens the ardor of the precipitous ecstasy, yet, on the other, it also creates "más fuego de amor." He explains the anomaly by observing that "en el amante el amor es llama que arde con apetito de arder más" (CE. XIII, 12). Implicitly, the flame of love in this strophe resembles that of Santa Teresa's ecstatic experience, one which causes both pleasure and pain. Tempering the soul's joy at reunion with the Amado is the physical wrenching occasioned by ecstasy, which San Juan alludes to in the commentary, as well as the realization that the brief moment of union cannot last. As the analogy intimates, love is a flame which burns with a desire to burn even more intensely.

When the mystic soul reaches the interior bodega of the unitive state, San Juan reiterates fire imagery to convey the essence of the experience. Spiritual marriage is at heart an ineffable experience, the saint asserts, yet he grasps for elemental comparisons to explain the union achieved between soul and God. The transforming union is "como si dijéramos agora la vidriera con el rayo del sol, o el carbón con el fuego, o la luz de las estrellas con la del Sol" (CE. XXVI, 4). Underlying each of these comparisons is the interrelationship of all the imagery developed in the works of the poet, for present in the glass is the mirror in all of its complex symbolism while the carbon made one with the fire recalls the green log of the Noche now purified of its imperfections and thus capable of becoming fire.

Culminating the series of prefatory references to fire and flame in the Cántico is the "llama que consume y no da pena" which San Juan presents as the ultimate goal of the mystic quest. Quite simply, the llama symbolizes the Holy Spirit, who completes and perfects the love of the soul and God. The Bride anticipates the transformation wrought in eternity by a total sharing of love between God and the soul, which, since perfect, can consume yet give no pain. While the mystic continues in an earthly existence some residue of pain, like the ashes from a fire, remains. In the glory that is to come the soul will know the perfection of love it tastes in the final state of mystical progress, that of transforming union.

Although the Noche oscura and the Cántico espiritual introduce the flame of love, it is in the poem and commentary of the Llama de amor viva that "the concrete symbol of flame may be regarded as the culminating symbol of the soul purified by love and raised to the transformation of a flame within the Fire and Light of God through light."[24] In the prologue to the commentary, San Juan states clearly that he wishes to deal with transforming union. He repeats the simile of the wood transformed by fire, which he first presented in the Noche, in order to explain that "en este encendido grado se ha de entender que habla el alma aquí ya transformada y calificada interiormente en fuego de amor, que no sólo está unida en este fuego, sino que hace ya viva llama en ella" (Ll. Prol., 4). When he passes to a strophe-by-strophe explanation of the poem, he elaborates on the underlying mystical message it transmits.

Virtually taking up where he left off in the Cántico, San Juan again equates the llama with the Holy Spirit who both consumes and transforms the soul by love. He discerns a dual symbolism in the action of the Spirit in the soul. On the one hand, fire consumes and transforms it "en suave amor." On the other, the interior fire causes the soul itself to "echa[r] llama [que] baña al alma en gloria y la refresca en temple de vida divina". The flames the soul produces are its acts of devotion, a comparison the author reinforces by having recourse once more to the wood consumed and transformed by fire. Unlike the green wood of the purgative state, the "madero" of union is "embestido en fuego, y los actos de esta alma son la llama que nace del fuego de amor" (Ll. I, 3-4). The Holy Spirit so imbues the mystic with grace that the two are as one in the acts of love produced.

The first strophe of the poem includes not only the personification of the flame of love through the poetic recourse of apostrophe, but also allusion to other imagery of mystical union utilized elsewhere by the poet. The flame wounds ("hieres") the soul "tiernamente . . . en el más profundo centro." Unlike the Bride's plaintive cry at the start of the Cántico, that which initiates the Llama is one of pleasurable pain in complete union with the object of the soul's love. In the commentary as well, San Juan interrelates the llama with other symbols of union developed in his earlier compositions. He recalls the Samaritan woman whose desire for the "agua viva" mirrors the soul's enjoyment of the "llama viva". He combines the touch of the flame with the wound of love it inflicts on the soul by citing the Bride of the Canticle who "se enterneció tanto, que se derritió" (Ll. I, 7). In rapid succession he juxtaposes the flame with the palace, games of love, the profoundest center, the stone, mansions and clear crystal, and the loving embrace. He next returns to a fire analogy, likening the operation of the Holy Spirit in the soul to "ascua encendida" inasmuch as "se afervora el fuego, que no solamente está encendida, sino echando llama viva" (I, 16), a simile which echoes the "carbón con el fuego" of the Cántico. By drawing on such varied analogies to explain the transforming nature of the union symbolized by the flame, San Juan overlays the significance of the llama with encrustations of mystical symbolism, subtly emphasizing the intricate interconnection of all of his symbols.

As he concludes the commentary of the first strophe, the author summarizes the entire stanza in prose. Addressing the Holy Spirit as flame, he states that it "traspas[a] la sustancia de [su] alma y la cauteriz[a] con [su] glorioso ardor" (Ll. I, 39). In choosing the verb cauterizar, San Juan finds a synonym for the hieres of the first strophe which also anticipates the effects of the llama enumerated in the second. As the poem continues, the flame metastasizes into the cauterio, llaga, mano and toque of the second as well as the lámparas de fuego of the third. In a fourfold apostrophe, the poet ties the effects of the flame to their origin both by parallel construction and by association to the delicate wounding of the first strophe. Underlying the analogies he draws in the Llama is the descriptive phrase first used in the Cántico to characterize the flame: "que consume y no da pena."

Addressing the flame as "cauterio suave," "llaga regalada," "mano blanda," and "toque delicado" in the second strophe, the poet continues a sense of pain inflicted on the soul that is yet assuaged by the tenderness of the Lover's action. The cautery perfectly captures the effect of the flame's touch, while the resulting wound follows logically both from cauterio and the verb herir. The personified flame and cautery next take on human form in the "mano blanda," which symbolizes both the power and affection of the soul's Lover. Finally, the "toque delicado" completes the circle by tying the action of the hand to the wounds, and, by association, to the living flame. The amorous vocabulary of symbolic death which concludes the first strophe ("acaba ya si quieres / Rompe la tela deste dulce encuentro") here gives way to the oxymoronic dying life metaphor of mystical poetry. San Juan thus condenses the effect of the soul's encounter at its most profound center in a series of exclamatory phrases that casts the experience in wholly mystical terms. As Barnstone remarks, the key to the poem's meaning is the initial exclamation, which avoids the banality of conventional love lyrics by juxtaposing the adjective living with flame rather than with love. It becomes "a sign of a human and mystical love pattern: an equation of death and life, of pain and joy."[25] Subsequent strophes develop the mystical sense of the poem further. While the fire of God is all-consuming, nevertheless, it does not eradicate the soul but, rather, transforms, clarifies, and enriches it. The poet establishes the basis for the paradox from the beginning of the work, first by addressing the Spirit as the living flame of love then by softening its effect on the soul by remarking that it "tiernamente hier[e]." The pleasure-pain paradox continues in the second strophe when the poet softens the effects of the cautery and wound by describing each in turn as "suave" and "regalada." As he explains in the commentary, since the cautery was soft, then, logically, the wound "ha de ser conforme el cauterio; y, así llaga de cauterio suave será llaga regalada" (Ll. II, 6).

In the commentary, San Juan develops the underlying Trinitarian nature of the symbols he employs. Just as the llama of the initial apostrophe represents the Holy Spirit, so, too, the cauterio and llaga, which are the flame's effects, also symbolize the third person of the Trinity. The "mano blanda" is a symbol of the Father, while the "toque" is the Son. Having established these correspondences at the outset, San Juan devotes the remainder of the commentary to an explanation of their interaction as the fuego de amor which consumes and transforms the mystical soul.

Both the cautery and the wound inflicted on the soul by the flame fittingly represent the Holy Spirit since "así como en el cauterio está el fuego más intenso y vehemente y hace mayor efecto que en los demás ígnitos, ansí en el acto de esta unión, por ser de tan inflamado fuego de amor más que todos los otros, por eso le llama [al Espíritu Santo] cauterio respecto de ellos" (Ll. II, 2). San Juan has already associated the Holy Spirit with

the flame so that, according to his rationale, the effects
wrought on the soul also symbolize the Paraclete. Juxtaposing
the "cauterio del fuego material" with "la llaga del cauterio de
amor," the author points out that the first may be assuaged only
with a salve different from the flame which induced the wound.
In contrast, the second is paradoxically cured by the application
of the very cautery which caused the wound in the first place.
Thus, the more the soul is wounded by love, the greater its love
becomes until it is transformed wholly into a veritable, yet
delectable, wound of love, in which state "está toda sana de
amor" (Ll. II, 7). Since the source of flame, cautery, and wound
is an infinite fire of love, the resulting wound is necessarily
"regalada".

In comparison to his interpretation of the cauterio and
llaga, San Juan's explanation of the mano and toque is brief.
The hand represents not only the power of the Father but also his
boundless generosity in bestowing gifts on the soul through the
instrumentality of both the Spirit as well as the Son in the form
of the "toque delicado". The interlocking symbolism of hand,
touch, wound, and cautery which inflame the soul with love
captures in graphic imagery the power, generosity, and delicacy
of the relationship between the mystic and the Trinity.

In his final reference to fire in the Llama, San Juan
addresses the lámparas de fuego in the last apostrophe of the
poem. Linked structurally to the earlier exclamations, the
invocation of the lámparas de fuego both continues fire symbolism

while also altering it in subtle yet significant ways. From the dominant sense of wounding and the concomitant pleasure-pain it produces, the poet next focuses on related properties of fire especially as manifested by lamps. They give light and heat. Also continued in this strophe is the sense of depth and interiority which the poet has stated explicitly in "el más profundo centro" of the first and intimated in the "matando muerte" of the second. The lamps of the third strophe emblazon "las profundas cavernas del sentido" heretofore darkened. In the final strophe, the soul addresses its lover familiarly, remarking on his delicate and amorous action "en [su] seno".

In the commentary San Juan equates the "lámparas de fuego" with the divine attributes revealed to the soul in transforming union. Detailing the comparison further, he likens each lamp to one of the attributes of God capable of enlightening the soul with suprasensible knowledge. Illuminated by the knowledge it receives, the soul is concomitantly inflamed by love. In simplest terms, the author says that to know God is to love him. Conversely, the mystic is to act in love because of that knowledge. San Juan cites Moses' vision of God on Mount Sinai to support his point, a familiar Biblical example of ineffable communication for mystical writers.

Although each lamp represents a particular attribute of God, the author stresses that all act in concert, so that each "abrasa en amor, ayudando también el calor de la una al calor de la otra y la llama de la una a la llama de la otra." The end result is that all form a single light and a single fire. The separate manifestations the flame has assumed through the course of the poem here converge in one image, which, while apparently plural in form ("lámparas"), is, in fact, a single source of heat and light to the soul. The three persons of the Trinity are one God with whom the mystic enjoys transforming union. As San Juan puts it: "todo se dice en esta palabra: que el alma está hecha Dios de Dios por participación de El y de sus atributos, que son los que aquí llama lámparas de fuego" (<u>Ll</u>. III, 8).

Even as the individual lamps converge to form a single flame and fire, so, too, do all of the elements of San Juan's poetic cosmos coalesce in the commentary. Awestruck by the significance of the union he has attempted to describe, the author first poses a rhetorical question to the soul: " ¿Quién dirá, pues, lo que sientes, ¡oh dichosa alma!, conociéndote así amada y con tal estimación engrandecida?" (<u>Ll</u>. III, 7). Attempting a reply, San Juan has recourse to a number of Old Testament citations evocative of much of his other imagery. Thus, he describes the soul as "engolfada e infundida," then calls it "el pozo de las aguas vivas que corren con ímpetu de el monte de Libano (Cant. 4, 15)" (<u>Ll</u>. III, 7). When he goes on to equate the "lámparas de fuego" with the "aguas vivas del espíritu," he joins two contrary elements as one just as he previously had done at the start of the commentary. What follows is further interconnection of imagery, for San Juan claims that the spirit of God partakes of the characteristics of both fire and water because:

en cuanto está escondido en las venas de el alma está
como agua suave y deleitable hartando la sed al
espíritu, y en cuanto se exercita en sacrificio de amar
a Dios es llamas vivas de fuego, que son las lámparas
del acto de la dilección y de las llamas que arriba
alegamos del Esposo en los Cantares (8, 6). (Ll. III,
8)

Having equated the flames with the living waters, the author

next discusses the significance of the descriptive phrase "en

cuyos resplandores," the resplendence of the lamplight playing on

the interior walls of the figurative caverns. The "resplandores"

symbolize the "noticias amorosas" transmitted to the soul by the

divine attributes represented by the lamps. The soul not only

receives the effects of the resplandores through enlightenment,

but shares intimately in their action by shining in turn with the

graces it receives. It is "transformada [y] hecha

resplandores." San Juan again interrelates the properties of

fire with another of the elements to explain transforming union:

y así diremos que es como el aire que está dentro de la
llama, encendido y transformado en la llama porque la
llama no es otra cosa que aire inflamado, y los
movimientos y resplandores que hace aquella llama ni
son sólo del aire ni sólo del fuego de que está
compuesta, sino junto de el aire y del fuego, y el
fuego los hace hacer al aire que en sí tiene
inflamado. (Ll. III, 9)

Given the symbolic association of the Holy Spirit with both fire

and air, the author aptly manifests the interpenetration of both

elements in the interior of the soul in his choice of "aire

inflamado" to characterize the amorous communications transmitted

to the mystic in transforming union.

Later in the commentary, San Juan completes the cycle when

316

he explains the significance of the "cavernas profundas" in terms
of their interior illumination. He systematically ties each of
the other elements to fire in the context of the Llama de amor
viva, achieving an effect which Icaza describes:

> Thus the four elements, of which in the sixteenth
> century it was thought all things were composed, are
> joined and fused into fire itself, probably with the
> implication that this fire symbolizes the burning love
> which alone remains when the other spiritual
> 'elements,' faith and hope, have given way to vision
> and possession.[26]

San Juan himself alludes to the purpose of his interconnection of
elemental imagery in the commentary when he explains that God
bestows mystical favors on chosen souls in order to lead them to
eternal life. The soul thus led realizes the proper end of its
creation and existence. So, too, do flame, air, earth, and water
seek their proper sphere in order to achieve the harmony of
creation envisioned by the sixteenth-century mind. The mystic
truly realizes the permanent union he constantly strives to
attain in this life only when he finally is able to "entrar en el
centro del espíritu de la vida perfecta en Cristo" (Ll. III, 10).
The foretaste of heaven exemplified by the divine epiphanies of
the Old Testament is within the purview of the mystic as well.
What San Juan hints at in the "bosques y espesuras" of the
Cántico espiritual, he makes clear in the Llama de amor viva when
he elucidates the pinnacle of the mystic experience by conjoining
the essential elements of creation as one. In transforming
union, the mystic shares in the life of the deity who makes
possible that very creation.

If man as microcosm embodies each of the four elements in a mixture which defines individual temperaments and personalities, he mirrors not only the cosmic spheres defined by the elements, but, in their entirety, the Creator and Mover of the spheres as well. The spheres are "todos los orbes celestes y los elementales" (p. 546) as Covarrubias defines them which make up the cosmovision first outlined by Plato and refined by Plotinus. What both Santa Teresa and San Juan discover in their individual mystical journeys and seek to translate into comprehensible terms is a cosmovision at once awesome yet simple:

> ils expriment de la manière la plus réaliste que les éléments du cosmos sont composés de la même substance et que cette substance n'est vraiment substance, c'est-à-dire divine, que par une opération radicale ou s'abolissant les uns dans les autres ils renaissent transfigurés: leur transfiguration est la manifestation de l'Amour, la réalisation de la vie (mystique).[27]

Thus, nourished by the water of faith, alternately cooled and fanned to ardor by the breath of the Holy Spirit, ultimately inflamed and illumined by the living flame of divine love, they find within the very ground of their being, where creature and Creator may truly be one.

Chapter 7

NOTES

[1] Otis Green, Spain and the Western Tradition, II, pp. 31-74, traces the literary history of the concept in Spanish literature.

[2] Cirlot, p. 95. The author goes on to cite Bachelard and Jung on the specific qualities of each element.

[3] Etymologiae, XIV, 1, i and Covarrubias, p. 961.

[4] Dicken, Crucible, pp. 237-38.

[5] The pictorial representation of the ascent of Mount Carmel is itself the center of some disagreement. Dicken, Crucible, pp. 238-44, maintains that it is the work of a later editor and never that of San Juan. Fr. Nöel-Dermot, O. C. D., "The 'Mount of Perfection' of St. John of the Cross, as presented by Diego de Astor," Mount Carmel, 7-8 (1959-1961), 77-83, while not refuting Dicken's claim, lends it tacit support by his descriptions of Diego de Astor's drawings and those of others. On the other hand, Eulogio de la Virgen del Carmen, O. C. D., San Juan de la Cruz y sus escritos (Madrid: Ediciones Cristiandad, 1969), pp. 173-84, staunchly defends the authenticity of San Juan's creation of the diagram by tracing it through numerous editions. San Juan's comments in the Subida (I, 13, x) seem to support Fr. Eulogio's contention.

[6] A. Bartlett Giamatti, The Earthly Paradise and the Renaissance Epic (Princeton: Princeton University Press, 1966), pp. 53-4.

[7] Helmut Hatzfeld, "Las profundas cavernas. The Structure of a Symbol of San Juan de la Cruz," in Estudios literarios sobre mística española, p. 297.

[8] See Fray Luis de León, El Cantar de los Cantares in Obras completas castellanas, I, Cap. 4, 16, p. 141.

[9] Etymologiae, XIII, 12, i. Covarubias, p. 51.

[10] Gaston Bachelard, L'Eau et les reves (Paris: Librarie Jose Cortin, 1963), p. 8.

[11] Alonso, La poesía de San Juan de la Cruz, p. 48.

[12] Maria Bertina Giovanni, "Teresa de Avila y el sentido de la naturaleza," RHM, 31 (1965), 74.

[13] Helmut Hatzfeld, Saint Teresa of Avila (New York: Twayne, 1969), p. 39.

[14] Cirlot, p. 274.

[15] Ewer, p. 150.

[16] Margit Frenk Alatorre, Entre folklore y literatura: lírica hispánica antigua, Jornadas, No. 68 (México: Colegio de México, 1971), p. 55.

[17] Bachelard, L'Eau, p. 20.

[18] The comparison is not unique to San Juan, but first appears in the works of Hugh of St. Victor. See the Selected Spiritual Writings, pp. 184-85.

[19] Covarrubias, p. 611.

[20] Susan Langer, Philosophy in a New Key (Cambridge: Harvard University Press, 1942), p. 145.

[21] Gaston Bachelard, The Psychoanalysis of Fire, trans. Alac C. M. Ross (Boston: Beacon Press, 1964), p. 55.

[22] P. de Surgy, "Les Degrés de l'échelles d'amour de saint Jean de la Croix," RAM, 27 (1941), 339.

[23] Baldesar Castiglione, The Book of the Courtier, trans. Charles S. Singleton (Garden City, N.Y.: Doubleday, 1959), Bk. IV, 62, pp. 346-47.

[24] Icaza, The Stylistic Relationship, p. 64.

[25] Willis Barnstone, "Mystico-Erotic Love in '0 Living Flame of Love'," RHM, 37 (1972-1973), 256.

[26] Icaza, The Stylistic Relationship, p. 57.

[27] Morel, Le Sens, III, p. 143.

CONCLUSION

By studying the imagery utilized by Santa Teresa and San
Juan to describe the various stages of mystical progress, a
pattern of interrelationship between individual images emerges
which enunciates the complete mystical message each writer
attempts to transmit. Both authors reveal individual preferences
in terms of specific images or methods of employing them, even as
both reflect the divergent background and circumstances in which
they compose their works. On the surface, Santa Teresa and San
Juan manifest two apparently distinct yet ultimately related
views of how a soul achieves mystical union. To simplify their
different approaches to union, however, is to oversimplify;
because, in essence, they present the obverse and reverse of the
same mystical coin. At the heart of virtually all mystical
discourse is paradox, so that apparently antithetical ways of
describing progress to union become, in fact, complementary means
of speaking of the same thing.

On the surface, Santa Teresa's imagery stresses a positive
sense of completion in her mystical works. For example, the two
dominant Teresian metaphors for mystical progress--irrigation of
the garden of the soul and passage through the mansions of the
interior castle--focus on movement toward peaceful fulfillment
and repose. Although she does not ignore purgation with its
sometimes negative connotations, yet her underlying message

emphasizes the via positiva rather than the via negativa.   Thus,
her tendency to amass seemingly disparate images within the
context of a single work, or, indeed, a single paragraph,
testifies to a penchant for embracing virtually the whole of
creation as a manifestation of the Creator she claims to join in
mystical union.   A colloquial and elliptical style underscores a
highly personal, almost impressionistic approach to union present
in her works. In similes and metaphors, her language is vivid,
direct, and familiar; hence perfectly suited to both her
temperament and the audience for whom she writes.

At first glance, San Juan's view of the mystical life
appears to contrast with that of Santa Teresa's by emphasizing
the via negativa especially in the gradual deprivation of first
the senses, both physical and spiritual, and then the spirit
which marks the Subida-Noche diptych. By emptying the soul of
all that is not God, San Juan asserts that the mystic may find
God. Thus, the graphic depiction of the paths to the summit of
Mount Carmel found as the frontispiece of the Subida shows the
most direct to be that of nada. Similarly, San Juan's overriding
image of night, which grows progressively darker as the soul
nears union, also seems to stress a way of denial rather than one
of all-embracing fulfillment. In the Subida and the Noche,
therefore, San Juan systematically removes creatures and creation
from the mystic's path, so that he may eventually emerge into the
dazzling light of the Llama's "más profundo centro." His is a
way of depuration which frees the mystic soul from all that is

not God, both externally in the works of creation and internally in the essence of its being. Between the purifying message of the Subida-Noche and the purified vision of the Llama, however, one finds San Juan's Cántico espiritual, where the mystical landscape teems with the whole of creation in a veritable canticle of praise of God and soul searching for and finding union.

San Juan's poetry achieves a lyrical embrace of all creation even greater than that manifested by Santa Teresa in her prose. While his prose style often reveals a more sustained and systematic approach to the mystical life indicative of the author's scholarly training, yet he, too, amasses images at times seeking by sheer numbers and associations to clarify a particular truth about the mystic way. He differs from Santa Teresa in the integrated nature much of his imagery assumes throughout all of his mystical treatises. Although his mystical theology is systematically structured in the prose commentaries, yet the lyrical is never far from the surface even there. Drawing on Biblical, patristic, or mystical authorities to elucidate or substantiate his message, San Juan attests to his theological training. At the same time, by integrating classical, and literary motifs into the context of his works, he immeasurably broadens and enriches both mystical and secular literature.

The apparent diversity of the many images utilized by both mystics thus appears as many facets of a single, simple message. Progress to mystical union is a paradoxical exercise on the part of the soul. It turns from the variety of creation in which God's presence is revealed to pursue this elusive God in an interior journey to the figurative center of its soul. As it abandons created things as well as its own passions, desires, and will, it approaches the transcendent reality of mystical union with the Creator. By leaving all, it possesses all. By turning from creation, it finds the Creator. From the many words of creation the mystics distill the one Word, God.

ABBREVIATIONS

BH	Bulletin Hispanique
BHS	Bulletin of Hispanic Studies
BICC	Boletín del Instituto Caro y Cuero
BRAE	Boletín de la Real Academia Española
CHA	Cuadernos Hispanoamericanos
FMLS	Forum for Modern Language Studies
HR	Hispanic Review
JHP	Journal of Hispanic Philology
JMRS	Journal of Medieval and Renaissance Studies
LdD	Letras de Deusto
LR	Lettres Romanes
MLN	MLN formerly Modern Language Notes
MLQ	Modern Language Quarterly
MLR	Modern Language Review
NDEJ	Notre Dame English Journal
NRFH	Nueva Revista de Filología Hispánica
PSA	Papeles de Son Armadans
QIA	Quaderni Ibero-Americani
RAM	Revue d'Ascetique et Mystique
REH	Revista de Estudios Hispánicos
Ren	Renascence
RF	Romanische Forshungen
RFE	Revista de Filología Española
RFH	Revista de Filología Hispánica

RHM	Revista Hispánica Moderna
RHS	Revue d'Histoire de la Spiritualité
RIE	Revista de Ideas Estéticas
RPh	Romance Philology
RyF	Razón y Fe

BIBLIOGRAPHY

Primary Texts

Juan de la Cruz, San. Cántico espiritual. Ed. Eulogio Pacho.
Madrid: Fundación Universitaria Española, 1981.

---. Cántico espiritual. Poesías. Ed. Cristóbal Cuevas
García. Madrid: Alhambra, 1979.

---. El Cántico espiritual, según el ms. de las Madres
Carmelitas de Jaén. Ed. Matías Martínez Burgos. Madrid:
Espasa-Calpe, 1969.

---. Le Cantique spirituel de saint Jean de la Croix, docteur de
l'église. Notes historiques, texte critique, version
française. Prologue by Dom Philippe Chevalier, O. S. B.
Paris: Desclée de Brouwer, 1930.

---. Le Cantique spirituel de saint Jean de la Croix, docteur de
l'église. Traduction du texte espagnol. Ed. Dom Philippe
Chevalier, O. S. B. Paris: Desclée de Brouwer, 1933.

---. The Complete Works of Saint John of the Cross. Trans. and
ed. E. Allison Peers from the critical edition of Fr.
Silverio de Santa Teresa, O. C. D. 3 vols. London: Burns
and Oates, 1945.

---. Obras de San Juan de la Cruz doctor de la iglesia. Ed. Fr.
Silverio de Santa Teresa, O. C. D. 4 vols. Burgos: Monte
Carmelo, 1929.

---. Poesía. Ed. Domingo Yndurain. 2nd ed. Madrid: Cátedra,
1984.

---. Poems of St. John of the Cross. Trans. Roy Campbell. New
York: Grosset & Dunlap, 1967.

---. The Poems of St. John of the Cross. Trans. John Frederick
Nims. 3rd ed. Chicago and London: University of Chicago
Press, 1979.

---. Vida y obras de San Juan de la Cruz. Biografía de
Crisógono de Jesús, O. C. D. Rev. ed. Matías del Niño Jesús,
O. C. D. Ed. Lucinio Ruano, O. C. D. 7th ed. Madrid:
Editorial Católica, 1973.

Teresa de Jesús, Santa. Camino de perfección. Ed. José María
Aguado. 2 vols. Madrid: Espasa-Calpe, 1969.

---. The Complete Works of St. Teresa of Jesus. Trans. and ed.
E. Allison Peers from the critical edition of P. Silverio de
Santa Teresa, O. C. D. 3 vols. London: Sheed and Ward,
1946.

---. Interior Castle. Trans. and ed. E. Allison Peers. Garden
City, N. Y.: Doubleday and Co., 1961.

---. The Life of Teresa of Jesus. Trans. and ed. E. Allison
Peers from the critical edition of P. Silverio de Santa
Teresa O. C. D. Garden City, N. Y.: Doubleday and Co., 1960.

---. Las Moradas. Ed. Tomás Navarro Tomás. Madrid:
Espasa-Calpe, 1968.

---. Obras completas. Transcripción, introducción y notas de
Efrén de la Madre de Dios, O. C. D. y Otger Steggink, O.
Carm. Madrid: Editorial Católica, 1972.

---. The Way of Perfection. Trans. and ed. E. Allison Peers.
Garden City, N. Y.: Doubleday and Co., 1964.

Other Texts

Alciati, Andres. Los emblemas de Alciato. Tr. en rhimas
Españolas. Lyon: Mathia Bonhome, 1549.

Aquinas, St. Thomas. The Summa contra Gentiles of St. Thomas
Aquinas. Trans. the English Dominican Fathers. 5 vols.
London: Burns, Oates & Washbourne, 1924.

---. Summa Theologiae. Latin text and English translation. 60
vols. [Cambridge]: Blackfriars, 1964-1976.

Augustine, [Saint]. Augustine: Earlier Writings. Trans. John H.
S. Burleigh. Vol. VI of The Library of Christian Classics.
Philadelphia: The Westminster Press, 1953.

---. The Confessions of St. Augustine. Trans. Rex Warner. New
York: New American Library, 1963.

---. Expositions on the Book of Psalms. Trans. by Members of
the English Church. In A Library of Fathers of the Holy
Catholic Church, anterior to the division of east and west.
Oxford: John Henry Parker; London: F. and J. Rivington,
1853.

Bernard of Clairvaux, St. On the Song of Songs. Sermones in
Cantica Canticorum. Trans. and ed. A Religious of C. S. M.

V. London: A. R. Mowbray and Co.; New York: Morehouse-Gorham, 1952.

---. Saint Bernard on the Love of God. Trans. Rev. Terence L. Connolly, S. J. Trappist, Ky.: Abbey of Gethsemani, 1943.

The Bestiary. A Book of Beasts. Trans. and ed. T. H. White. New York: G. P. Puntam's Sons, 1960.

Biblia sacra iuxta Vulgatam Clementiam. Ed. Alberto Colunga, O. P. and Laurentio Turrado. 4th ed. Madrid: Editorial Católica, 1965.

Bonaventure, Saint. The Enkindling of Love also called the Triple Way. Ed. William I. Joffe. Paterson, N. J.: St. Anthony Guild Press, 1956.

---. The Mind's Road to God. Trans. George Boas. New York: The Liberal Arts Press, 1953.

Calderón de la Barca, Pedro. Obras completas. Vol. III. Autos sacramentales. Madrid: Aguilar, 1967.

El Cantar de los Cantares. 3rd ed. Trans. Fray Luis de León. Madrid: Espasa-Calpe, 1958.

Le Cantique des Cantiques. Ed. A. Robert et al. Paris: J. Gabalda, 1963.

Castiglione, Baldesar. The Book of the Courtier. Trans. Charles S. Singleton. Garden City, N. Y.: Doubleday, 1959.

The Cloud of Unknowing and the Book of Privy Counseling. Ed. William Johnston, S. J. Garden City, N. Y.: Doubleday, 1973.

Covarrubias Orozco, D. Sebastián. Tesoro de la lengua castellana o española. Madrid: Turner, 1977.

Dionysius the Areopagite. The Divine Names and the Mystical Theology. Ed. and trans. C. E. Rolt. London: S. P. C. K., 1940.

Erasmus, Desiderius. El Enquiridión o manual del caballero cristiano. Ed. Dámaso Alonso. Prólogo Marcel Bataillon. La Paraclesis o exhortación al estudio de las letras divinas. Ed. Dámaso Alonso. Madrid: Revista de Filología Española, 1971.

Garcilaso de la Vega. Obras completas con comentario. Ed. crítica Elias L. Rivers. Columbus, Ohio: Ohio State University Press, 1974.

Góngora, Luis de. _Poems of Góngora_. Ed. R. O. Jones.
Cambridge: Cambridge University Press, 1966.

Gracián, Baltasar. _El Criticón_. 8th ed. Madrid: Espasa-Calpe,
1943.

Hilton, Walter. _The Scale of Perfection_. Ed. Illtyd Trethowan,
Monk of Downside. St. Meinrad, Indiana: Abbey Press, 1975.

Hugh of St. Victor. _The Divine Love. The Two Treatises De laude
Caritatis and De Amore Sponsi ad Sponsam_. Trans. Religious
of C. S. M. V. London: A. R. Mowbray & Co., 1956.

---. _Selected Spiritual Writings_. Trans. Religious of C. S. M.
V. New York: Harper & Row, 1962.

Isidorus of Seville, Saint. _Etymologiarum sive originum. Libri
XX_. Ed. W. M. Lindsay. 2 vols. Oxonii: Clarendoniano,
1911.

Juana Inés de la Cruz, Sor. _Obras completas_. Ed. Francisco
Monterde. Mexico: Porrúa, 1969.

Laredo, Bernadino de. _The Ascent of Mount Sion; Being the Third
Book of the Treatise of That Name_. Trans. E. Allison
Peers. London: Faber & Faber, 1952.

Llull, Ramon. _Antología de Ramon Llull_. Trans. Ana María de
Saavedra and Francisco de P. Samaranch. 2 vols. Madrid:
Dirección General de Relaciones Culturales, 1961.

Loyola, San Ignacio de. _Obras completas_. Ed. P. Cándido de
Dalmases, S. J. Madrid: Editorial Católica, 1952.

Luis de Granada, V. P. M. Fray. _Obras_. Vol. VI of _Biblioteca de
Autores Españoles_. Ed. D. Buenaventura Carlos Aribau.
Madrid: 1944.

Luis de León, Fray. _De los nombres de Cristo_. Madrid:
Espasa-Calpe, 1957.

---. _Obras completas castellanas_. Vol. I. Ed. Félix García, O.
S. A. Madrid: Editorial Católica, 1977.

---. _La poesía de fray Luis de León_. Ed. Oreste Macrí.
Salamanca: Anaya, 1970.

The Metaphysical Poets. Ed. Helen Gardner. Baltimore, Md.:
Penguin Books, 1966.

Migne, Jacques Paul, ed. _Patrologiae cursus completus, seu
bibliotheca universalis . . . omnium SS. patrum, doctorum,
scriptorumque ecclesiasticorum. Series Latina. A_

Tertulliano ad Innocentium III. Parisiis: Migne, 1844-1865. 221 vols.

Origen. The Song of Songs. Commentary and Homilies. Ancient Christian Writers 26. Trans. R. P. Lawson. Ed. Johannes Quaten and Joseph Plumpe. Westminster, Md.: The Newman Press; London: Longman's Green & Co., 1957.

Osuna, Francisco de. Tercer abecedario espiritual. Ed. Melquiades Andrés. Madrid: Editorial Católica, 1972.

Plato. Phaedo. Trans. F. J. Church. New York: The Liberal Arts Press, 1951.

---. Phaedrus. Trans. W. G. Helmbold and W. B. Rabinowitz. New York: Bobbs-Merrill, 1956.

---. Timaeus. Ed. and trans. John Warrington. London: Dent; New York: Dutton, 1965.

Pliny. The Natural History of Pliny. Trans. John Bostock and H. T. Riley. 6 vols. London: Henry G. Bohn, 1855.

Quevedo y Villegas, Francisco de. Obra poética. Ed. José Manuel Blecua. 3 vols. Madrid: Castalia, 1969.

Richard of Saint-Victor. Selected Writings on Contemplation. Trans. Clare Kirchberger. London: Faber & Faber, 1957.

Rolle, Richard. The Fire of Love. Trans. Clifton Wolters. Baltimore, Md.: Penguin, 1971.

Ruysbroeck, Jan van. The Adornment of the Spiritual Marriage. The Sparkling Stone. The Book of Supreme Truth. Trans. C. A. Wyschenk Dom. Ed. Evelyn Underhill. London: John M. Watkins, 1951.

---. The Seven Steps of the Ladder of Spiritual Love. Trans. F. Sherwood Taylor. London: Dacre Press, 1952.

Theobaldus Episcopus. Physiologus. Ed. P. T. Eden. Leiden und Koln: E. J. Brill, 1972.

La vida de Lazarillo de Tormes y de sus fortunas y adversidades. Ed. R. O. Jones. Manchester: Manchester University Press, 1963.

332

Critical Sources

Academia Española, Real. Diccionario de autoridades. Edición
    facsímil. 3 vols. Madrid: Gredos, 1964.

---. Diccionario de la lengua española. 19th ed. Madrid:
    Espasa-Calpe, 1970.

Actas del Congreso Internacional Teresiano. Salamanca 4-7
    Octubre, 1982. Ed. Teófanes Egido Martínez, et al. 3 vols.
    Salamanca: Universidad de Salamanca, 1983.

Actas del Primer Congreso Internacional de Hispanistas. Oxford:
    Oxford University Press, 1964.

Actas del Quinto Congreso Internacional de Hispanistas. II.
    Bordeaux: PU de Bordeaux, 1977.

Alatorre, Margit Frenk. Entre folklore y literatura: lírica
    hispánica antigua. Jornadas No. 68. México: Colegio de
    México, 1971.

Alonso, Dámaso. "La caza de amor es de altanería. Sobre
    precedentes de una poesía de San Juan de la Cruz." BRAE 26
    (1947): 63-79.

---. La poesía de San Juan de la Cruz (desde esta ladera). 6th
    ed. Madrid: Aguilar, 1966.

---. Poesía española; ensayo de métodos y límites estilísticas.
    Madrid: Gredos, 1971.

Andrés Martín, Melquiades. Los Recogidos. Nueva visión de la
    mística española (1500-1700). Madrid: Fundación
    Universitaria Española Seminario "Suárez", 1975.

Anshen, Ruth Nanda, ed. Language: An Enquiry into its Meaning and
    Function. New York: Harper and Bros., 1957.

Aranguren, José Luis L. San Juan de la Cruz. Madrid: Ediciones
    Júcar, 1973.

Arintero, Juan G. Cuestiones místicas. Madrid: Editorial
    Católica, 1956.

Asensio, Eugenio. Poética y realidad en el Cancionero peninsular
    de la Edad media. Madrid: Gredos, 1957.

Asín Palacios, Miguel. Obras escogidas. I. Madrid: C. S. I. C., 1933.

---. "El símil de los castillos y moradas del alma en la mística islámica y en santa Teresa." Al-andalus 11 (1946): 263-74.

L'Autobiographie dans le monde hispanique. Actes du Colloque international de la Baume-les-Aix, 11-13 Mai 1979. Etudes Hispaniques 1. Aix-en-Provence: Université de Provence, 1980.

Bacarisse, Salvador, et al., eds. What's Past Is Prologue: A Collection of Essays in Honour of L. J. Woodward. Edinburgh: Scottish Academic Press, 1984.

Bachelard, Gaston. L'Eau et les reves. Essai sur l'imagination de la matière. Paris: Librairie José Corti, 1963.

---. The Psychoanalysis of Fire. Trans. Alac C. M. Ross. Boston: Beacon Press, 1964.

Bainton, Roland H. "Man, God, and the Church in the Age of the Renaissance." The Renaissance. New York: Harper and Row, 1953. 77-96.

Ballestero, Manuel. Juan de la Cruz: De la angustia al olvido. Bacelona: Península, 1977.

Barnstone, Willis. "Mystico-Erotic Love in 'O Living Flame of Love'." RHM 37 (1972-1973): 253-61.

Baruzi, Jean. "Introduction à des recherches sur le langage mystique." Recherches Philosophiques (1931-1932): 66-82.

---. Saint Jean de la Croix et le problème de l'experience mystique. 2nd ed. Paris: Alcan, 1931.

Bataillon, Marcel. Erasmo y España. Estudios sobre la historia espiritual del siglo XVI. México-Buenos Aires: Fondo de Cultura Económica, 1950.

---. "Sur la genèse poétique du Cantique spirituel de saint Jean de la Croix." BICC 5 (1949): 251-63.

---. "La tortolica de 'Fontefrida' y del Cántico espiritual." NRFH 7 (1953): 291-306.

Bell, Aubrey F. G. Castilian Literature. Oxford: Clarendon Press, 1938.

---. Luis de Leon: A Study of the Spanish Renaissance. Oxford: Clarendon Press, 1925.

Benassy-Berling, Marie-Cécile. Humanisme et religion chez Sor Juana Inés de la Cruz. Paris: Editions Hispaniques, 1982.

Bergua, José, ed. Refranero español. Colección de ocho mil refranes populares, ordenados, concordados y explicados precedida del Libro de los proverbios morales de Alonso de Barros. 7th ed. Madrid: Ediciones Ibéricas, 1968.

Berthelot, Andre. "Sobre: la 'Oncena lira' del Cantico espiritual de San Juan de la Cruz." PSA 86 (1977): 115-26.

---. "Sur la traduction de la poesia de S. Jean de la Croix." RHS 53 (1977): 117-28.

Bertini, Giovanni Maria. "Teresa y el sentido de la naturaleza." RHM 31 (1965): 71-177.

Blecua, José Manuel. "Los antecedentes del poema del 'Pastorcico' de San Juan de la Cruz." Sobre poesía de la edad de oro. Madrid: Gredos, 1970. 96-99.

Bonnard, Maryvonne. "Les Influences réciproques de sainte Therese et saint Jean de la Croix." BH 37 (1935): 129-48.

Bouyer, Louis, Cong. Orat. "'Mysticism': An Essay on the History of a Word." Mystery and Mysticism. London: Blackfriars, 1956. 119-37.

Bowra, C. M. Inspiration and Poetry. Cambridge: Cambridge University Press, 1951.

Bremond, Henri. Prayer and Poetry; a Contribution to Poetical Theory. Trans. Algar Thorold. London: Burns Oates & Washbourne, 1927.

Brenan, Gerald. St. John of the Cross; his life and poetry. Trans. of poetry by Lynda Nicholson. Cambridge: Cambridge University Press, 1973.

Bruno, Fr., O. C. D. St. John of the Cross. Ed. Fr. Benedict Zimmerman, O. C. D. New York: Sheed and Ward, 1932.

Butler, Dom Edward Cuthbert. Western Mysticism. London: Constable, 1951.

Cahill, Tierney J. "The Symbol of the Flame in the Works of San Juan de la Cruz." M. A. thesis. Catholic University of America, 1950.

Calvert, Laura. "The Widowed Turtledove and Amorous Dove of Spanish Lyric Poetry: A Symbolic Interpretation." JMRS 3 (1973): 273-301.

335

Camón Aznar, José. Arte y pensamiento en San Juan de la Cruz. Madrid: Editorial Católica, 1972.

Campo, Agustín del. "Poesía y estilo de la Noche oscura." RIE 3 (1943): 33-48.

Castela, Lucien. "Mystique et autobiographie: La Vida de sainte Thérèse." L'Autobiographie dans les monde hispanique. Actes du Colloque international de la Baume-les-Aix, 11-12-13 mai 1979. Etudes Hispaniques 1. Aix-en-Provence: Université de Provence, 1980. 139-54.

Celaya, Gabriel. Exploración de la poesía. Barcelona: Seix Barral, 1971.

Centenary of Saint Teresa. Carmelite Studies. Ed. John Sullivan, O. C. D. Washington, D. C.: ICS Publications, 1984.

Chevalier, Dom Philippe, O. S. B. "Le Cantique spirituel a-t-il été interpolé?" BH 24 (1922): 307-42.

---. "Le Cantique spirituel interpolé." Vie Spirituelle-Supplément 14 (1926): 109-62; 15 (1927): 69-109; 22 (1930): 1-11, 80-89; 28 (1932): 29-50.

Chorpenning, Joseph. "The Literary and Theological Method of the Castillo interior." JHP 3 (1979): 121-33.

---. "Reading St. Teresa of Avila's Life Today." Spirituality Today 36 (1984): 196-209.

---. "St. Teresa's Presentation of Her Religious Experience." Centenary of St. Teresa. Washington, D. C.: ICS Publications, 1984. 152-88.

Cinco ensayos sobre Santa Teresa de Jesús. Madrid: Editorial Nacional, 1984.

Cirlot, J. E. Dictionary of Symbols. Trans. Jack Sage. New York: Philosophical Library, 1962.

Concha, Victor G. de la. El arte literario de Santa Teresa. Barcelona: Editorial Ariel, 1978.

Conger, George P. Theories of Macrocosmos and Microcosmos in the History of Philosophy. New York: Columbia University Press, 1922.

Corominas, Joan. Breve diccionario etimológico de la lengua castellana. 3rd ed. Madrid: Gredos, 1976.

336

Crisógono de Jesús, Fr., O. C. D. San Juan de la Cruz, el Hombre, el Doctor, el Poeta. 1st ed. Barcelona: Labor, 1935.

---. San Juan de la Cruz, su obra científica y su obra literaria. Madrid: Mensajero de Santa Teresa y San Juan de la Cruz, 1929.

IV Centenario de Santa Teresa (1582-1982). Número extraordinario. Letras de Deusto 24 (Jul-Dic 1982).

Cuevas García, Cristóbal. "El significado alegórico en el Castillo teresiano." LdD 24 (Jul-Dic 1982): 77-97.

Cummins, John G. "Aqueste lance divino': San Juan's Falconry Images." What's Past in Prologue: A Collection of Essays in Honour of L. J. Woodward. Eds. Salvador Bacarisse, et al. Edinburgh: Scottish Academic Press, 1984. 28-32.

Curtius, Ernst Robert. European Literature and the Latin Middle Ages. Trans. Willard R. Trask. New York: Harper and Row, 1953.

Daniel de la Inmaculada, Fr., O. C. D. "La estética en los místicos." El Monte Carmelo 63 (1955): 287-310.

Danielou, Jean. Les Symboles chrétiens primitifs. Paris: Editions du Seuil, 1961.

D'Arcy, M. C. The Mind and Heart of Love. New York: Meridian Books, 1956.

Dicken, E. W. Trueman. The Crucible of Love. A Study of the Mysticism of St. Teresa of Jesus and St. John of the Cross. New York: Sheed and Ward, 1963.

---. "The Imagery of the Interior Castle and Its Implications." Sancta Teresia a Iesu. Doctor Ecclesia. Roma: Edizioni del Teresianum, 1970. 198-218.

Dictionnaire de spiritualité, ascétique et mystique, doctrine et histoire. Eds. Marcel Viller, S. J., et al. Paris: Gabriel Beauchesne et Fils, 1937.

Diego, Gerardo. "La naturaleza y la inspiración poética en S. Juan de la Cruz." Revista de Espiritualidad 27 (1968): 311-19.

Disandro, Carlos A. Tres poetas españoles. San Juan de la Cruz, Luis de Góngora, Lope de Vega. La Plata: Ediciones Hostería Volante, 1967.

D'Ors, Eugenio. Estilos del pensar. Madrid: Ediciones y Publicaciones Españolas, n. d.

Duchaussoy, Jacques. Le Bestiaire divin ou la symbolique des animaux. Paris: Le Courrier du Livre, 1972.

Dunbar, H. Flanders. Symbolism in Medieval Thought and Its Consummation in the Divine Comedy. New York: Russell and Russell, 1961.

Duvivier, Roger. "De l'ineffabilité mystique à la confusion critique? Un débat de méthode à propos de la genèse du Cántico espiritual". Estudios de historia, literatura y arte hispánicos ofrecidos a Rodrigo A. Molina. Ed. Wayne Finke. Madrid: Insula, 1977. 109-27.

———. "L'Histoire des écrits de saint Jean de la Croix." LR 31 (1977): 343-52.

Eco, Umberto. Art and Beauty in the Middle Ages. Trans. Hugh Bredin. New Haven and London: Yale University Press, 1986.

Efrén de la Madre de Dios, O. C. D. and Otger Steggink, O. Carm. Santa Teresa y su tiempo. 3 vols. Salamanca: Universidad Pontífica, 1982; 1984.

Emeterio de Jesús María, Fr., O. C. D. "La poesía sanjuanista en la evolución del sentimiento cósmico." El Monte Carmelo 43 (1942): 477-520.

Enciclopedia de la Biblia. Barcelona: Ediciones Garriga, 1963.

Estudios de historia, literatura y arte hispánicos ofrecidos a Rodrigo A. Molina. Ed. Wayne Finke. Madrid: Insula, 1977.

Etchegoyen, Gaston. L'Amour divin: Essai sur les sources de sainte Thérèse. Bordeaux: Feret et Fils, 1923.

Eulogio de la Virgen del Carmen, Fr., O. C. D. El Cántico espiritual. Trayectoria histórica del texto. Paris: Desclée, 1967; Roma: Edizioni del Teresianum, 1967.

———. "La clave exegética del Cántico Espiritual." Ephemerides Carmeliticae 9 (1958): 307-37; 11 (1960): 312-51.

———. San Juan de la Cruz y sus escritos. Madrid: Ediciones Cristiandad, 1969.

Ewer, Mary Anita. A Survey of Mystical Symbolism. London: S. P. C. K.; New York: Macmillan, 1933.

Fawcett, Thomas. The Symbolic Language of Religion. London: SCM Press, 1970.

338

Ferguson, George. Signs and Symbols in Christian Art. London: Oxford University Press, 1974.

Ferguson, John. Encyclopedia of Mysticism and Mystery Religions. New York: Crossroad, 1982.

Fernández Leborans, María Jesús. Luz y oscuridad en la mística española. Madrid: Cupsa Editorial, 1978.

Florisoone, Michel. Esthetique et mystique, d'après sainte Thérèse d'Avila et saint Jean de la Croix. Paris: du Seuil, 1956.

Fowlie, W. A. Clowns and Angels. New York: Sheed and Ward, 1943.

Franklin, James C. Mystical Transformations. The Imagery of Liquids in the Work of Mechtild von Magdeburg. Rutherford, N. J.: Farleigh Dickinson University Press, 1978.

Frutos Cortés, Eugenio. Creación filosófica y creación poética. Madrid: José Porrúa Turanzas, 1976.

García Lorca, Francisco. De Fray Luis de León a San Juan. La escondida senda. Madrid: Castalia, 1972.

Garrido, Pablo M., O. Carm. Santa Teresa, San Juan de la Cruz y los Carmelitas españoles. Madrid: Universidad Pontífica Fundación Universitaria Española, 1982.

Garrigou-Lagrange, Rev. R., O. P. Christian Perfection and Contemplation according to St. Thomas Aquinas and St. John of the Cross. Trans. S. M. Timothea Doyle, O. P. St. Louis: B. Herder Book Co., 1944.

Gaskell, G. A. Dictionary of All Scriptures and Myths. New York: The Julian Press, 1976.

Giamatti, A. Bartlett. The Earthly Paradise and the Renaissance Epic. Princeton: Princeton University Press, 1966.

Gilson, Etienne. The Spirit of Medieval Philosophy. Trans. A. H. C. Downes. New York: Chas. Scribner's Sons, 1940.

Gimeno Casalduero, Joaquín. "La 'Noche oscura' y la 'Llama de amor viva', de San Juan de la Cruz: Composición y significado." CHA 346 (1979): 172-81.

---. "El pastorcico de San Juan y el pastorcillo de las redondillas." HR 47 (1979): 77-85.

Grant, Patrick. Literature of Mysticism in Western Tradition. New York: St. Martin's Press, 1983.

Green, Otis H. Spain and the Western Tradition. The Castilian Mind from El Cid to Calderón. 4 vols. Madison: University of Wisconsin Press, 1963.

Groult, Pierre. Los místicos de los países bajos y la literatura espiritual del siglo XVI. Trans. Rodrigo A. Molina. Madrid: Fundación Universitaria Española, 1976.

---. Les Mystiques des Pays-Bas et la littérature espagnole du seizième siècle. Louvain: Uystpruyst, 1927.

Guillén, Jorge. Language and Poetry. Some Poets of Spain. Cambridge: Harvard University Press, 1961.

---. Lenguaje y poesía. Madrid: Alianza, 1972.

---. "Poesía de San Juan de la Cruz." PSA 20 (1961): 22-44.

Guillén, José. "La poética en el Cántico espiritual." Revista de Espiritualidad 1 (1942): 438-47.

Gunn, Giles B., ed. Literature and Religion. New York: Harper & Row, 1971.

Haduch, Sr. Mary Casimira, C. S. S. F. "Classification of Some Symbols in 'La noche oscura del alma' of San Juan de la Cruz." M. A. thesis. Catholic University of America, 1956.

Hahn, Juergen. The Origins of the Baroque Concept of Peregrinatio. Studies in the Romance Languages and Literatures 131. Chapel Hill, N. C.: University of North Carolina Press, 1973.

Hall, James. Dictionary of Subjects and Symbols of Art. New York: Harper & Row, 1974.

Harper, Ralph. Human Love. Existential and Mystical. Baltimore, Md.: Johns Hopkins Press, 1966.

Hatzfeld, Helmut. "Los elementos constituyentes de la poesía mística." Actas del Primer Congreso Internacional de Hispanistas. Oxford: Oxford University Press, 1964. 319-325.

---. Estudios literarios sobre mística española. 2nd ed. Madrid: Gredos, 1968.

---. "The Influence of Ramón Llull and Jan van Ruysbroeck on the Language of the Spanish Mystics." Traditio 4 (1947): 337-97.

---. Santa Teresa de Avila. New York: Twayne, 1969.

340

———. "Two Types of Mystical Poetry. Illustrated by St. Teresa and St. John of the Cross ('Vivo sin vivir en mí')." American Benedictine Review 1 (1951): 421-62.

Highet, Gilbert. The Classical Tradition. Greek and Roman Influence on Western Literature. London: Oxford University Press, 1949.

Homenaje a Casalduero: Crítica y poesía. Eds. Rizel Pincus Sigele and Gonzalo Sobejano. Madrid: Gredos, 1972.

Hondet, Jean-Gabriel, O. S. B. Les Poèmes mystiques de saint Jean de la Croix. Paris: Editions du Centurion, 1966.

Hoornaert, Rodolphe. Saint Teresa in Her Writings. Trans. Rev. Joseph Leonard. London: Sheed and Ward, 1933.

———. Sainte Thérèse, écrivain; son milieu, ses facultés, son oeuvres. Bruges: Desclée de Brouwer, 1922.

Hornedo, R. M. de, S. J. "El humanismo de san Juan de la Cruz." RyF 129 (1944): 133-50.

Howe, Elizabeth Teresa. "'Alma región luciente' of Fray Luis de León." REH 15 (1981): 425-51.

———. "Donne and the Spanish Mystics on Ecstasy." NDEJ 13 (1981): 28-44.

———. "The Mystical Kiss and the Canticle of Canticles: Three Interpretations." American Benedictine Review 33 (1982): 302-11.

———. "St. Teresa's Meditaciones and the Mystic Tradition of the Canticle of Canticles." Ren 33 (1980): 47-64.

Huizinga, Johan. Homo Ludens. A Study of the Play-Element in Culture. Boston: Beacon Press, 1950.

Icaza, Rosa Maria. The Stylistic Relationship between Poetry and Prose in the Cántico espiritual of San Juan de la Cruz. Washington, D. C.: Catholic University Press, 1957.

Inge, William Ralph. Christian Mysticism. New York: Meridian Books, 1956.

Introducción a la lectura de Santa Teresa. Ed. Alberto Barrientos. Madrid: Editorial Espiritualidad, 1978.

Izquierdo Duque, Sor Magadalena. Santa Teresa de Jesús, metáforas y símbolos. Madrid: Ediciones Iberoamericanas, 1963.

341

James, William. The Varieties of Religious Experience. New York: New American Library, 1963.

Jiménez Duque, Baldomero and Luis Morales Oliver. San Juan de la Cruz. Conferencias pronunciadas en la Fundación Universitaria Española los días 9 y 11 de diciembre de 1975 con motivo del Tercer Centenario de su beatificación. Madrid: Fundación Universiaria Española, 1977.

Jiménez Salas, Maria. Santa Teresa de Jesus: bibliografía fundamental. Madrid: C. S. I. C., 1962.

Jennings, E. "Poetry and Mysticism: On Re-reading Bremond." Dublin Review 234 (1960), 84-90.

Jones, R. O. The Golden Age: Prose and Poetry. The Sixteenth and Seventeenth Centuries. Vol. 3 of A Literary History of Spain. London: Ernest Benn; New York: Barnes and Noble, 1971.

Juan de Jesús María, Fr., O. C. D. "El díptico Subida-Noche." Sanjuanistica. Rome: Teresianum, 1943. 27-82.

Kantorowicz, Ernst H. The King's Two Bodies. A Study in Medieval Political Theology. Princeton: Princeton University Press, 1957.

Kilkenny, Eugene F. "Analysis of the 'Cántico espiritual' of San Juan de la Cruz in the Light of the Biblical Canticum Canticorum." M. A. thesis. Catholic University of America, 1950.

Krynen, Jean. Le Cantique spirituel de saint Jean de la Croix commenté et refondu au XVIIe siècle: un regard sur l'histoire de l'exégese du Cantique du Jaen. Acta Salamanticensia: Filosofía y Letras III. Salamanca: Universidad de Salamanca, 1948.

Langer, Susan. Philosophy in a New Key. A Study in the Symbolism of Reason, Rite and Art. Cambridge: Harvard University Press, 1942.

Lewis, C. Day. The Poetic Image. London: Jonathan Cape, 1947.

Lewis, C. S. The Discarded Image. An Introduction to Medieval and Renaissance Literature. Cambridge: Cambridge University Press, 1964.

Lida [de Malkiel], María Rosa. "Transmisión y recreación de temas greco-latinos en poesía lírica española." RFH 1 (1939): 20-63.

342

---. <u>La tradición clásica en España</u>. Barcelona: Ariel, 1975.

Lobera Serrano, Francisco and Norbert v. Prellwitz. "Sulla poetica di San Juan de la Cruz: <u>En una noche oscura</u> (la parte: Analisi delle strofe I-IV)." <u>Studi Ispanici</u>. Pisa, Italy: 1979. 81-104.

López Baralt, Luce. "Huellas del Islam en San Juan de la Cruz: En torno a la 'Llama de amor viva' y la espiritualidad musulmana israqui." <u>Vuelta</u> 45 (1980): 5-11.

---. "Para la génesis del 'pájaro solitario' de San Juan de la Cruz." <u>RPh</u> 37, iv (1984): 409-424.

---. "San Juan de la Cruz: una nueva concepción del lenguaje poético." <u>BHS</u> 55 (1978): 19-32.

---. <u>San Juan de la Cruz y el Islam</u>. Río Piedras, P. R.: Universidad de Puerto Rico-Recinto de Río Piedras, 1985.

---. "Santa Teresa de Jesús y Oriente: El símbolo de los siete castillos del alma." <u>Sin Nombre</u> 13, iv (July-Sept 1983): 25-44.

López Estrada, Francisco. "Una posible fuente de San Juan de la Cruz." <u>RFE</u> 28 (1944): 473-77.

Louth, Andrew. <u>The Origins of the Christian Mystical Tradition. From Plato to Denys</u>. Oxford: Clarendon Press, 1981.

Lovejoy, Arthur O. <u>The Great Chain of Being. A Study of the History of an Idea</u>. Cambridge: Harvard University Press, 1964.

Luis de San José, Fr., O. C. D. <u>Concordancias de las obras y escritos de Santa Teresa de Jesús</u>. 2nd ed. Burgos: El Monte Carmelo, 1965.

---. <u>Concordancias de las obras y escritos del doctor de la iglesia, San Juan de la Cruz</u>. Burgos: El Monte Carmelo, 1948.

Macdonald, Inez Isabel. "The Two Versions of the Cántico Espiritual." <u>MLR</u> 25 (1930): 165-84.

McInnis, Judy B. "Eucharistic and Conjugal Symbolism in <u>The Spiritual Canticle</u> of Saint John of the Cross." <u>Ren</u> 36 (1984): 118-38.

Maio, Eugene A. <u>St. John of the Cross: the Imagery of ERos</u>. Madrid: Playor, 1973.

343

Maldonado Arenas, Luis. Experiencia religiosa y lenguaje en San Teresa. Madrid: PPC, 1982.

Maldonado de Guevara, Francisco. "Guirnalda y covelada. La estrofa 15 del primer 'Cántico espiritual'." Clavileño 5 (1954): 22-29.

Mancho Duque, María Jesús. El símbolo de la noche en San Juan de la Cruz. Estudio léxico-semántico. Salamanca: Universidad de Salamanca, 1982.

Maritain, Jacques. Creative Intuition in Art and Poetry. New York: Meridian, 1955.

---. Distinguish to Unite or the Degrees of Knowledge. Trans. Gerald B. Phelan. New York: Chas. Scribner's, 1959.

Maritain, Jacques and Raïssa. The Situation of Poetry. New York: Philosophical Library, 1955.

Marlay, Peter, "On Structure and Symbol in the 'Cántico espiritual'." Homenaje a Casalduero. Madrid: Gredos, 1972. 363-69.

Márquez Villanueva, Francisco. "El símil del castillo interior: sentido y génesis." Actas del Congreso Internacional Teresiano. Salamanca: Universidad de Salamanca, 1983. 495-522.

May, Rollo, ed. Symbolism in Religion and Literature. New York: George Braziller, 1960.

Medieval Mystical Tradition and St. John of the Cross. Westminster, Md.: Newman Press, 1954.

Méndez Plancarte, Alfonso. San Juan de la Cruz en México. México: FCE, 1959.

Menéndez Pelayo, Marcelino. San Isidoro, Cervantes y otros estudios. Madrid; Espasa-Calpe, 1941.

Menéndez Pidal, Ramón. La lengua de Cristóbal Colón, el estilo de Santa Teresa, y otros estudios sobre el siglo XVI. Madrid: Espasa-Calpe, 1942.

Merton, Thomas. The Ascent to Truth. New York: Harcourt, 1951.

Millet, Louis, et al. Le Symbole. Recherches et débats 29. Paris: Librarie Arthème Fayard, 1959.

Milner, Max. Poésie et vie mystique chez saint Jean de la Croix. Paris: Editions du Seuil, 1959.

344

Moncy, Agnes. "Santa Teresa y sus demonios." PSA 36 (1965): 149-66.

Morales, Jose L. El Cántico espiritual de San Juan de la Cruz. Su relación con el Cantar de los Cantares y otras fuentes escriturísticas y literarias. Madrid: Editorial de Espiritualidad, 1971.

---. "Paralelismo entre fray Luis de León y san Juan de la Cruz." Revista de Espiritualidad 27 (1968): 345-51.

Morales Borrero, Manuel. La geometría mística del alma en la literatura española del siglo de oro. Notas y puntualizaciones. Madrid: Universidad Pontificia de Salamanca and Fundación Universitaria Española, 1975.

Morel, Georges. Le Sens de l'existence selon saint Jean de la Croix. 3 vols. Paris: Aubier, 1960.

---. "La Structure du symbole chez saint Jean de la Croix." Le Symbole. Ed. Louis Millet et al. Paris: Libraire Arthème Fayard, 1959. 66-86.

Morel Fatio, Alfred. "Les Lectures de sainte Thérèse." BH 10 (1908): 17-67.

Moreno, Salvador. "La música en San Juan de la Cruz." CHA 53 (1963): 54-66.

Morgan, Hon. Evan. "Some Aspects of Mysticism in Verse." Essays by Divers Hands Being the Transactions of the Royal Society of Literature of the United Kingdom. Ed. John Bailey. IX. London: Oxford University Press, 1930. 103-24.

Morón Arroyo, Ciriaco. "'I will give you a living book': Spiritual Currents at Work at the Time of St. Teresa of Jesus." Centenary of Saint Teresa. Washington, D. C.: ICS Publications, 1984. 95-112.

---. "Mística y expresión: la originalidad cultural de Santa Teresa." Crisis 20 (1973): 211-42.

Murray, Rosalind. "Saint John of the Cross." Month. New Series 7 (1952): 149-61.

Musurillo, Herbert, S. J. Symbolism and the Christian Imagination. Baltimore: Helicon Press, 1962.

Mystery and Mysticism. A Symposium. London: Blackfriars, 1956.

Nelson, Lowry. Baroque Lyric Poetry. New Haven and London: Yale University Press, 1961.

Nöel-Dermot, Fr., O. C. D. "The 'Mount of Perfection' of St. John of the Cross, as presented by Diego de Astor." Mount Carmel 7-8 (1959-1961): 77-83.

Olabarrieta, Sr. Miriam Thérèse, S. C. N. The Influence of Ramon Llull on the Style of the Early Spanish Mystics and Santa Teresa. Washington, D. C.: The Catholic University Press, 1963.

---. "Simple Imagery and Meaning in the Poems of St. John of the Cross." M. A. thesis. Catholic University of America, 1954.

O'Reilly, Terence. "The Literary and Devotional Context of the 'Pastorcico'." FMLS 18, iv (1982): 363-70.

Orozco Díaz, Emilio. Manierismo y barroco. Madrid: Cátedra, 1975.

---. Mística, plástica y barroco. Madrid: Cupsa Editorial, 1977.

---. "La palabra espíritu y materia en la poesía de San Juan de la Cruz." Escorial 9 (1942): 315-35.

Ottonello, Pier Paolo. Bibliografia di S. Juan de la Cruz. Roma: Teresianum, 1967.

Pablo, Daniel de. Amor y conocimiento en la vida mística. Madrid: Fundación Universitara Española, 1979.

---. Dinámica de la oración; acercamiento del orante moderno a Santa Teresa de Jesús. Madrid: Editorial de Espritualidad, 1973.

Pardo Bazán, Emilia. Homenaje literario a Santa Teresa de Jesús. Lecciones de literatura. Cuatro españolas. Madrid: Ibero-Aermicana, 1914.

Parker, Alexander A. "Metáfora y símbolo en la interpretación de Calderón." Actas del Primer Congreso Internacional de Hispanistas. Oxford: Dolphin Book, Co., 1964. 141-60.

Paschal of the Blessed Sacrament, Fr., O. C. D. "A Visual Aid to the 'Interior Castle'." Ephemerides Carmeliticae 13 (1962): 566-75.

Peers, E. Allison. Handbook to the Life and Times of St. Teresa and St. John of the Cross. London: Burns and Oates, 1954.

---. Mother of Carmel. A Portrait of St. Teresa of Jesus. London: SCM Press, 1945.

346

---. St. John of the Cross and Other Lectures and Addresses 1920-1945). London: Faber and Faber, n. d.

---. Saint Teresa of Jesus and Other Essays and Addresses. London: Faber and Faber, 1953.

---. Spririt of Flame. A Study of St. John of the Cross. Wilton, Conn.: Morehouse-Barlow, 1946.

---. Studies of the Spanish Mystics. 2nd ed. rev. Vol. I. London: SPCK; New York: Macmillan, 1951.

Pelisson, Nicole. "Les Noms divins dans l'oeuvre de sainte Thérèse de Jesus." Etudes sur Sainte Thérèse. Ed. Robert Ricard. Paris: Centre de Recherches Hispaniques, 1968. 57-185.

Perella, Nicolas J. The Kiss Sacred and Profane. Berkeley and Los Angeles: University of California Press, 1969.

Peterkiewicz, Jerzy. The Other Side of Silence. The Poet at the Limits of Language. London: Oxford University Press, 1970.

Plé, A. "Mysticism and Mystery." Mysticism and Mystery. London: Blackfriars, 1956. 1-17.

Poitrey, Jeannine. Vocabulario de Santa Teresa. Madrid: Universidad Pontificia de Salamanca and Fundación Universitaria Española, 1983.

Polo de Bernabé, José Manuel. "Tensión metafórica y transmisión del lenguaje poético: de Garcilaso a San Juan." REH 16 (1982): 275-85.

Poveda Arino, José María. La psicología de Santa Teresa de Jesús. Madrid: Rialp, 1984.

Praz, Mario. Studies in Seventeenth Century Imagery. Vol. I of Studies of the Warburg Institute. London: The Warburg Institute; University of London, 1939.

Preminger, Alex, ed. Encyclopedia of Poetry and Poetics. Princeton: Princeton University Press, 1965.

Probst, J. H. "Místicos ibéricos. El beato Ramón Llull y San Juan de la Cruz." Estudios franciscanos 52 (1951): 209-23.

Queiros, A. "A naturaleza na poesía de S. João da Cruz." Broteria 35 (1942): 155-65.

Religious Experience and Truth. A Symposium. Ed. Sidney Hook. New York: NYU Press, 1961.

The Renaissance. Six Essays. New York: Harper & Row, 1953.

Ricard, Robert. Estudios de literatura religiosa española. Madrid: Gredos, 1964.

---. Etudes sur Sainte Thérèse. Paris: Centre de Recherches Hispaniques, Institut d'Etudes Hispaniques, 1968.

---. "Quelques remarques sur les Moradas de sainte Thérèse." BH 47 (1945): 187-98.

---. "Saint Jean de la Croix et l'image de la 'buche enflammée': Contributions à l'étude d'un theme symbolique." LR 33 (1979): 73-85.

---. "Sobre el poema de San Juan de la Cruz 'Aunque es de noche'." Clavileño 6, xxxv (1955): 26-29.

Richards, I. A. Principles of Literary Criticism. New York: Harcourt, Brace & Co., 1925.

Rico, Francisco. El pequeño mundo del hombre. Varia fortuna de una idea en las letras españolas. Madrid: Castalia, 1970.

Rivers, Elias. "The Vernacular Mind of St. Teresa." Centenary of Saint Teresa. Washington, D. C.: ICS Publications, 1984. 113-129.

Rodríguez, Leandro. "Christo en el 'centro' del alma según S. Agustín y Santa Teresa." Revista de espiritualidad 91 (1964): 171-85.

Rogers, Edith. "The Hunt in the Romancero and Other Traditional Ballads." HR 42 (1974): 133-171.

Roig, Rosendo. "De la visión del infierno a la visión del primer carmelo. Comentario estilístico del capítulo XXXII del Libro de la vida de Santa Teresa." LdD 24 (1982): 59-75.

Ros, Fidele de. "La 'palomica' des Moradas: papillon ou colombe?" BH 46 91944): 233-36.

Rosenmeyer, Thomas G. The Green Cabinet. Theocritus and the European Pastoral Lyric. Berkeley and Los Angeles: University of California Press, 1969.

Rossi, Rosa. Teresa de Avila. Biografía de una escritora. Trans. Marieta Gargatagli. Barcelona: Icaria, 1984.

Rougemont, Denis de. Love in the Western World. Trans. Montgomery Belgion. Rev. ed. New York: Harper & Row, 1956.

Rowland, Beryl. Animals with Human Faces. Knoxville, Tenn. University of Tennessee Press, 1973.

---. Birds with Human Souls. Knoxville, Tenn.: University of Tennessee Press, 1978.

Royo Marín, Antonio, O. P. Doctoras de la iglesia. Doctrina espiritual de Santa Teresa de Jesús y Santa Catalina de Siena. Madrid: Editorial Católica, 1970.

Rudder, Robert S. "Santa Teresa's Mysticism: The Paradox of Humility." Hispania 54 (1971): 341-45.

Ruffinatto, Aldo. "Los códigos del eros y del miedo en San Juan de la Cruz." Dispositio 4 (1979): 1-26.

Ruiz de San Juan de la Cruz, Fr. Frederico. "Cimas de contemplación: exégesis de 'Llama de amor viva'." Ephemerides Carmeliticae 13 (1962): 257-98.

Sabino de Jesús, Fr., O. C. D. San Juan de la Cruz y la crítica literaria. Santiago de Chile: Tall. Graf. S. Vicente, 1942.

Saenz, Hilario S. "Notas a la glosa 'Vivo sin vivir en mí' de Santa Teresa y de San Juan de la Cruz". MLQ 13 (1952): 405-408.

Sainz Rodríguez, Pedro. Espiritualidad española. Madrid: Rialp, 1961.

---. Introducción a la historia de la literatura mística en España. Madrid: Editorial Voluntad, 1927.

Salinas, Pedro. Reality and the Poet in Spanish Poetry. Trans. Edith Fishtine Helman. Baltimore, Md.: Johns Hopkins Press, 1966.

Salstad, M. Louise. "The Garden of God: Metamorphoses of Paradise in Religious Verse of Sixteenth-Century Spain." Durham University Journal 71 (1979): 197-212.

Sánchez Moguel, Antonio. El lenguaje de Santa Teresa de Jesús. Juicio comparativo de sus escritos con los de San Juan de la Cruz y otros clásicos de su época. Madrid: Clásica Española, 1915.

Sancta Teresia a Iesu. Doctor Ecclesia. Roma: Edizioni del Teresianum, 1970.

Sanjuanistica: studia a professoribus facultatis theologicae Ordinis Carmelitarum Discalcatorum quarta a nativitate S. Joannis a Cruce universalis Ecclesiae doctoris celebritate volvente edita. Roma: Collegium Int. SS. Teresiae a Jesus et Joannis a Cruce, 1943.

Sarmiento, Edward, ed. Concordancias de las obras poéticas en castellano de Garcilaso de la Vega. Columbus, Ohio: Ohio State University Press, 1970.

Santa Teresa y la literatura mística hispánica. Actas del I Congreso Internacional sobre Santa Teresa y la mística hispánica. Madrid: Ediséis, 1984.

Schoff, W. H., ed. The Song of Songs. A Symposium. Philadelphia: Commercial Museum, 1924.

Serrano Plaja, Arturo. "Dos notas a San Juan de la Cruz." CHA 242 (1970): 1-12.

---. Los místicos. Buenos Aires: Editorial Atlántida, 1943.

Setién de Jesús María, Fr. Emeterio G. Las raíces de la poesía sanjuanista y Dámaso Alonso. Burgos: El Monte Carmelo, 1950.

Silberer, Dr. Herbert. Problems of Mysticism and Its Symbolism. Trans. Smith Ely Jelliffe. New York: Samuel Weiser, 1970.

Sloman, Albert E. "Calderón and Falconry: A Note on Dramatic Language." RPh 6 (1953): 299-304.

Smitheram, [Mary] Lou Hale. "The Symbol of Night in the Works of Santa Teresa de Jesús and San Juan de la Cruz." Diss. University of California: Santa Barbara, 1977.

Spitzer, Leo. "Classical and Christian Ideas of World Harmony: Prolegomena to an Interpretation of the Word Stimmung." Traditio 2 (1944): 409-64; 3 (1945): 307-64.

---. A Method of Interpreting Literature. New York: Russell and Russell, 1967.

Spurgeon, Caroline F. E. Shakespeare's Imagery and What It Tells Us. Cambridge: Cambridge University Press, 1935.

Stowe, Everett M. Communicating Reality through Symbols. Philadelphia: Westminster Press, 1966.

Strolle, Jon M. "The Names of God in Saint Teresa." Literary Onomastics Studies 4 (1977): 115-30.

Studia Mystica. 8, ii (1985).

Surgy, P. de. "Les Degrés de l'échelle d'amour de saint Jean de la Croix." RAM 27 (1951): 237-59; 327-46.

---. "La Source de l'échelle d'amour de saint Jean de la Croix." RAM 27 (1951): 18-40.

Symons, Arthur. "The Poetry of Santa Teresa and San Juan de la Cruz." Contemporary Review 75 (1899): 542-51.

Tatarkiewicz, Wladyslaw. History of Aesthetics. Vol. II of Medieval Aesthetics. Ed. C. Barrett. Mouton, The Hague; Paris: Polish Scientific Publishers, 1970.

Teresa Maria Benedicta of the Cross, Sr., O. C. D. The Symbols of the Animals, Flowers, and Fruits in the Poetry of the Spiritual Canticle of St. John of the Cross. Salamanca: 1972.

Thompson, Colin P. "The Authenticity of the Second Redaction of the Cántico espiritual in Light of Its Doctrinal Additions." BHS 51 (1974): 244-54.

---. The Poet and the Mystic. A Study of the Cántico espiritual of San Juan de la Cruz. Oxford: Oxford University Press, 1977.

Tillich, Paul. "The Religious Symbol." Rollo May, ed. Symbolism in Religion and Literature. New York: George Braziller, 1960. 75-98.

---. "The Word of God." Ruth Anshen, ed. Language: An Enquiry into Its Meaning and Function. New York: Harper and Row, 1957. 122-33.

Trueblood, Alan S. "La mariposa y la llama; motivo poético del siglo de oro." Actas del Quinto Congreso Internacional de Hispanistas. II. Bordeaux: PU de Bordeau, 1977. 829-37.

Ulanov, Barry. "Shakespeare and Saint John of the Cross: De contemptu mundi." Sources and REsources: the Literary Traditions of Christian Humanism. Westminster, Md.: Newman Press, 1960. 150-87.

Unamuno, Miguel de. "Avila de los caballeros." Por tierras de Portugal y de España. Madrid: Renacimiento, 1911. 173-83.

---. "De mística y humanismo." En torno al casticismo. Vol. I of Obras completas. Madrid: Escelicer, 1966.

---. Niebla (Nívola). Madrid: Espasa-Calpe, 1914.

Underhill, Evelyn. Mysticism. New York: E. P. Dutton and Co., 1961.

Urban, William Marshall. Language and Reality: The Philosophy of Language and the Principles of Symbolism. London: George

Allen and Unwin; New York: Macmillan, 1939.

Urbano, Fr. Luis, O. P. "Las alegorías predilectas de Santa Teresa de Jesús." Ciencia Tomista 27 (1923): 52-71.

———. "Las analogías predilectas de Santa Teresa." Ciencia Tomista 29 (1924): 350-70.

Valera y Alcalá Galiano, Juan. "Las escritoras en España y elogio de Santa Teresa." Nuevos escritos críticos. Madrid: M. Tello, 1888.

Valverde, José M. Estudios sobre la palabra poética. Madrid: Rialp, 1952.

Vega, Angel Custodio. Cumbres místicas. Fray Luis de León y S. Juan de la Cruz. Madrid: Aguilar, 1963.

———. La poesía de Santa Teresa. Madrid: Editorial Católica, 1972.

Vilnet, Jean. Bible et mystique chez saint Jean de la Croix. Paris: Desclée de Brouwer, 1949.

Vossler, Karl. La poesía de Santa Teresa. Madrid: Editorial Católica, 1972.

Wardropper, Bruce W. "The Color Problem in Spanish Traditional Poetry." MLN 75 (1960): 415-21.

———. Historia de la poesía lírica a lo divino en la cristiandad occidental. Madrid: Revista de Occidente, 1958.

Warnke, Frank J. European Metaphysical Poetry. New Haven and London: Yale University Press, 1974.

———. Versions of Baroque. European Literature in the Seventeenth Century. New Haven and London: Yale University Press, 1972.

Watkin, Edward Ingram. The Philosophy of Mysticism. London: Grant Richards, 1920.

Weatherby, Harold L. The Keen Delight: The Christian Poet in the Modern World. Athens: University of Georgia Press, 1975.

Welch, John, O. Carm. Spiritual Pilgrims. Carl Jung and Teresa of Avila. New York: Paulist Press, 1982.

Wellek, Rene and Austin Warren. Theory of Literature. 3rd ed. New York: Harcourt, Brace and World, 1970.

Weston, Jessie L. From Ritual to Romance. Garden City, N. Y.:
    Doubleday, 1957.

Whittlesey, E. S. Symbols and Legends in Western Art. New York:
    Chas. Scribner's Sons, 1972.

Williams, George Walton. Image and Symbol in the Sacred Poetry
    of Richard Crashaw. South Carolina: University of South
    Carolina Press, 1963.

Wilson, E. Faye. "Pastoral and Epithalamium in Latin
    Literature." Speculum 23 (1948): 35-57.

Wilson, E. M. "The Four Elements in the Imagery of Calderón."
    MLR 31 (1936). Rept. in Spanish and English Literature of
    the 16th and 17th Centuries. Cambridge: Cambridge
    University Press, 1980. 1-14.

---. "Spanish and English Religious Poetry of the Seventeenth
    Century." Journal of Ecclesiastical History 9 (1958):
    38-53.

---. Spanish and English Literature of the 16th and 17th
    Centuries. Cambridge: Cambridge University Press, 1980.

Wilson, Margaret. San Juan de la Cruz: Poems. London: Grant &
    Cutler, 1975.

Zurmuehlen, Franck Bernhard. [Brice, Fr., C. P.]. Teresa, John
    and Thérèse: A Family Portrait of Three Great Carmelites.
    New York: F. Pustet, 1946.